Marketing Research

Dr. P. Sathyapriya

Published by:

biztantra

Ideas for Tomorrow!

An Imprint of dreamtech PRESS

ISBN: 978-93-5119-775-1

Reprint Edition: 2021

Printed at: Nisha Enterprises

Preface

This book is written to serve as a marriage between theory and application of Marketing Research. The key objective of the book is to introduce research methods and its applications in the field of marketing. This book covers the basic concepts and its application with case studies specific for marketing problems. Quantitative and qualitative methods of research are discussed elaborately. Every analysis explained in the book is augmented with a case using SPSS. Navigation guide to go through the steps using SPSS is explained throughout. It will help any beginner in using statistical software to advance through effortlessly. Basic knowledge of statistics and understanding of marketing research problems will help the readers to utilize the contents in a better manner.

P. Sathyapriya

About the Book

About the Book

The first part of the book from chapters 1 through 6 explains the basic research methodology. The book starts with an introduction about marketing research and the process involved in performing research. It is followed by a discussion on research design and sampling design with the data collection methods and techniques. The data collection is guided with formulation of questionnaire and development of scales. Process of coding and tabulating of the data with testing the reliability and validity of the scales is elaborated in Chapter 7. Once data is ready for analysis, SPSS (Statistical Package for Social Sciences) is introduced for quantitative analysis. Second part of the book from chapters 7 through 11 brings out the application of SPSS for simple statistical methods. Testing of hypothesis with simple statistical tools like t-test, ANOVA, chi-square and correlation is discussed. Chapter 12 through 15 explains the multivariate statistical tools. It includes application of regression, discriminant, conjoint analysis, factor analysis, cluster analysis, perceptual mapping and multidimensional scaling for marketing problems. Every analysis elaborates a case, its appliance with SPSS and final discussion of the results and the decision to be made. The last part of the book brings out the qualitative research methods, data collection methods and data analysis. This is followed by a chapter on report writing. Additional exercises to work out are given with questions to be discussed for every chapter. It is a comprehensive book that brings out the basic methods of doing marketing research.

About the Book

[illegible]

About the Author

About the Author

Dr. Periyasamy Sathyapriya is presently Professor in Marketing and Strategy at ICFAI Business School (IBS), Hyderabad. Earlier, she was Professor at Alliance School of Business, Alliance University, Bangalore. She obtained her Masters in Business Administration and Doctorate from Coimbatore Institute of Management and Technology in the area of Marketing. She is an alumnus of the prestigious Faculty Development Programme from IIM Ahmedabad. She has about nine years of academic experience, teaching marketing courses. An ardent researcher, she has published notable research papers in national and international conferences and seminars.

As an academician, Dr. Sathyapriya has designed curriculum for Management courses and has been a member on doctoral research committees. She offers training and consultancy to the corporate world in the area of Marketing Research, focusing on application of Marketing Research tools and techniques to find solutions to real world issues. She is actively involved in research initiatives in the areas of understanding consumer behavior and service gaps.

As a teacher scholar, Dr. Sathyapriya's thirst for knowledge led her to attend various workshops and faculty programmes. She also had the honor of being the resource person and chair person for similar programs and has won research excellence awards.

Acknowledgements

Acknowledgements

All things are possible with the blessings of Almighty. HIS blessings made me an author. I would thank Saibaba for giving me the strength and little knowledge to write this book. I would like to quote:

"Those blessings are sweetest that are won with prayer and worn with thanks."

— *Thomas Goodwin*

Many people deserve my thanks for the motivation and contribution in bringing this book. First I would thank my employers for extending the resources to complete the book. I took up the initiative to write the book when I worked with School of Business, Alliance University. I thank the administrators and faculties at School of Business, Alliance University, Bangalore. I thank Dr. Madhukar Angur, Chancellor, Alliance University, Dr. J. Mahender Reddy, Vice Chancellor, IFHE University for the facilities provided in the university. I completed my book after joining IBS, Hyderabad. I thank the Director Dr. Narasimhaiah Gorla, Dean Prof. C.V. Kumar and the Area Coordinator Dr. G. Radhakrishna from IBS Hyderabad for their support in the academic arena.

I bow my head to thank my gurus Dr. K.A. Chinnaraju and Dr. P. Natarajan, Administrators at Coimbatore Institute of Management and Technology for their continuous support and guidance. My friends are my strength. To mention a few, I am grateful to my friend Prof. P. Asha (Professor at School of Business, Alliance University, Bangalore) who was with me throughout my writing. Her thoughtful comments and suggestions as my reviewer are gratefully acknowledged. I acknowledge the contribution of Mr. R.P. Suganesh, working with TCS, in sharing his insights about marketing research and the case studies. I sincerely thank the continuous motivation given by Mr. Yoginder Singh, Editor of Biztantra publications.

My thanks are due to my family members. First I am grateful to my spouse Mr. S. Kanagachalam who motivated me to take up this work. Without his efforts the book would not have started nor completed. I would also appreciate the interest and curiosity shown by my son S.K. Sasivarnan to publish this book. I thank my parents and my in-laws for their moral support.

P. Sathyapriya

Acknowledgements

Brief Contents

Detailed Contents

CHAPTER 13: Decision Making Models 163

CHAPTER 14: Data Reduction Techniques 183

CHAPTER 15: Brand Positioning Methods 205

CHAPTER 16: Qualitative Approaches 223

Chapter 17: Report Writing 231

Index 239

Chapter 1

Marketing Research

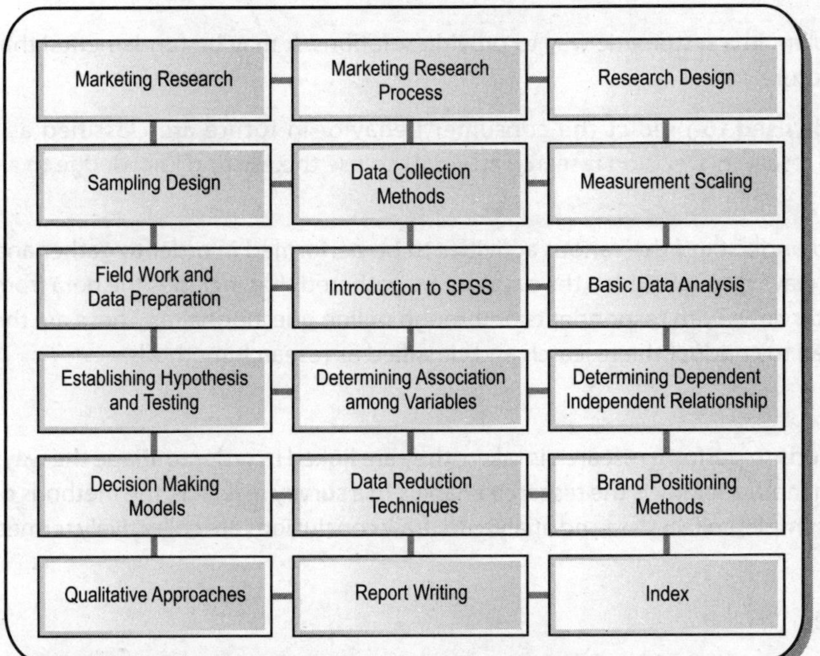

Outline

Chapter Structure

- Introduction to Marketing Research
- Definition of Marketing Research
- Importance of Marketing Research
- Role of Marketing Research in Managerial Decision Making
- Classification of Marketing Research
- Marketing Research Services
- Review Questions

Chapter Overview

Chapter one introduces the basic terms used in marketing research, definition of marketing research, and its importance. It explains the role of marketing research and its extensive usage for managerial decision making. It also brings in the classification of marketing research methods and the research firms that engages in marketing research activities.

INTRODUCTION TO MARKETING RESEARCH

Marketing research has emerged as a part of marketing if it the decision regarding the product attributes, line extension, pricing strategy, promotional mix decisions, competitor analysis, consumer investigation or distributor strategies Research conducted in marketing may be problem solving or decision making or predictive in nature. It may be performed internally in the marketing or research department of the organization or outsourced to a research firm or agency. With intense competition and changing consumer need, it has become imperative for marketers to make decisions logically driven through research.

In social research, the terminologies used to elaborate the research process are: Research methods, Research methodology, Theoretical perspective and Epistemology.

Research Methods

Research investigates the problem in a systematic way to provide solutions. It may be fundamental that seeks solution for problem in future.

For instance, those methods used to predict the consumer behavior in future are classified as fundamental or basic or pure research. Decision research attempts to use the existing knowledge to a given problem.

In research, the initial step is to understand the various activities to be performed in order to gather and analyze data. This includes the ways through which the data can be gathered that includes the data from internal records, data bases, interviews with respondents or through online questionnaires. These are the methods or techniques involved to conduct the research and classified as research methods.

Research Methodology

Once the decision on the methods to perform research is taken, they are linked in order to shape the ways to derive conclusions. Research methodology is the research enabler. In a survey research, the methods or the ways employed to identify sample, collect data and analyze to draw conclusions are collectively termed as Research Methodology.

Theoretical Perspective

If the methodology is laid down, a number of assumptions underlying the methodology are brought out. The logic behind the assumptions can be explained, based on the existing theories of human behavior. For example, when in-depth interviews are conducted, assumptions are made on language, inter-subjectivity and communication. These assumptions are made based on existing theories and researchers' experience and views about human nature.

Epistemology

Every event and object exists in the world, already. Researchers identify, explain and justify the part of knowledge explored – researchers discover. For example, if there is a problem among the garment exporters, a researcher identifies the problems, explores it and may suggest solutions to overcome the same. This may be achieved through a survey conducted with the help of the questionnaire. Epistemology brings out the theory of knowledge existing with the help of appropriate methodology.

Scientific knowledge can be proven by logical reasoning, by experience or experimentation. Research, either conceptual or empirical is carried out to establish such knowledge. Social scientists perform conceptual researches and empirical studies to benefit from the outcomes of these two levels.

DEFINITION OF MARKETING RESEARCH

Marketing research involves application of research methods for marketing problems. Problem involves decision making situation. Thus marketing research addresses the problem or the situation, involves collection of data, and analyzes data to make appropriate decisions.

It may be to understand the market opportunities, explore the competitors and their position in the market place, study the expectations of the consumers, their existing and latent needs, effectiveness of marketing mix elements, or policy implications.

American Marketing Association defined Marketing Research as follows:

"Marketing research is the function that links the consumer, customer, and public to the marketer through information - information used to identify and define marketing opportunities and problems; generate, refine, and evaluate marketing actions; monitor marketing performance; and improve understanding of marketing as a process. Marketing research specifies the information required to address these issues, designs the methods for collecting information, manages and implements the data collection process, analyzes, and communicates the findings and their implications."

Marketing research thus involves decision making that is responsive to customer needs and increased profits of the organization. It includes the data collected and decisions made to produce and transfer the goods and services that satisfy the customer and positions with a competitive edge in the market place. Decision making is made more systematically by involving the research methods. It is performed by systematically exploring the situation, understanding the problem and assuming solution, gathering data, coding, tabulating and analyzing to make inferences and verify solutions.

Market research explains the research conducted in a specific market place and marketing research involves the research performed for any marketing problem and the results of which are generalised.

For example, HUL conducting research in the rural markets of North Karnataka (Karnataka is a state in the southern part of India) to identify the opportunities for detergent powders is market research. The research pertains to the specific area or market place. If the same research is conducted to understand the rural consumer behaviour towards the consumption of detergent powders, it is marketing research as the research does not confine to a specific market. Thus market research is the research conducted in a small market place and marketing research is performed in a broader perspective.

IMPORTANCE OF MARKETING RESEARCH

The central focus of marketing is to understand customers and deliver value to them. This can be product oriented, including identifying right products for the consumers at right price to be delivered on right time with complete information on promotion made. On the other hand it can be service oriented, delivering the service as per the perceived satisfaction of the customers. More and more understanding of the customers, competitors, and the market place is essential for the marketers to face the challenge. This understanding is obtained with a close observation, interaction with customers or other stakeholders and analyzing the responses to make decisions that is achieved with marketing research techniques. Thus research becomes an integral part of marketing. In specific, the importance of marketing research is listed below.

1. MR is important to decide the product or technology that is to be made available to the consumers.
2. To explore the segments that exists and the right targets to concentrate upon.
3. To understand the factors to be concentrated to position the brand in the minds of the target consumers.
4. The packages that can be made available in a rural vs. urban market.
5. Price at which the products can be made available at different retail outlets.
6. The promotion mix that is to be decided to reach consumers effectively.
7. Personnel required at the frontline and the training needs of the salesmen.
8. To understand the effective ways to maintain the relationship with the customers.
9. The extent of after sale service and promises that brings in new customers and retains the existing ones.
10. To understand the trends in buying behaviour that reveals the opportunities ahead or problems to be addressed immediately.
11. To decide the amount that can be spent on marketing activities that will reap better returns.
12. To decide the strategies to be formulated to utilise the opportunities or to solve the problem.

Ultimately research enhances the efficiency of the marketers and leads to profitability of the organization.

ROLE OF MARKETING RESEARCH IN MANAGERIAL DECISION MAKING

Marketing research reduces the uncertainty and facilitates better marketing decisions from the Information collected. Uncertainties may exist with a problem or in understanding the opportunities. The researchers will get to know the problem as sales performance or symptoms of the problems like customers going dissatisfied from the stores. If the problem is sales performance, researchers should have interaction with the sales men to understand the exact problem. Is it with the product performance, competitors, salesmen, etc? Understanding of the problem clearly reduces uncertainty and ambiguity in understanding the nature of the problem. If the problem is clear, marketing research techniques helps researchers to make decisions from the alternatives available.

Marketing research helps to understand 'what' is to be done, 'why' it is to be done and 'how' the results are incorporated in the business.

For instance, the problem of reduced sales in a restaurant can be solved with marketing research techniques. The understanding of the reasons for decline in sales, exploring the reasons to enhance the sales performance, and the strategies to be adopted by the restaurant in near future, will help the marketers to draw methodologies and make decision to solve the problem. This effort is essential to understand the need to solve the emerging problem that may reflect on the performance of the organization in the future.

CLASSIFICATION OF MARKETING RESEARCH

The type of marketing research depends on the research purpose, the data to be collected, analyzed and processed. Based on the type of data collected, marketing research can be broadly classified as qualitative and quantitative research. With respect to methodology the research can be pure or basic research, conclusive research, descriptive research, exploratory research, experimental research and causal research. Based on the decision to be made about the marketing mix elements, research can be product research, pricing research, promotion research, market research and distribution research. The research conducted in real settings may sometimes not fall under any category and include the characteristics of more than one type.

Qualitative Research

Research is performed to study the behaviour of consumers/distributors in the market place to study the abstract components. So they are qualitative in nature. The reasons behind consumer behaviour, motives and desires underlying the human are studied with non-numeric data collected.

For instance, reasons for consumers choice of a brand or motivation to visit a retail outlet can be studied with are qualitative research. It explores the human behaviour and deals with behavioural science. It requires expertise from the part of the researcher and applied in the area of consumer behaviour studies.

Quantitative Research

Research conducted generally deals with understanding the behaviour of variables and measuring them. It involves collection of data or usage of measurement scales that will be coded and quantified further.

For instance, sales performance of the firm can be studied from the historical data of sales available in the organization and from the interest expressed by the consumers in future buying measured on scale. This type of data is further analyzed using statistical techniques to draw conclusion.

Basic Research

Researches done in order to evolve theoretical foundations are basic research. It results in cost minimization model, motivation model, effective distribution model, etc. It is the result of advance knowledge with the researcher and the results are generalized about the human behaviour.

Conclusive Research

It is more a solution oriented research for the emerging problem in the business.

For instance, if the advertisement campaign is not appealing, study conducted to explore the reasons and features expected in a successful advertising campaign will solve the problem. A conclusive research is more problem focused and brings in solution to the immediate problem and may sometimes incidentally contribute to the development of theoretical knowledge.

Descriptive Research

Descriptive research is performed for a problem that is clearer and the characteristics of the problem can be described.

For instance, the shopping behaviour of the consumers can be studied and described with survey techniques. It is more an enquiry to understand the facts in a better way. Simple statistical tools are used to describe. Hypothesis can be stated and it may or may not the proved. Research conducted to understand the perception of youth towards a brand is another example that can be of descriptive.

Analytical Research

Analytical research formulates hypothesis, probes into the problem, analyze the situation to make critical evaluation. Based on the analysis made, the hypothesis will be proved or disproved. It also studies the relationship that exists among the variables.

For instance, in understanding the shopping behaviour of the consumers, the variables influencing the shopping behaviour is studied and the extent of the influence is established.

Exploratory Research

The problem encountered in the market place will not have clarity always. There will be less data available about the problem. Exploratory research makes an enquiry about the unfamiliar problem to have clarity in the problem, understand the variables influencing the problem. It aids in formalizing the research problem.

For example, the organization may have problem with the marketing strategies. But the marketing strategies may not be clearly classified by the marketers and the reasons for the problem may not be clear. The messy situation calls for research to clearly understand the research problem and identify variables influencing them to understand the relationship that exist. It is not a final research and generally followed by a descriptive or causal research.

Experimental Research

Experimental research measures the impact of one variable on another in some specific situation.

For example, productivity of the sales men depend on his background knowledge, type of product, training imparted and experience. The relationship between these variables can be studied by conducting experimentation. Different types of training can be imparted and the impact can be studied; training can be imparted to one group and the other group kept idle, the impact of training can be studied.

Causal Research

The relationship among the variables studied may exhibit certain behaviour. Some variables may directly influence our problem and some of them will influence but as an intervening variable. Understanding of the movement of these variables is studied by causal research. It explores the independent variables and the variables influencing these independent variables and the extent of their influence and brings clarity in establishing causal relationship.

For instance, in understanding the behaviour of online shoppers, it is necessary to understand the construct and the relationship it has with the dependent variables. Construct may be the price which is influenced by the distribution, promotion and cost of production. There may be single or more than one construct that influences dependent variable, online shopping behaviour.

Product Research

It includes study carried out to understand the right product/service to be produced that satisfies the customer. It also explores the future demand that may exist with advanced technology and innovation. It includes brand equity research, brand association research, brand attribute research, brand name testing research, segmentation research, positioning research, and concept testing research.

For example, research done by P & G to introduce Olay (Anti ageing skin care solution) in the Indian market includes the exploratory research conducted to understand the acceptance of the product among Indian women. Product Research activities include testing the acceptance of the concept of a product or service to provide solutions to customers, understanding the right segment to target, the position to create in the minds of the customers with the choice of right name for the product, association of consumers with the brand name, etc.

Price Research

Pricing research includes the research performed to understand the right price that creates competitive position and also retains profits for the firm. Price policies, product line pricing and response to price changes are the end results of Price research. Price elasticity research helps to understand the behaviour of consumers to every change in price and aids in price formulation. Conjoint analysis, brand price trade off models help in identifying right price for the brand.

Promotion Research

It includes research pursued to understand the right promotion mix to be delivered to the customers that satisfies them. Advertising research is conducted to understand the reach and the effectiveness of a channel in promoting the products. It also includes copy testing or pretesting done to understand the success of the advertisement before its launch and post testing done to understand the success of the advertisement that reflects in consumer purchases. Ad tracking research helps to measure the effectiveness of an ad in attracting audience attention, interest, desire and purchase behaviour can be studied in promotional researches. Commercial eye tracking research helps to understand the attractiveness of ad that reflects in their visual behaviour including expansion of eyes, pupil, etc.

Market Research

A better understanding of marketing environment is essential for every business man. It includes recognizing the demand and its pattern that exists in the market place, change in the trend that exists, movements of competitors, better understanding of market structure, and yet others. Research carried out to understand this phenomenon is market research. It explains the feasibility of the product/service made available in a market place. Coolhunting research is performed to observe the market to understand the changes happening in society, culture, etc., that aids in market prediction. Test marketing technique helps the marketer to understand the behaviour of consumers in a small selected market place that helps for generalizations.

Distribution Research

The decision about the channels of distribution depends on the cost involved and the right time with which the consumers can be reached effectively. Store audits are done to explore the effective display of products in retail outlets. Channel behaviour researches bring in the behaviour of channel members, their relationships and performance. Distributor channel audit helps the marketers to understand the retailers and wholesalers behaviour that gets reflected on the consumers.

Other Types of Research

Researches can also be classified based on the way it is conducted or usage of technology. Research conducted to understand consumer satisfaction, factors considered by consumers in decision making and buying, variables that motivate a consumer, etc. are some of them in marketing. Test marketing is done to introduce the new product or brand in a sample market and study the performance. Online panel researches and viral marketing research helps the marketers to understand the expectations of consumers with usage of innovative technology for better reach. Mystery shoppers help in observing consumers at their purchase points that gives better understanding of their behaviour.

Choice of the type of research depends on the problem studied and methods employed to study the problem.

MARKETING RESEARCH SERVICES

Marketing research service is offered internally or externally for the firms. Internal services include the research service provided by the research department of the firm and external research service include the service offered by the exclusive research firms for the marketing problems faced by the organization.

Internal Research Service

Firms with higher sales volumes may establish their own research department. It will increase their fixed costs of material and research personnel. An individual or a team in marketing department of an organization may also be assigned the responsibility of research. The primary role of such department or team is to address the problems to serve the industrial or ultimate consumers.

External Research Service

All firms may not afford to establish their own research department. So they outsource their research to research service firms. There are different types of such firms who are categorized based on the service offered. The types of research firms include:

Full Service Firms: Full service research firms conduct the complete research for the marketing problems. The service rendered by these firms starts from identifying the research problem from the management problem defined. It also includes services of designing the research, collecting and analyzing the data, making the report and presenting to the marketers to make decisions.

For example, Amplitute Research Firm offers full service through mails, telephone, and online survey. They conduct market research surveys, employee surveys, customer satisfaction and feedback surveys. Similarly Polaris Market Research, a full service marketing research firm does researches on customer satisfaction and loyalty, customer retention, brand research, new product development and sales force performance. Impetus Research is another service firm that offers full service concentrating on both qualitative and quantitative researches in market place. Majestic MRSS, a full service research firm specializes in multi country research. West Group Research firm also offers full service research for the clients in hospital, education, recreation and insurance sectors. Other full service research firms are: TNS-Global, The Kantar Group (TKG), which includes Milward Brown group, Research International, IMRB International, Light Speed Research, The Ziment Group, and Mattson Jack Group. The full service research firm may offer syndicated service, standardized service, customized service or online service.

Syndicated service firms offer same information or data to a syndicate/group of firms. It is more economical to collect the data and offer as and when a firm needs.

For example, Outsource2India (O2I) gathers and sells common data designed to serve information needs that could be shared by a number of customers. Syndicated sources included data on household or consumer obtained through survey, purchase and media panels and electronic scanner services. Reports are available on basis of customers product lines and sales territories. Nielson Media Research's radio and television ratings are available in series of quarterly reports detailing video and television usage in three screens – TV, Internet and Mobile.

Standardized service firms collect data as a syndicate firm but offer as per the requirement of an individual firm. Standardized methods of collecting the data are adopted. It provides customized service from the available syndicate data. TNS NIPO offers standardized services in consumer and business-to-business (B2B) markets, locally and internationally.

Customized service firms offers service to suit the specific research need. It is costlier compared to the other research services as the process is exclusive for each client. Burke is known for its full service custom marketing research. Their core research areas are customer loyalty, sales force research and relationship researches.

Online service firms offers service through internet and mobile. Specialist firms offer online full research service. These days almost all research firms extend online research.

For example Burke's Digital Dashboard online reporting solution provides real time access to online survey findings. Burke's also moderates online focus groups. Similarly RNB Research provides online panel to survey.

Limited/Part Service Firms

Limited service firms offer one or some of the marketing research activities. It may be to formulate the research design, develop the questionnaire, or to collect the data, or to make analysis and draw conclusions.

Field service firms specialize in primary data collection. These firms operate in a specific geographic area to collect the data in that area. Data will be collected through interviews, questionnaire, as mystery shoppers or mall-intercept surveys. Phone/Mail service firms specialize in collecting data through telephones or mobile phones and through mails.

Market segment specialist service firms collect data from one or some market segments. For instance data collected from specific segment or group like children, house wife, Hispanics, etc. is done by market segment specialist firms. This service is required if the research is conducted in specific to understand the behaviour of this segment or to compare the behaviour across segments. Test market research are also conducted by these firms.

Specialized research methods firms provide exclusive service like multivariate data analysis, conducting only focus group discussion, performing ethnographic researches, etc. Any of the full service research firms offer these limited services on request.

Review Questions

1. Define research and explain its importance.
2. Explain the importance of marketing research.
3. Discuss the role of marketing research in managerial decision making.
4. What are the different types of research?
5. Explain the services offered by research firms.

Chapter

2

Marketing Research Process

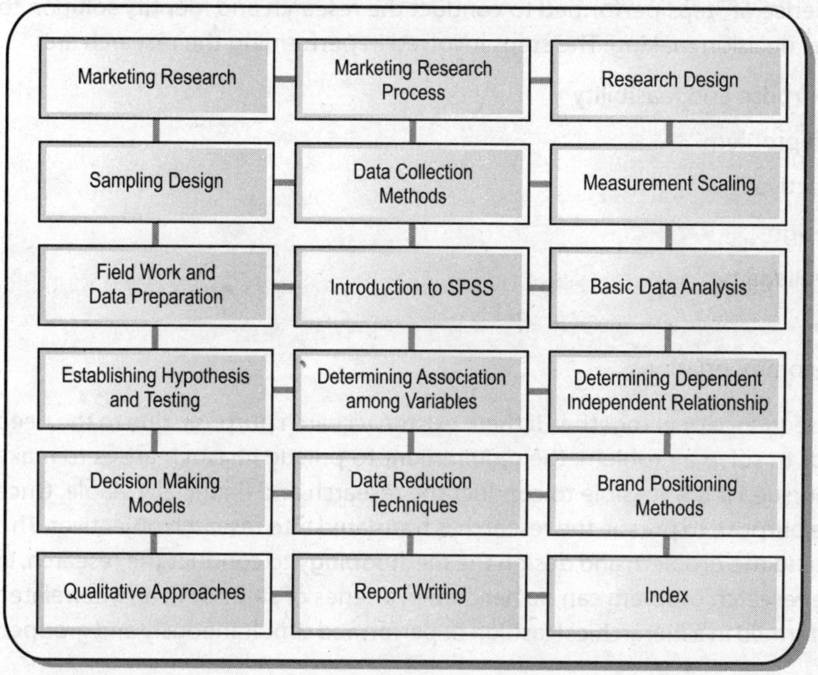

Outline

Chapter Structure

- Introduction
- Research Process
- Problem Identification and Definition
- Developing Research Objectives
- Establishing Research Questions and Hypothesis
- Formulating the Research Design
- Sampling Design
- Data Collection Methods
- Results and Discussion
- Report Preparation
- Review Questions

Chapter Overview

Chapter two explains the process involved in performing a marketing research. This chapter brings the sequence of steps to be followed in performing a research activity, methodology involved, and the method of reporting the research output for enhancing the process of decision making.

INTRODUCTION

Research involves identifying solutions to the existing problems. It probes into the situation to scientifically evolve solutions or explanations of the problem studied.

If there exist a decision making situation, analyse what to do?

How to do? – perform research to analyse the available alternatives or make adhoc decisions?

The process involved in performing research includes series of steps.

RESEARCH PROCESS

Research process includes sequence of steps performed to conduct the research and identify solution to the problem, and result in better decision making. The steps involved in performing the research are:

1. Explore the research purpose and feasibility
2. Formulate the research problem
3. Establish research objectives
4. Formulate research design
5. Establish validity and reliability
6. Analyze the data
7. Make decisions and recommendations

These steps can be achieved in sequence or in together. If there exists a research purpose, due to the need created to explore a situation or to solve a problem, the requirement to pursue research arises to make decision. But research can be pursued if it is feasible to conduct the research and financially viable. Once the feasibility is established, the purpose to pursue the research is translated into research objectives. This helps the researcher to understand the problem and design the methodology to conduct the research. In order to arrive at a solution, the research problem can be handled in a series of steps or in an interrelated manner. These steps can be performed in a hierarchical fashion or performed simultaneously and grouped under major heads as follows:

PROBLEM IDENTIFICATION AND DEFINITION

Identifying the problem and formulation from research perspective requires a lot of understanding of the exact problem. It requires translation of management problem into a research problem.

For instance, the management problem will be to introduce a new advertisement that has to be translated into a research problem that is to test the acceptance of the new advertisement among the target consumers that will result in purchase behaviour. Once the problem is identified in clear sense, the purpose of the research can be brought out and the working hypothesis can be developed.

The value of the outcome of the research should necessarily be higher than the cost involved in pursuing such research.

For instance, if the problem is to understand the consumer's acceptance to a new product, the product can be tried in a test market and the feasibility of the product success can be determined. In this case, the time involved, the amount spent to pursue the research should be comparatively less to cover in the cost. If the research problem identified is feasible then the objectives that flow to solve the research problem can be established.

DEVELOPING RESEARCH OBJECTIVES

The objective of the research provides the direction of research.

For example, in order to understand the acceptance of the new advertisement, the objectives formulated will be to understand the impact of advertisement on consumers. Formulation of specific objectives will help to identify the information required and methods to follow to pursue the research. Clear and stated objectives will help the researcher to achieve specific outcomes. The objectives formulated explain why a research is conducted, and what will be the outcome. It sets the direction of the research. For instance, the objective to study, the impact of new advertisement and its effect on consumer buying decisions help to understand clearly what the purpose of pursuing the research is.

ESTABLISHING RESEARCH QUESTIONS AND HYPOTHESIS

In understanding the research problem questions can be raised.

For example, to study the impact of new advertisement, the research questions raised can be:

- Is there difference in the new advertisement as perceived by the consumers?
- Does the new advertisement result in purchase decision?

Formulation of these research questions explain what research is done in a questioning format. If the research questions are raised, hypothesis if any will be stated. Hypotheses are the assumed solution for the research problem stated. The hypothesis can be stated assuming that the mean of the sample is same as the mean of the population or there exists no difference between the mean of two different samples. The hypothesis stated is null hypothesis that is proved or disproved in the research. If the null hypothesis is not true, the alternate hypothesis will hold good.

For instance, in the example to study the impact of new advertisement, the null hypothesis formulated will be:

H_0: There is no difference perceived by the consumers between the old and new advertisements (or) the mean ratings of the old advertisement and the new advertisement are the same.

H_A: There is difference between the old and new advertisements as perceived by the consumers (or) the mean ratings of the old advertisement and the new advertisement vary.

Once hypothesis is formulated research design will be formulated and decision about the methods to collect data will be done.

FORMULATING THE RESEARCH DESIGN

Research design helps to structure the research in a more logical and sequential form. It brings in the ways to perform the research. The three basic types of research designs are: exploratory, descriptive and experimental/causal designs. If the research is new or the research is conducted in a new environment, a clear understanding of the problem or the variables influencing the problem may not be arrived at. This can be solved by exploring the situation and understanding the problem with clarity. In these situations exploratory research is performed. If the research problem is clear, solutions to the problem is sought with a descriptive or causal research. Thus the exploratory research helps in answering 'what' the research is about. If this is clear, it leads to descriptive research. Description of the market or the environment or the people involved is required and pursued with a descriptive research design. It may be to study the perception of consumers, the profile of consumers, the interest or the reason for a consumer to prefer a brand. It explains 'what' the problem is. If there is increase or decrease in sales 'why' there is an increase or decrease? The reasons for the behaviour will also be brought out in a descriptive research. In answering 'why' the problem has occurred, the relationship between the variables will be understood that develops the causal research design.

For instance, the increase or decrease in sales and its effect by advertisement, sales promotion, price, and competitor's policies can be understood in a better way by establishing causal relations. These relations may be direct or indirect and bring out a causal chain explaining the impact of independent variables on dependent variable and the influence of intervening variables.

If the method to perform the research is finalized, the data that is to be collected, sources of collecting the data, and the respondents from whom data is to be collected etc., will be planned.

SAMPLING DESIGN

Sampling design explains the sampling method to be adopted, sample size and the sampling frame from where data is to be collected. Sampling frame explains the place or the population from where the sample will be selected. If the study is to understand the college students' opinion about the new brand of shirts introduced in youth segment, if the study is conducted in Chennai, the college goers in Chennai include the population from whom study will be conducted. Collecting data from all college goers may not be feasible as it will involve more amount of time and money. So a representation of the population, sample is selected to collect data and generalize their opinion about the population. This requires careful choice of the sample.

Sampling Method

The sample can be selected by adopting probability sampling method or non-probability sampling method. If every member of the population has equal chance to be selected as a sample, it is probability sampling method. If every member of the population don't get equal opportunity to be selected as a sample, it is non-probability sampling. In conducting the research among youth, the researchers may understand that every member selected as the sample may not be sincere to reveal their opinion. So they may use certain criteria to select these samples.

For instance, only those studying in selected engineering colleges may be considered as the sample as the researchers found that these students more serious and truthful with their experience. In this case, all the college goers don't get equal chance to be selected as the sample. Thus the selection of research methods depends on the research problem and the situation in which it is solved.

Probability sampling methods are the following:

Simple Random Sampling: This method of sampling ensures randomness in selection of sample and is applied if the population is known. It is performed with random table or by lottery method. In using random table, list the population and assign numbers consecutively (start numbering in five digits / seven digits). Select a part of random table and check the availability of the numbers assigned for the population in the selected part. The number assigned for the population that is also available in the random table, will be considered as the sample. In case of lottery method, the names or the numbers assigned for the population is written down in a chit and the required number of chits is drawn randomly. This method of selection is more objective and ensures normal distribution of the sample.

Sequential Sampling: In sequential sampling, the selection of the first sample is made using random sampling method. Then every 5th or 8th member of the population is drawn as the sample. For this purpose, the population can be arranged in ascending or descending order. This method can be practiced even if the size of the population is not known.

For instance, if the data is to be collected with the consumers visiting a shopping mall, every 5th member visiting the mall can be considered as the sample. When starting the process, the choice of the first member is made at random. The process will be continued till we arrive at the required sample size.

Stratified Sampling: If the population studied is huge, the sample selected may sometimes not represent the sub groups that exist.

For instance, if the study is conducted to understand consumer's perception toward a retail brand in India, the sample collected should represent the consumers from all regions. To ensure this, consumers from north, east, west, and south can be grouped together to form four clusters. Random sampling method can be executed to select sample from these clusters. This ensures good representation of sample from all parts of India brings in more validity for generalization. This method will be more appropriate if the population is large and it is heterogeneous in nature. The groups formed are called strata's and each stratum is unique in its nature. Members having similar attributes are grouped in each stratum.

Cluster Sampling: In case of huge population that is homogeneous, selecting sample using random sampling method will take time and involve more cost. Cluster sampling will provide a better solution for sample selection. In this method, the population is grouped and the groups are similar. Random sampling is made to select few groups depending on the sample requirement.

Area Sampling: If the sampling is made in a geographical area, it is called as area sampling.

For example, the study to understand the standard of living of people in a state, require sample from all districts, representing different thaluks and villages. The geographical area in this example, village is selected at random and all households in that specific village is studied.

Multi-stage Sampling: Any sampling method practiced for more than once in selecting sample for a study, is called multi stage sampling.

For example, in the example discussed in the previous method, random sampling will be used to select thaluks from each district. This is the first stage of sampling. If the villages in each thaluks are again selected at random, the sampling is done for the second time to narrow down the villages to study. This may continue to select few households in the selected villages.

Thus sampling method may not be always used at one stage to select the sample. It is continued for two or three stages depending on the requirement to narrow down the population studied. This ensures the adoption of multi stage sampling.

The non-probability sampling methods are:

Convenience Sampling: In convenience sampling method, any member of population whom the researcher feels comfortable and easy to approach is selected as the sample. The researchers may not always have time and resources to approach the population at random. In such situation, convenience sampling will be adopted. But it may not be the representation of the population. But in certain situations this sampling method will be appropriate. For instance, if the population is homogeneous and selection any of the members may not disturb the randomness of response, convenience sample is good to practice.

Quota Sampling: If the selection of sample should satisfy certain criteria, quota sampling is adopted. For instance, in the sample of consumers selected of the study, there may be restriction in selecting sample in different age categories.

For example, if 40 percent of them should be of youth category between 16 to 23 years of age; 20 percent of them in middle age category between 23 to 40 years of age; 30 percent of them in adult category between 40 to 58 years of age; and 10 percent in senior citizen category above 58 years of age. Quota for each category is fixed. So the sample will be selected only to the extent of quota available. After selection of this number, remaining members of the population don not have the chance to participate as the sample.

Judgemental Sampling: The expert choice made in selecting the sample will hold equally well if it is logical and objective. In this method of judgmental sampling researcher may find some logical reason to select the sample or he may derive it based on the literatures reviewed or based on the expert opinion. But there will be some strong reason to substantiate that they are the right representation of the population. This method is practiced if the researcher knows the population and its characteristics and is clear to choose the right representation of them.

Snow Ball Sampling: Snowball sampling is practiced if the population is not known and only one or two members of the population is known. The known members act as the reference from whom the remaining sample is identified and approached.

For example, aids patients are not known in public. So a laboratory who like to know the feedback on usage of certain drug for aids patients can have the list either from doctors treating aids patients or some NGO's (non-governmental organizations) aiding them. The list of patients visiting a doctor or aided by an NGO will become the sample size for the research.

Sample Size Determination: Statistically there are formulas to determine the sample size. But there are no hard and fast rules to select the required sample size. Any size that represents the population and is normally distributed will be appropriate. Sample selected will be normally distributed if it is large or true representation of the population. Size of the sample also depends on the resource available for the research. It includes the time and money available at the disposal of the researcher. Too large the sample, more accurate the prediction about the sample but it increases the cost of research. So a bridge between the size estimation and the cost is to be evolved by the researcher. It also depends on the size of the population, acceptable level of significance, and acceptable level of error.

Once the sampling method is decided and sample is drawn in required size, the right method and instrument to collect the data is to be decided.

DATA COLLECTION METHODS

Data required for the research may be primary or secondary. Secondary data are that information that exists and collected as per the requirement of the current research. It includes the data that about the industry collected from data bases or public domains, data pertaining to a firm collected from internal database, and the database maintained by the ministry, associations and research firms. The Primary data is the data collected for the first time exclusively for the specific research need. There are different methods adopted for data collection. It includes:

Observation: In understanding the consumer behaviour in a retail store, the researcher may observe the behaviour of consumers visiting the retail outlet during a specific time and record such information. This information can further be processed and analyzed to make decisions.

Questionnaire: Questionnaire is an important tool used to collect data from the respondents. It can be a structured or unstructured questionnaire. If the questionnaire is formal with complete list of questions in a prescribed sequence, it is structured questionnaire. Such structured questionnaires are used to collect the opinion of the respondents of similar phenomenon or on same scales of measurement. This approach may not be possible for all types of researches. If a researcher likes to understand the variables influencing the customer choice towards a retail store, the variables can be listed and the extent of influence is measured on a scale. It is a structured questioning method. In an unstructured method, the variables are revealed by the respondents and give flexibility for the respondents to share their views without any limitation or restriction. Such questionnaire has more open-ended questions.

Mailed Questionnaire: Sending questionnaires online through online survey or by mail is common approach to data collection. These questionnaires are available in the online web stores that help consumers to fill in whenever they visit such websites. The web links are also mailed to respondents personally to fill in.

Personal Interview Schedule: Personal interview is the most reliable method of data collection. It requires list of questions prepared and ready to be raised with the respondents. The interviewer has the challenge in recording the responses as revealed by the respondent and interpreting it. So it is commonly practised by expert researchers. The list of questions may be structured or unstructured. In unstructured interviews, the respondent is free to explain the reason for the behaviour and the interviewer can draft the questions based on the flow of the response.

Telephonic Interview: Telephonic interviews are carried out if the questions to be raised are less in number and the responses are short like a multiple choice question.

Once the instrument of data collection is finalized, the validity of the instrument is ensured.

Validity of the Instrument

If the instrument is ready for data collection, the validity is ensured by reinforcing the contents / variables measured and the flow or the order of their arrangement. This is done by enquiring about the validity with a small sample as a pilot study. Based on the response about the questionnaire, further corrections are made. Validity can also be ensured with a discussion with the experts or by reviewing the literatures. The data collected from the sample respondents considered for pilot study can be tested with Croanbach's alpha score to ensure reliability. If the Cronbach's alpha score for the scales used to measure opinion or perception or satisfaction is above 0.6, then the scale is reliable to collect data and draw conclusion. Once the validity and reliability of the instrument is established, the questionnaire / interview schedule is used for data collection.

RESULTS AND DISCUSSION

If the data is ready, the next phase is to code the data, classify into groups and enter them. It can be entered in an excel sheet or an SPSS input file for further analysis. The tools used for data analysis depend on the objectives formulated for the research problem.

If the objective is to understand the difference if there exists among the respondents of two cities towards the new brand of television, independent t-test will be the appropriate statistical tool to adopt. The results are drawn based on the significance of p-value.

If the p-value is less than 0.05 at 95 percent confidence level or 5 percent level of significance, it is concluded that there exists difference in the perception of people in two cities towards the new brand of television. The the results of data analysis helps the researcher to draw conclusion and make decisions. The decisions are generally made at 5 percent or 1 percent level of significance. In rare cases decisions are made at 10 percent level of significance.

REPORT PREPARATION

Once the data analysis is complete, they are arranged in the order of the objectives and presented with the chapters in an organized manner. It starts with an introductory chapter (giving the introduction about the study, objectives or purpose of the study, research questions and scope of the study), followed by the literature reviews, research methodology (explaining the sampling design, research design and data collection methods) and data analysis with a results and conclusion made. The report prepared will include the annexure of questionnaire or interview schedule used data collection and any other information relevant to the work. The report is prepared in simple and understandable language so that it explains the concepts and addresses the problem with clarity and rationality.

Review Questions

1. Explain the research process.
2. What are the methods of sampling?
3. Explain the process of developing objectives, research questions and hypothesis with example.
4. Explain the types of research design.
5. What are the methods of data collection?
6. Explain the process involved to conduct the research in understanding the satisfaction of customers with the new brand of toothpaste.

Chapter 3

Research Design

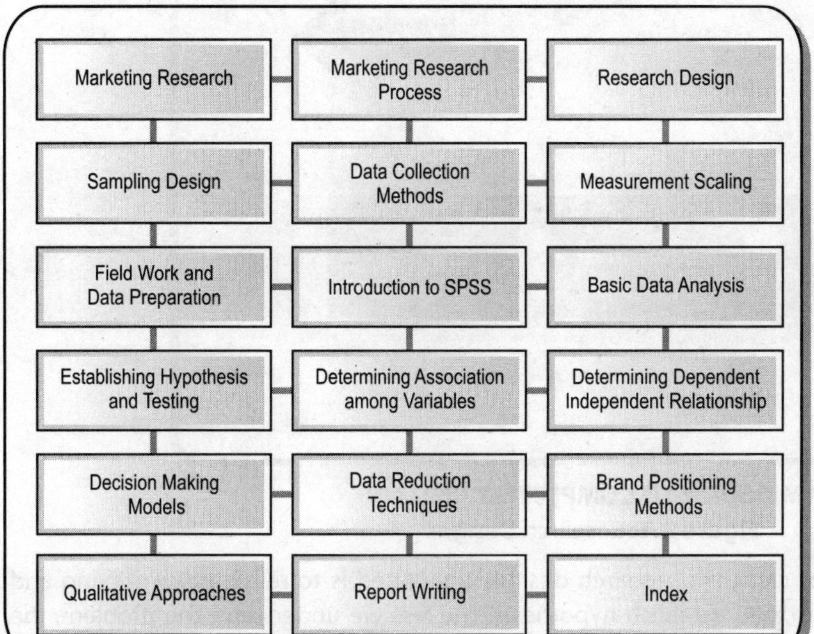

Outline

Chapter Structure

- Introduction
- Exploratory Research Design
- Descriptive Research Design
- Causal Research Design
- Review Questions
- Recommended Readings

Chapter Overview

Chapter three explains in detail the basic research designs used in marketing research and its application in specific situations. The chapter discusses the different stages of research and application of the three basic types of research design.

INTRODUCTION

Once the research problem is identified, the objectives and hypothesis are stated, the next phase is to finalize the research design. A research design is the plan of methods and techniques in conducting the research. The choice of research design depends on the research problem studied and the purpose and methods of doing research. Research design is the blue print of the research project. It explains the population studied, sampling frame, sampling method, sample size, data collection method, and the tools planned for analysis. It gives the framework of the research to be pursued or a plan for investigation into the problem. Based on the purpose and the decision required for the problem, the research design can be broadly classified as exploratory, descriptive, and causal.

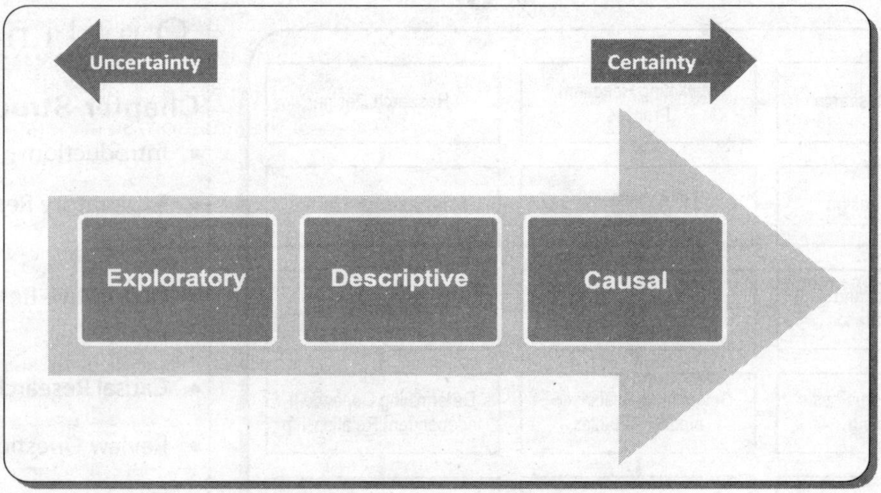

AMBIGUITY TO COMPLETELY CERTAIN

Figure 3.1: Research Designs

If the problem of research is not clear, the research design formulated is to result in identifying and formulating the research problem, and establish hypothesis. The less we understand the problem, the more exploratory the design becomes. If the research problem is clear and the situation is to be described and measured with the variables involved, it involves descriptive research design. In describing and understanding the problem, the variables may exercise an association and relationship. This requires an establishment of causal research design to determine and establish such relationship.

EXPLORATORY RESEARCH DESIGN

The purpose of formulating an exploratory research design is to identify and formulate the problem in order to derive alternative courses of action. Since the research problem is not clear, the hypothesis is not formulated and tested. Predetermined set of procedures are not followed instead unstructured or informal method is adopted to explore. So there is more flexibility in conducting research. The researcher seeks to understand the problem situation and formulate objectives and hypothesis with clear insights. The results of the research will further lead to future research initiatives.

Searching for Secondary Information: Search for literatures to identify similar problem situations and the ways in which the problem is approached and explored. It may be by searching external or internal resources. Internal resources include company records, and internal data bases. External resources include published databases, government records, journals and magazines. The search of literatures will help the researchers to focus the problem. For instance, the reduction in sales of a brand can be explored from the previous history of its trend, seasonal index and business cycles. But it may not help them understand the current situation exactly. It requires observation into the problem situation.

Observing the Problem Situation: Examining the situation will help the researchers to learn the nature of the problem and the variables influencing. This requires going back to the case and investigating the background of the problem. For example, to understand the reason for lesser sales performance of the new brand of a refrigerator, the situation should be clearly examined. This will help the researcher to understand the independent variable that influences the sales. It may be price, advertising, sales promotion, dealer promotion, store display, brand name itself or the performance of the product. Since the investigation happens after the problem, it may lead to subjective interpretation of the situation. So understanding the problem from the persons involved or from the experts will help to formulate the problem more precisely.

Interviewing the Individuals Involved or with the Experts: It is highly desirable to understand the problem from the individuals involved. In the case of decline in sales, the sales persons and the customers can be interviewed to understand the problem situation. Unstructured interviews or questionnaire will help the researcher to find the involved. Focus group discussion is another technique that is commonly used at exploratory stage. The group consists of 8 to 12 members discussing about the problem to understand the background reasons and evolve solutions. A moderator makes the focus group to concentrate the discussion around the problem. Such discussions are useful for the problems related to new products, generation of new ideas to market or position the existing products, developing creative advertising and merchandising. The discussion will happen for about an hour to share the opinion, attitude and information about the problem situation.

Exploratory research design results in understanding the problem situation precisely. So in many situations it is qualitative in nature. The techniques adopted to collect data include observation, focus group discussion, investigation, personal interviews, open end surveys, video conferencing and projective techniques like word association tests, sentence completion tests, role play, Thematic Apperception Test, and depth interviews. These methods of data collection are further discussed in Chapter 5. Simulation of the problem situation will also help to understand the research problem and its components. Simulation creates a prototypical situation, its effect, and investigating with it happens.

DESCRIPTIVE RESEARCH DESIGN

Describing the market behaviour or situations is accomplished with a descriptive research design. Descriptive research is a structured research design where the research problem is clearly defined; objectives and hypothesis are formulated; and data collected to make analysis and draw conclusions. The hypothesis stated will be proved or disproved with the analysis made. The research will clearly explain what the problem is, why it has happened, how to solve it. Descriptive research design is carried out as a quantitative research in general. It is more of a preplanned and organized research design. Planning is done with respect to information to be collected, methods and sources of data collection, tools and techniques to be adopted for analysis, and procedures to draw conclusion. This design is appropriate to perform product, price, promotion, distribution and market research studies.

For example, to introduce the new brand of car in the premium segment, the marketer first identifies the customer, their preferable outlets in buying a car, features of the car and the price, service outlets expected, and the media that communicates. This research can be performed by establishing descriptive research design. The results convey the description of the market and identifying the variables influencing the performance of the car in the segment. Association among the variables is studied that helps in future predictions. The performance of the car can be understood with the sales that exist. Prediction of the sales performance can be established with the variables influencing. In this case sales performance is the dependent variable that depends on the influence of the independent variables like price, brand, features, services, etc. Associations are used to infer and make predictions and not to establish relationship of causality. Descriptive designs can be cross sectional or longitudinal.

Cross Sectional Design: It is adopted if the research is to be conducted once and during a specific period of time.

For instance, in understanding the sales performance, the variables influencing sales can be studied with the extent of its influence. The variables influencing sales may be sales promotion, advertising, sales men performance, and competitor's strategies. The impact of these independent variables on dependent variable (sales) is studied during the period of survey. It can also result in the predictions made with the data collected during that point of time. On conducting cross sectional research for a specific time period, predictions may not hold good as the behaviour of independent variables and its impact on sales are not studied continuously. It results in longitudinal research designs.

Longitudinal Research Design: The research studies can be continued after regular intervals. In predicting the performance of sales, if the sales performance is studied after every 6 months it is longitudinal in nature. The continuation of the research work for a long period adopts longitudinal research design. Longitudinal research designs measures the performance of the same sample repeatedly for a specific time period. If a sample is observed for a long period, they are representatives of the population, forming a sample panel for observation. These panels will be selected to represent different segments, demographics and geographic. This makes the continuous study to represent the opinion of the total population.

For example, an FMCG brand studying the consumers preference towards their brand, will select the consumer panel who represent different segments like housewife, working, students, etc from different places of the city with different income level and age group. Consumer panel may also be interviewed to understand the reason for brand preference. For this purpose, standard or unstandardized questions can be used. It can be the same questions every time or it may vary with time. It depends on the research requirements. In order to understand the brand preferences or brand switching behaviour, same questions are asked at regular intervals to know the brand preferred and reasons for the same. In case of market tracking studies, longitudinal studies are generally preferred. It helps the researcher to understand the changes in the brand preference, price, market share and its impact on consumer behaviour.

CAUSAL RESEARCH DESIGN

In establishing relationship among variable, causality may exist. It is the result of cause and effect relationship that comes in reality.

For example, if advertisement is effective, it results in increased sales. The effectiveness of advertisement may depend on the celebrity used or music, jingles, story, screen play, etc. There exists relationship among all the variables. The increase in sales is not controllable and it is a dependent variable. Effectiveness of advertisement is an independent variable which is decided by the marketers. This will have the effect of variables like celebrity, music, story, etc., which are called as extraneous variable. These extraneous variables may have some effect on the dependent variable, sales. These relationships are brought out in causal research design.

Causality is brought out clearly with the experimentations done with the dependent and independent variables. Experiments can be field experiments or laboratory experiments. It brings into limelight the impact of extraneous variables. Causal research designs are well established by Structural Equation Modeling.

Field Experiments

In case of field experiments, the behaviour of dependent and independent variables are studied in the real setting.

For instance, behaviour of consumers studied in super markets, retail shops, shopping malls, etc are field studies. If the preference towards a new ad copy is to be studied, the ad copy can be displayed in a retail outlet to understand its effect on consumers who visit. This brings the variables consumers look into in an ad copy, the variables that may influence the preference but not directly like the time of visit of the consumers, etc.

Field studies bring more validity for the experimentation made. But it is more time consuming. **Test marketing** is another type of field experimentation carried out. Firms like to understand the consumer preferences will select a sample city or place to test the product. The sample place select to test the product should be representative enough to ensure validity of the results. If the product is accepted in the test markets, it ensures the acceptance in the whole geographical region.

For example, air lines test marketing the acceptance of snack variety with few flights around the globe, new FMCG (Fast Moving Consumer Goods) test marketed for its acceptance in a sample city, etc.

Laboratory Experiments

Laboratory settings study the behaviour of dependent variable with the manipulated behaviour of dependent variable. It controls the impact of extraneous variable to a greater extent. Different types of experimentation made in a controlled setting are:

Time-series Experiment: In time series experimentation, a group of test units or a panel of consumers is observed over a period of time in a controlled setting. The behaviour of consumers is recorded continuously with regular time periods to understand the trend that exists.

For example, in brand preference studies, the preference studied continuously with regular intervals helps the marketers to understand the trend in the preference exerted by the consumers.

Before – After Research Design without Control Group: The behaviour of experimental units can be studied without any experimentation and with experimentation and the difference is studied.

For instance, in understanding the preference of consumers towards a product, the preference can be measured on a scale ranging from strongly agree to strongly disagree (Refer Likert Scale in Chapter 6). If sales promotion is the experimentation done, it is introduced after measuring the preference of consumers towards the product. The preference of consumers towards the product is measured again in the same scale. The difference in the preference before sales promotion and after sales promotion reveals the impact of sales promotion (the experimentation done).

After only Research Design with Control Group: In this type of experimentation there will be two groups of respondents. One group undergoes experimentation (Experimental group) and another group without any experimentation (Control group). The difference in the performance of two groups after treatment will reveal the effect of experimentation.

For example, if the effect of sales promotion is to be studied, on group without utilizing sales promotion and another with sales promotion are considered. The difference in the preference of two groups of consumers is studied.

Before – After Research Design with Control Group: In this design, two groups experimental group and control group exist. Experimental group undergo treatment and control group remains the same. Before beginning the treatment or experimentation, the two groups are measured. Then treatment is introduced only for the experimental group. After the treatment, the behaviour of the two groups is again measured. The effect of the treatment is given by the difference in the behaviour of the two groups (experimental and control). The behaviour of the experimental group is revealed by the difference in the performance before and after treatment. Similarly the behaviour of the control group is studied before and after the treatment given to the experimental group.

For example, in case of sales promotion, one group of respondents is offered sales promotion and another group don't avail sales promotion. The preference of both the groups before and after introduction of sales promotion is studied and the difference across the group reveals the impact of sales promotion.

Thus an experimental research design makes scientific investigation to manipulate and control the behaviour of independent variables to understand the variation caused in dependent variables and others. The validity of this research design increases with the control of extraneous variables and the extent of generalization of the outcome.

Review Questions

1. Explain research design.
2. What are the different types of research designs?
3. Explain the types of experimental research designs.
4. What are the types of descriptive research design?
5. Explain the application of an exploratory research design.
6. A leading soft drink manufacturer decided to understand the effectiveness of store promotion. Two stores in Delhi were selected for the study. New promotion was introduced in one retail store and the other retail store continued with the existing promotion. Store display, sales men support, in store promotion, with the sales performance was studied for 10 days. They observed an increase in the sales of the retail store with new promotion.

   What is the appropriate research design to understand is there a significant increase in the sales with the new promotions made?

Recommended Readings

The recommended readings lists the research articles that demonstrate the six research designs discussed elaborately in the chapter.

1. "Factors Affecting 'Internet Marketing' Campaigns with Reference to Viral and Permission Marketing" Shukla, Timira; Institute of Chartered Financial Analysts of India (Hyderabad). *The ICFAI Journal of Management Research.* Hyderabad: Jan 2010; Vol. 9, Issue 1; p. 26.
2. "Veterans Returning From War in to the Classroom: How Can Colleges Be Better Prepared To Meet Their Needs?" Zinger, Lana; Cohen, Andrea; *Contemporary Issues in Education Research.* Littleton: Jan 2010; Vol. 3, Issue. 1; p. 39.
3. "Determinants of Online Shopping: Examination of an Early-Stage Online Market" Liebermann, Yehoshua; Stashevsky, Shmuel; *Canadian Journal of Administrative Sciences.* Halifax: Dec 2009; Vol. 26, Issue 4; p. 316.
4. "Does Consumers' Demographic Profile Influence Online Shopping?: An Examination Using Fishbein's Theory/EST-CE QUE LE PROFILE DÉMOGRAPHIQUE DES CONSOMMATEURS INFLUENCE LES ACHATS

EN LIGNE?: UNE EXPERTISE EN UTILISANT LA THÉORIE DE FISHBEIN" Hashim, Afizah; Ghani, Erlane K; Said, Jamaliah; *Canadian Social Science.* Montreal: Dec 31, 2009; Vol. 5, Issue 6; p. 19.

5. "Consumer Privacy Concerns and Preference for Degree of Regulatory Control: A Study of Mobile Advertising in Japan" Okazaki, Shintaro; Li, Hairong; Hirose, Morikazu; *Journal of Advertising.* Armonk: Winter 2009; Vol. 38, Issue 4; p. 63.

6. "Effects of Interactivity on Website Involvement and Purchase Intention" Jiang, Zhenhui; Chan, Jason; Tan, Bernard C Y; Chua, Wei Siong; *Journal of the Association for Information Systems.* Atlanta: Jan 2010; Vol. 11, Issue 1; p. 34.

Chapter 4

Sampling Design

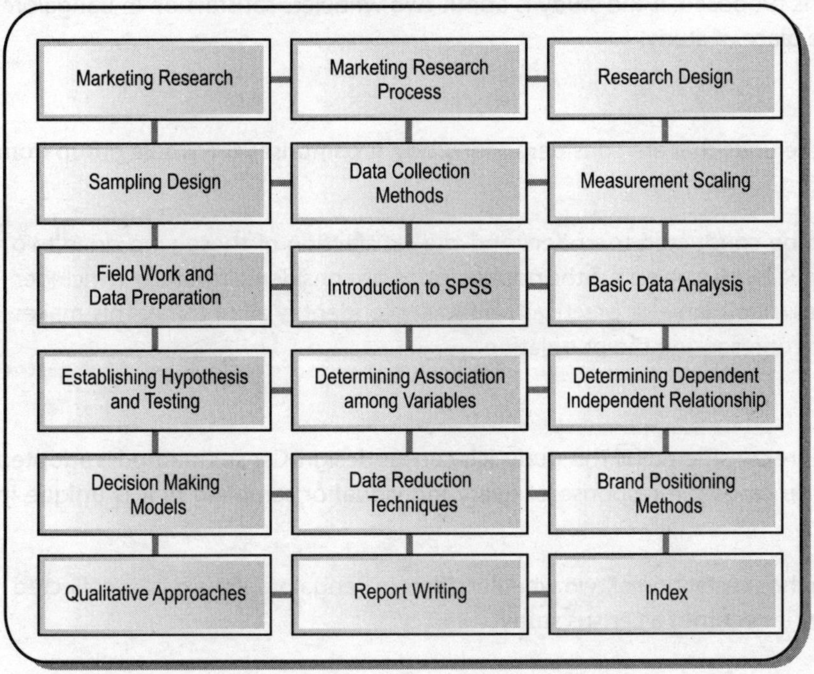

Outline

Chapter Structure

- Introduction
- Sampling Process
- Sampling Methods
- Sample Size Determination
- Sampling Errors
- Review Questions

Chapter Overview

Chapter four discusses the sampling process in an elaborate manner. It explains the sequence of steps followed in selecting a sample. The different methods of sampling, the errors that occur in sampling and cautions to make. The chapter also brings in the method of determining the sample size to select the adequate number of sample for the study.

INTRODUCTION

Research in marketing begins and ends with consumers. Consumers are the members in the universe from whom the research begins and ultimately the results of the research target to identify and satisfy consumer needs. This requires identification of the right members of the universe to begin the research. Sampling design explains the method or process used to draw the members of the universe, the sample, in order to conduct the study. It explains the sampling frame, the sampling method, and the sample size to be selected. This is done because it is not practically possible to conduct the study on the whole of the population. Some of the terms that explain the sampling process clearly are discussed below.

Universe

Universe is the place the study is proposed. If the study is about two wheelers satisfaction in Bangalore, Bangalore is the universe or the place of study.

Population

It includes the whole frame or the units that are considered for study. It comprises the whole group from whom information is to be sought.

For instance, if the study is to be conducted to understand the satisfaction of those who drive two wheelers, then all those who drive two wheelers are the population to be considered for study. It includes a large number and sometimes indefinable or practically difficulty to identify all of them. This makes the researcher to draw sample representing the population.

Census

If all elements of the population are considered for the study, it is census design. Census method is adopted if the sampling unit is small or in cases the response of every individual or sampling unit is unique in nature.

For example, in understanding the satisfaction of two wheeler riders in Bangalore, if the data is collected from all the two wheeler riders, it becomes a census study.

Sample

Sample is the representation of the population drawn with any of the sampling methods in order to conduct the study. It is the small division or illustration of the population. Sample will help the researcher to draw inferences about the population studied. It saves the time and cost involved in collected the data from the whole population. Parameter estimations (information about population) are made from the statistical inferences made from the information collected from the sample. These generalizations hold well if the sampling method is accurate and represents the population.

Sampling Frame

Sampling frame includes the criteria with which the sample is selected. For instance, if the satisfaction towards the two wheelers is studied in Bangalore, then the sampling frame is Bangalore. If the study is conducted among the teen agers, then teen agers in Bangalore is the sampling frame. It is the elements of the population that explains the population. If the study is conducted among specific club members, then it becomes the sampling frame.

Sampling Distribution

It includes the distribution of sample considered for study. A representative or repeat sampling will ensure normal distribution of the sample. More the sample is normally distributed; it ensures better representation of the population. This is because, population generally is distributed normally any number of sample that is normally distributed will better represent the characteristics of population.

SAMPLING PROCESS

If it is decided to collect the data from a sample, the process involved in sampling is to be understood. Once the sampling frame and the sampling method is decided, the sample will be identified and selected. It involves the following steps:

- Identify the population to be studied. Define the characteristics of the population that will further help to identify sample with similar characteristics. Clear understanding of population as to who, where and when are to be recognized.

For example, to understand the satisfaction of customers, it is required to understand the type of customers, loyal or all customers during a period of time, or with specific income or age category, specific geographic area, and more specific the extent and time.

- If the population is identified, the size of the population will become clear. It helps the researcher to decide to select all the members or representative members of the population. The decision regarding census or a sample depends on the sampling unit or the universe considered for the study and the sample size. If the sampling unit is small and the population is less in number, census survey is possible.

For instance, in introducing a discount sample and to understand the consumers preference to it, data can be collected with all those consumers availing it during the discount period. If the discount period is one month, it may not be possible to collect data from all consumers which require selecting a sample. Once the population is identified, the decision regarding the type of study – census or sample is made.

- Once the decision of the study is made, the method or type of sampling is to be decided. If the study requires an unbiased sample, it requires adoption of probability sampling method. If non probability sampling method is adopted, it depends on the expertise of the researcher in selecting the representative sample.
- Finalization of the sampling method also depends on the sample size. Sample size can be smaller if the sampling method is more objective. This happens with random sampling that gives the representation of the population objectively. In case of non-probability sampling method, increased sample size will reduce the bias of sampling method. Even a small sample will be

sufficient if it brings the characteristics of the population in the right manner. The size depends on the time, cost and the budget available with the researcher.

➢ The final stage is the actual selection of the sample with the method decided. There may be challenges in acquiring the decided sample size and executing an unbiased sampling method in reality. This should be overcome with the experience of the researcher.

For instance, in interviewing a customer, the accompanying person may be interviewed who may not represent the population. There may also occur non response error or refusal for participation from sample. This requires researcher to opt for alternate sample. In case of online questionnaires, required number of responses may not be reached. This may compel the researcher to reduce the sample size, or extend the sampling method in a different sampling unit.

SAMPLING METHODS

Method of sampling can be categorized under probabilistic and non-probabilistic methods. Probability sampling is an objective method of sampling where every member of the population has equal opportunity to be selected as the sample. It is more scientific and systematic in bringing in the representation from the population. Common methods of probability sampling are: simple random sampling, systematic sampling, stratified sampling, cluster sampling, area sampling and multi stage sampling. But every research may not be able to adopt probability sampling due to the constraint of resources. In such cases, non-probability sampling is adopted. Non-probability sampling will not allow each member of the population to have equal participation in being a sample. The methods of non-probability sampling include: convenient sampling, judgemental sampling, quota sampling and snow ball sampling.

Simple Random Sampling

Random sampling gives equal opportunity of selection of the population for the best representation. In this method, the population is listed and assigned with random numbers within the sampling frame. For instance, to understand the preference of consumers towards a retail outlet in an area, identify the households, assign them with numbers consecutively. Random number table is generated in Microsoft excel or an existing random table is used. Select a part of the table. Choose those numbers from the random table if they are in the assigned list of the population. This selection of sample from the population identified from the random table gives complete randomness in the sample selected. It is more objective and gives best representation of the population. If the population is comparatively small, the numbers or their names can be written in chits and lots can be picked up to identify the sample. This lottery method also gives randomness in the sample selected. This method of sampling is possible only if sampling frame is identified. So it has application in industrial marketing researches where the sample consists of limited number of dealers or intermediaries.

For example, understanding the effectiveness of supply chain from dealers is possible to conduct with random sampling. Application of this sampling method for consumer research is limited as the complete list of household in an area is generally not available.

Systematic Sampling

Simple random sample can be extended systematically with a known and equal probability of selection. In a population of 1000, there may be 100 members to be selected as the sample. For this purpose, every 10th member can be selected as the sample. To select the first person, simple random sampling can be adopted to bring randomness. Then the pattern of every 10th member continues. If the interval is 6 then, every 6th member of the population will be selected. This method is followed to select sample from a list of population e.g., from telephone directory, from mobile subscribers list, etc. It need not list the population and assign numbers. Instead, the method is adopted if there is an existing list in a pattern (ascending or descending) and sometimes even if the population size is unknown.

For instance, if the consumers visiting a shopping mall is to be interviewed, using systematic sampling, every 5th member entering the mall will be sample. The survey will continue till the required sample is attained. In this case, the population size may not be available. But randomness is brought in by selecting the members in a pattern.

Stratified Sampling

Stratification of the sample is done if there are more groups that exist in the population. In such cases right representation of the population is possible if sample is selected from all groups or stratum. Stratification increases the accuracy of representation with relatively small sample size representing all groups. The population is divided into different homogeneous groups or strata. Each group or stratum is different from one another. Stratum may be classified based on age, income, gender, geographical region, or with unique characteristics.

The sample is selected from each stratum with simple random sampling method. The decisions to be made before selection of sample include:

- bases of stratification,
- number of strata, and
- sample to be selected from each stratum.

Bases for stratification may be geographic, demographic, or socio-economic. It is important to form strata which have similarity in the characteristics of the population within the strata. But the characteristics of population between strata should be different. Limited members in each stratum will give more accuracy and representation. Decisions regarding the number of strata depend on the consistency within the population and the budget available to form more strata. Sample selected from each stratum may be proportionate or disproportionate to the size of the stratum. In case of proportionate stratified sampling, the sample selected is proportionate to the size of the population in each stratum. It may not be the case with disproportionate stratified sampling where equal representations from each stratum can be made irrespective of the size of the stratum.

For instance, to select 100 sample respondents from two strata of 800 male and 200 female, 80 male and 20 female respondents will make stratified proportionate random sample. If 50 male and 50 female respondents are selected from each stratum, it is disproportionate random sampling. In selection of these sample from each stratum, simple random sampling is adopted.

Cluster Sampling

Cluster sampling is adopted if the population is homogeneous and requires quick selection of a large sample. In this case, the population is grouped into clusters of small size. Simple random sampling is used to select few clusters to reach the required sample size. The characteristics of the population across clusters should be the same to have good representation.

For example, to select households in a large town, cluster sampling can be adopted. In this case, the whole town can be classified into different blocks or clusters that have the similar population. Few of these clusters can be selected using simple random sampling. This will help to identify the representative sample from a huge population.

Area Sampling

Area sampling is a random sampling done on geographical area. Geographical maps form the sampling frame. To select the sample across countries to study the multicultural perspectives, area sampling is adopted. The area to be studied is identified with names of states or cities or streets or villages. Random sampling is adopted to select few of this area from where data is collected. This method is adopted to study the success of policies and strategies across the nation.

Multi-stage Sampling

If any of the random sampling is performed with different levels or stages, it is multi-stage sampling.

For instance, in area sampling, after selecting few states, random sampling can again be used to select few places in the selected states. Further to select the sample in these places, random sampling can be further employed. Thus random sampling is used to select few states and few places in the selected states and few members from each place. Sampling is performed at three levels and classified multi-stage sampling. Multi-stage sampling is generally adopted in nation wise surveys.

Convenient Sampling

This is more ad hoc method of sampling. The samples that are accessible, easy to approach and collect data and those who will cooperate are identified as sample. This method brings best representation if it is used in a more homogeneous group.

For instance if the study is conducted in a city like Bangalore that has representation from all the states due to software firms, anyone selected in the city will bring in randomness. But if the researcher brings in his friends and relatives, it will have more bias. This method is used in case of "mall intercept surveys". In these surveys, the respondents will to participate and volunteering to be surveyed is considered as sample. This method of sampling is used in retail stores and consumer surveys. It will bring in more respondents in less time from a cooperating group of consumers. In order to bring better representation, sample size is relatively large in convenient sampling.

Judgemental Sampling

If the researcher is experienced in identifying the right sample, judgmental sampling that identifies the sample based on the judgment of the researcher will bring best representation of the sample. Sampling of this type is also called as 'Purpose Sampling'. Samples are drawn from the universe if assumed it will better bring in the behaviour of the population. But this method may have the bias of the researcher in identifying the right sample as it depends on the judgment of the researcher. So the expertise of the researcher in identifying the right sample will bring good representation of the population.

For instance, in order to launch a new brand, the firm may prefer to study the penetration strategies to be adopted. The research will target the competitors offering similar products and the prospective consumers. It is less costly in drawing samples than other methods. However a lot of assumptions are made about the sample drawn.

Quota Sampling

Quota sampling is used if the target sample requires specified number of respondents from different categories of the population. Quota sampling is if representation from all the sectors or categories is required as per the discretion of the researcher.

For example, in selecting 100 respondents from the different age groups, the researcher may decide to select 15 percent in age group less than 20 years and 35 percent in age group between 20 to 30 years and 40 percent in age between 30 to 40 years and 10 percent of age 40 years and above.

This condition of quota will be fixed based on the target sample for the research. If the research is to understand the behaviour of consumers towards different brands of big size cars, the quota specified will be appropriate. If the study proposes to understand the behaviour of youth in buying a mobile phone, the quota will consists of more youth in the age category of 15 years to 25 years. It is commonly used method of non-probability sampling as it gives better representation of the sample. This method will be successful in bringing in the right mix of the sample if the quotas are correctly fixed. It has more application in consumer opinion surveys as it has the flexibility in bringing the required category of sample.

Snowball Sampling

It is a referral or multiplicity sampling method. If the target sample is not known or not approachable, this method of sampling is adopted. Increasing the sample from one of few respondents to identify the sample is done.

For instance, to understand the satisfaction of services among foreign tourists, a travel agency may not be able to approach the foreign tourists and collect data. For this purpose, the reference of few tourists may help them to identify more samples. These referrals may extend to second level also. The referred sample will again refer more samples to target. This is continued till the required sample sized is enquired. This method is generally adopted if the characteristics of the population are rare and not easily identifiable or approachable. Snowball method increases sample with each level and increases the response rate and helps to identify the qualified respondents.

Panel Sampling

In consumer surveys, there may exist situation to understand the opinion of the same set of respondents continuously in regular intervals. Same respondents or sample units are surveyed on regular basis i.e. once a month or once a week. This is done from a fixed panel to understand the variation in the opinion of the respondents over different periods of time. The sample unit or the panel members may be selected with complete randomness. But if the same respondents are surveyed repeatedly, randomness may not continue. This is because in reality the target universe will change over time. The existing players may enter new segments and new players enter the market. So the representation of the universe may not continue with the selected panel members in long run. So it is more a non-probability sample after subsequent rounds of survey. This method is generally adopted in case of experimentation surveys that explore the change in behaviour of consumers with different treatments.

SAMPLE SIZE DETERMINATION

Sample size is appropriate if it makes best representation of the sample. The sample should be reliable enough to make appropriate prediction of the behaviour of the population. Rule of thumb states that even 30 respondents will best represent the population if selected with due diligence. Decision on the size of the sample depends on the variation in the responses. More the population is homogeneous; lesser the size of the sample preferred and heterogeneity in population requires increased sample size comparatively. The mathematical formula worked by statisticians is:

$$n = (\partial Z)^2 / (E)^2$$

where 'E' is the standard error that can be allowed in the study. It is the difference allowed between the sample mean and the population mean. 'μ' the population mean is given by $\bar{X} \pm E$. Z is the standard error of the confidence interval. In general, 95% confidence interval is considered which has a standard error of 1.96. Standard error of the mean, ∂ is given by allowable error 'E' divided by standard error of the confidence interval, 'Z'.

$$\partial = E / Z$$

For example, in a study to measure customer preference, seven point scale is used where '1' represents low level of preference and '7' represent high level of preference to the statements in the preference scale. The assumed level of confidence level is 95 percent with a standard error, Z of 1.96. Deviation of sample mean from population mean 'E' is not known and a rough approximation of 0.5 is made. Standard error of the mean '∂' is given by range divided by the mid-scale value 3. Range is given by the difference between the maximum and the minimumscale value (7-1 = 6).

$$\partial = 6 / 3 = 2$$

Hence $n = (2 * 1.96)^2 / (0.5)^2 = 61$ (approx.)

Therefore a sample size of 61 will estimate the customer preference measured on a 7-point scale at 95 percent confidence level with a deviation in the sample mean of 0.5 from the population mean.

In practice, the formulas are not followed and ultimately the experience of the researcher and the type of sampling helps him to have the right sample size. Sometimes it is decided by budget available.

SAMPLING ERRORS

Sampling error occurs generally if the sample is not the true representation of the population. Sampling errors can be reduced with adoption of random and unbiased selection of sample. Extent of sampling errors can be estimated in case of probability samples. Increased sample size and appropriate sampling method generally reduces sampling errors. This is basically the problem that occurs in the choice of the sample. Other than the error in sampling process, errors may occur due to nonresponse or selection of wrong sample.

Sampling method and size is the challenge that a researcher addresses. The modern methods of data collection using internet services may not use these traditional sampling methods. In such cases feedback questionnaires with existing customers orsending the questionnaire to selected audience or sending questionnaires to all possible respondents who visit during a specified period may be adopted.

Review Questions

1. Explain the terms 'census' and 'sample'.
2. Explain the process involved in selecting a sample.
3. Discuss the methods of sampling.
4. What is an appropriate sample size for a research study?

Chapter 5

Data Collection Methods

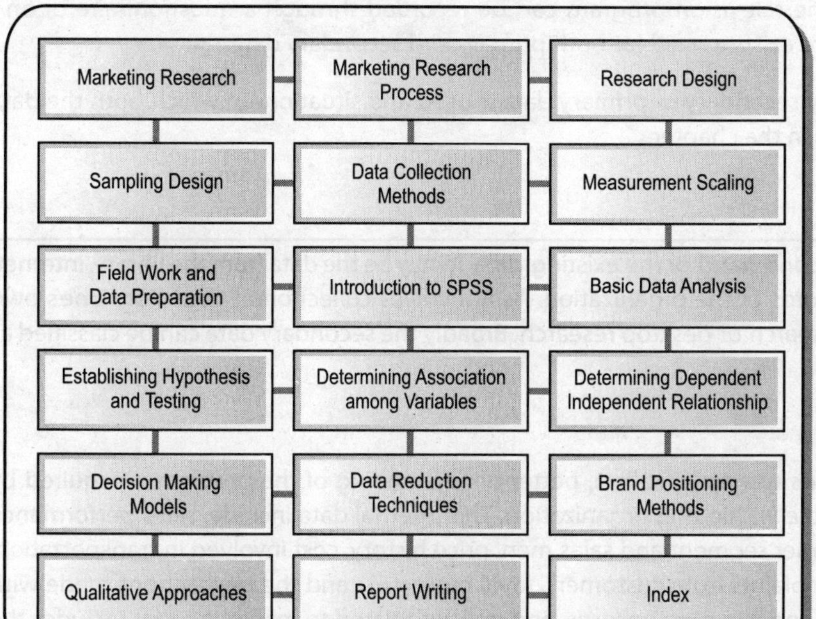

Outline

Chapter Structure

- Introduction
- Secondary Data
- Sources of Secondary Data
- Primary Data
- Data Collection Techniques
- Review Questions
- Sample Questionnaire

Chapter Overview

Chapter five elaborates the methods of collecting data. It includes the secondary sources and primary data collection methods. The chapter details the situation in which a specific method of data collection tool is used.

INTRODUCTION

Marketing research activities require data to make analysis and further lead to decision making. The data required may exist at different sources or may be required to be collected for the research. Collecting the existing data and using for the research is an easier task compared to the data that is to be collected further. The data existing is called the secondary data and the data to be collected fresh for the research purpose is called the primary data.

For instance, to understand the consumer's interest in viewing a program in television, both primary secondary data can be used. Consumer rating index prepared by research firms can be the secondary source that reveals the consumers interest. The secondary data available may not be updated or not customized. This situation will demand for primary data collection. The primary data to understand the consumer's opinion about the television program can be recorded through a questionnaire or an interview schedule. Thus there exists a need for both primary and secondary data.

There are situations where only secondary or primary data is used and situations in which both the data are used. It is further discussed in the chapter.

SECONDARY DATA

Secondary data refers to the 'second-hand' or the 'existing' data. It may be the data from the library, internet, data bases, or the internal records of the organization. As it involves collection of data from one's own desk, it is also called as 'desk research' or 'desktop research'. Broadly the secondary data can be classified as Internal and External.

Internal Secondary Data

If the research problem pertains to a specific firm, better understanding of the problem is acquired by going through the data available within that organization. This internal data include: sales performance by category, geography, customer segment and sales men, price history, cost involved in transportation, competitors performance, complaints from customers, loyal customers and the transactions made with them, web page visitors, stock and inventory records, and policies related to marketing that includes the advertising policy, pricing policy, etc. Internal data becomes the first hand information available for further enquiry.

For instance, if the sales are declining, the trend, seasonal index and cyclical index will help to understand the reason. If it is because of the trend, season or business cycle, the marketer can continue and withstand the situation. If not, the marketer should further probe the situation to identify reasons. The internal data is available through intranets in the organization to share across the departments and generally free of cost.

External Secondary Data

Data available from the resources outside the organization will also aid the researchers to address the problem.

The advantages and disadvantages in procuring and using secondary data for research purpose are as follows:

Advantages of Secondary Data

- Data is easily available as it exists already.
- Less time and cost is involved in collection.
- It doesn't require expertise to formulate the instrument of data collection.
- Secondary data is available for a length of period.

For instance, in understanding the sales performance, the data on the sales performance may exist for 10 years or 20 years in the organizational records. It provides the history of performance which may not be possible to record in a primary data collection.

Disadvantages of Secondary Data

- Data may not satisfy the needs of the specific research or it may not be sufficient enough.
- Availability of the secondary data is not assured unless we acquire it.
- Amount spent to search for secondary data will become waste if the data is not available. So it becomes costly as it is uncertain to predict the availability of the data.
- It may be outdated. For instance, data on consumer satisfaction, if outdated, is a waste data.
- Existing data may not be available in uniform format.

For instance, data collected on textile exports may not measure the same type of textiles for all years measured. For some years, it includes the exports only to quota countries, or both quota and non quota countries, or it may include different items of textile for different years. recorded. This will not be useful for further analysis.

- The units of measurement may vary with the records available. This again will lack uniformity in the data available, or readiness of the data is not assured.

SOURCES OF SECONDARY DATA

The secondary sources to access data include:

Government Sources: Government sources are authenticated and published source of historical data available for research. It includes data available with the respective ministries and departments. Data published by the trade associations, government organizations and agencies form a valid data base.

Online Sources: Online data is the major source of data for research. It includes the data available in the government websites, trade organizations and other websites. It gives wider access to the source of the data available through online directories and data bases. Online journals and databases provide solution for the data search.

Academic Sources: Academic sources include data available in library, databases maintained by institutions, and research reports that give exhaustive information of the problem addressed.

Industry Sources: Industry journals, reports and databases are valid source of secondary data. It gives updated information of the industry leaders, their strategies and competitors. For example, Auto car gives updated information of automobile industry.

PRIMARY DATA

Primary data is collected exclusively for the research. It is the fresh data collected during the research and it is required in the area of marketing.

For instance, secondary data about the sales performance of the brand will help us to project the trend that may continue. But the market place is dynamic and the trend may not continue if there is shift in the consumer purchase behaviour. This understanding is required for marketers to make decisions.

Advantages of Primary Data

- Data required for the research problem in specific can be collected.
- Data is fresh and collected for the purpose of research, so it is an updated or current data that assures the validity and reliability to a greater extent.
- Data can be collected in required format and style.

Disadvantages of Primary Data

- Data collection requires usage of appropriate tools that involve experts to draft questionnaire or schedule for the requirement of the research.
- It is not a readily available data. It involves more time to collect the data.
- It is costly to administer and collect the data.

DATA COLLECTION TECHNIQUES

Primary data used for the research is to be collected for the research purpose in specific. It involves different techniques of data collection that include: observation, interview, mail questionnaire. The choice of the technique depends on the research problem, resource availability and the expertise of the research in application.

Observation Method

Observation is a technique used in marketing research to understand the consumers in the shopping place. It is done to understand the consumer's behaviour at the point of purchase. There are different types of observation based on the method involved. It include: structured vs. unstructured, disguised vs. undisguised, qualitative vs. quantitative. It requires researcher to be present in person to collect the data. It is more subjective as the behaviour of the respondent is recorded as perceived by the observer or the researcher. This method is generally not adopted individually in conclusive researches.

Structured Observation vs. Unstructured: observation Observation may follow a pattern or a sequence in an orderly fashion. For instance consumers may be observed in the same order from entry to exit. This is done to bring in certain amount of consistency in observation. This method is more structured observation. Instead, the consumers visiting a specific section of the store may be observed at random without any criterion. It is an unstructured observation.

Disguised vs. Undisguised Observation: Observation may not be explained to the consumers in performing research. This method of observation is disguised and brings in the reality in field setting or test marketing. In experimental research, the respondents are observed knowingly. It is undisguised observation.

Qualitative vs. Quantitative Observation: The data collected during observation may be qualitative or quantitative. For instance, in observing the sales men effectiveness, number of units sold in a day is quantitative and the methods employed or the skills used to sell is qualitative observation.

Interview Method

Interview method of data collection stimulates responses from the interviewee or the respondent with the questions raised by the interviewer. There are various types of interviews conducted based on the amount of standardization used and involvement of the interviewer or the researcher. Based on the type or amount of standardization of questions raised to the respondents, the methods of interview can be classified as: structured, unstructured, semi-structured and indepth interviews. Based on the method used to interview, the types of interview are: personal, telephonic and online.

Structured Interview: Same set of questions may be required to be enquired with the sample respondents. This necessitates standardized or same questions to be raised to every respondent. This will help the researcher to aggregate the responses and draw conclusion. The structured interview schedule may have open ended questions or closed ended questions.

For example, the structured interview to understand the satisfaction of consumers in using an Airline service can be:

Sample Open ended Question:

What are the factors that make you feel satisfied in using an Airline service?

Or

Sample Close ended Question:

- Are you satisfied with the services of XYZ Airlines? Yes/No
- What are the services you are satisfied to a greater extent and the services satisfied to lesser extent?
- Ticket booking services - Satisfied to greater extent/Satisfied to lesser extent/Not satisfied
- Airport clearance services - Satisfied to greater extent/Satisfied to lesser extent/Not satisfied
- Reception services - Satisfied to greater extent/Satisfied to lesser extent/Not satisfied
- Food services - Satisfied to greater extent/Satisfied to lesser extent/Not satisfied
- Air hostess services - Satisfied to greater extent/Satisfied to lesser extent/Not satisfied

Structured interview is generally used for survey research for descriptive studies more specific to collect quantitative data. Interviewers read out the questions in the same order as given in the schedule and record the responses. The responses may be recorded manually by writing it in the schedule or tape recorded and coded later. Questions are very specific and offers fixed range of responses.

Unstructured Interview: Unstructured interviews are informal interviews. Questions depend on the interviewee and his/her response. The interview has list of problems to be addressed in the interview and probed in a casual way. Questions are phrased in accordance with the respondent. This method is generally adopted in qualitative researches in specific for ethnographic research.

For example, to understand the consumers opinion about merchandising in the shop floor of a retail outlet, the interviewer would start with informal interactions and explore with simple about the retail outlet, the goods and services available, method of arrangement, convenience to select the goods, etc.

Semi-structured Interview: An interview may demand certain structurization in the beginning and then continue in an informal style.

For instance, to understand the consumers opinion in the shop floor arrangement, certain questions like their frequency of visit, the products sought may be same and later to understand their opinion about the arrangement, the interviewer can proceed based on the products they buy.

In-depth Interview: In depth interviews are more a qualitative research technique, where the respondents are given indication about the problem or situation and they are guided by the interviewer to discuss more about the problem in specific. The respondent or the interviewee is encouraged to speak and it is recorded. This method of interviewing is adopted in behavioural researches ie. to understand buyer behaviour, motives behind buying and to study their perception. It requires expertise on the part of the interviewer. It brings out the underlying reasons for the behaviour of the respondents or the consumers involved in buying. The interview may require more amount of time as it probes the reasons for the behaviour in an unstructured fashion. So it is conducted with prior appointment of the interviewee or the respondents. To make the respondent comfortable it is required for the researcher to establish a rapport and then proceed with the interview process. Recording during these interviews can be done manually or with electronic device. Prior permission should be sought in using such mechanical devices and the extent of usage of such interviews for research. It is more appropriate method of data collection for exploratory researches.

Personal Interview: Face to face interview or personal interview is the most common method of interview. It gives the advantage for the researcher to understand the feelings, emotions of the respondents at the time of interview for each and every question posed. Personal interview are generally conducted on prior appointments. In case of mall intercept interviews, there may not be any appointments fixed but conducted with the consent of the respondents. The interviewer or the researcher should have a clear understanding of the questions posed and the order in which it is to be enquired with the respondent. To get better responses, the interviewer can establish a good rapport with the respondents. It can be structured or unstructured based on the purpose of the respondents. Interviewer should follow required etiquette in fixing appointments / seeking voluntary participation, dressing for the interview, in establishing friendly relationship for the smooth conduct of the process.

Telephone Interview: If the data to be collected is comparatively less and is more standardized, telephonic interview is more appropriate. It enables the researcher to make calls and seek the response. It reduces the time and money for travel as in case of personal interviews. These interviews are common in marketing research to understand the satisfaction in visiting a store, using a promotion scheme, utilizing a service, etc. It is generally used in feedback surveys. It also has relevance for announcing sales promotions or offers and discounts for regular and loyal customers, to announce the new schemes or services to the customers and in continuing customer relationship. This type of interview requires interviewers making calls and recording responses. It also has the challenge to identify the right respondent and the personal characteristics cannot be studied.

Online Interview: Usage of computers in interview is increasing with more usage of desktops and laptops with internet connections. Computer aided personal interviewing (CAPI) allows the interviewer to ask the question and the respondent to answer online. These responses can be easily recorded and further used for data analysis. It is economical with time and money and reach large amount of respondents easily. This is advantageous in understanding the cultural differences that may exist among the consumers of different countries which is not easy to study in person. These interviews can be conducted with those visiting the specific websites or approached the specific respondent online.

There are different types of data used for research and administered by various styles. Selection of the right method to collect data with the appropriate technique for collection depends on the expertise of the researcher and it results in accuracy and reliability of the data collected.

Questionnaire Method

Collecting data through questionnaire is the most common method of data collection. It lists the questions to raised to the respondents in a specific order. The questionnaire is then sent by post, mailed or sent through online for the respondents to answer. Based on the method of drafting the question and administering it, the questionnaires can be: structured, unstructured, open ended, closed ended and online questionnaire.

Structured Questionnaire: The questions related to the research problem are listed in a sequence that gives more clarity to respond. It can be open ended or closed ended. The questions raised are same for all the respondents. This method ensures better reliability in the data collected.

For instance, the questions asked in different formats may probe different types of responses that may be avoided in a structured questionnaire. Standardization is not only in the questions but also in the responses collected.

For example, the following question may bring various responses.

Do you shop here regularly?

The response may be Yes or No or Once in a month or Once in two weeks, etc.

In a structured questionnaire, the same question can be posed as follows:

How frequently you shop here?

- Once in a month

- Once in fifteen days
- Once in a week
- Once in two days
- Every day

This method of questioning not only standardizes the questions but also the responses.

Unstructured Questionnaire: The questions pertaining to the research are listed and may not have complete guidance to respond. It is more of an open ended question that gives choice for the respondent to return.

Open-ended Questionnaire: The questions raised are left with no choice but for the responded to fill in. It is more unguided form of questionnaire. But it reveals the right opinion. For instance, to identify the major factor that drives consumers in choosing a mobile service, the respondents can be left with a choice to fill in. The choice of factors may vary among customers. Such variations are captured in open ended questionnaires. For example,

Why do you buy Fast track watches?

Closed-ended Questionnaire: This method of data collection is frequently used as it provides guidance for the respondent to select from the choices available. This method of questioning is generally used in descriptive and causal researches. It can be dichotomous question like:

Are you satisfied with our service? Yes / No

It can also be multiple choice questions. For example;

What are the services you are satisfied with our Airlines?

- Ticket booking services
- Airport clearance services
- Hospitality services
- Other services

Online Questionnaire: Floating questionnaires through online is easy and economical method of data collection. This is gaining its importance as the usage of computers and internet connectivity is popularizing. It also can be sent to respondents across various countries or broader geographies.

Data to be procured for the research – primary or secondary depend on the nature and purpose of the research problem. The methods to collect data are decided based on the research design, expertise of the researcher and the resource available for data collection. Data collection if rightly performed will result in reliable outcome and better decision making.

Review Questions

1. What are the types of data available for marketing research?
2. What are different sources of secondary data?
3. Explain the methods to collect primary data.
4. What are the types of interview performed for data collection?
5. Prepare a structured questionnaire to measure the satisfaction of consumers with new types of pizzas introduced in Dominos.
6. What are the types of questionnaire used in marketing research?
7. Explain the appropriate data to be collected and method to collect for understanding the consumer's satisfaction with the online services offered by an airlines company.

Sample Questionnaire

The following questionnaire is drafted to understand the reasons for penetration of Dove Soap in the selected villages of South Karnataka. (This is the list of sample questions from an elaborate questionnaire).

1. Do you use Dove soap for bathing? If yes, proceed. If no, suspend the process
2. What influenced you to buy Dove? (Tick whichever option is applicable)
   - o Usage among friends
   - o Usage among neighbours
   - o Advertisements
   - o Features
   - o Bought for trial
   - o Any other (please specify) ________________
3. Do all the family members use Dove? Yes / No
4. If yes, how many members use Dove? (please specify) ______
5. If no, what are the reasons for other members for not using Dove? (please specify) ____
6. How frequently do you buy Dove soap? (Tick whichever option is applicable)
   - o Once in a week
   - o Thrice in a month
   - o Twice in a month

- o Once in a month
- o Any other (please specify) ____________

7. Have you seen the advertisement of Dove? Yes / No
8. If yes, which advertisement you like the best? (please specify) ____________
9. Is Dove soap available in your retail outlets? Yes / No
10. If no, how do you buy your soap? (please specify) ____________
11. Explain the extent of influence of the following factors to prefer Dove Soap.

Give your reasons in a scale where '1' means influence to a greater extent; '2' means influence to a nominal extent; '3' means neutral influence; '4' means not influencing; '5' means not influencing to a greater extent.

S. No	Factors	1	2	3	6	5
1	I prefer Dove for its white colour and purity					
2	I prefer Dove for its perceived quality					
3	I prefer Dove for its fragrance					
4	I prefer Dove for its long lasting feature					
5	I prefer Dove because it is good for skin					
6	I prefer Dove for the confidence the brand promises					
7	I prefer Dove for its advertisement					
8	I prefer Dove because it is available in my retail outlet					
9	I prefer Dove because it is good for all seasons					
10	I prefer Dove for its price					

12. Demographic details (Tick whichever option is applicable):
    1. Name:
    2. Age (in years): Less than 15 / 15 – 25 / 25 – 35 / 35 – 45 / 45 and above
    3. Gender: Male / Female
    4. Educational Qualification: No formal education / School level / College level / Professional / Any other (please specify) ____________
    5. Family size (Number of members): ______
    6. Family Income per month (in rupees):
       - o Less than 5,000
       - o 5,000 – 10,000
       - o 10,000 – 15,000
       - o 15,000 – 20,000
       - o 20,000 and above.

Chapter 6

Measurement Scaling

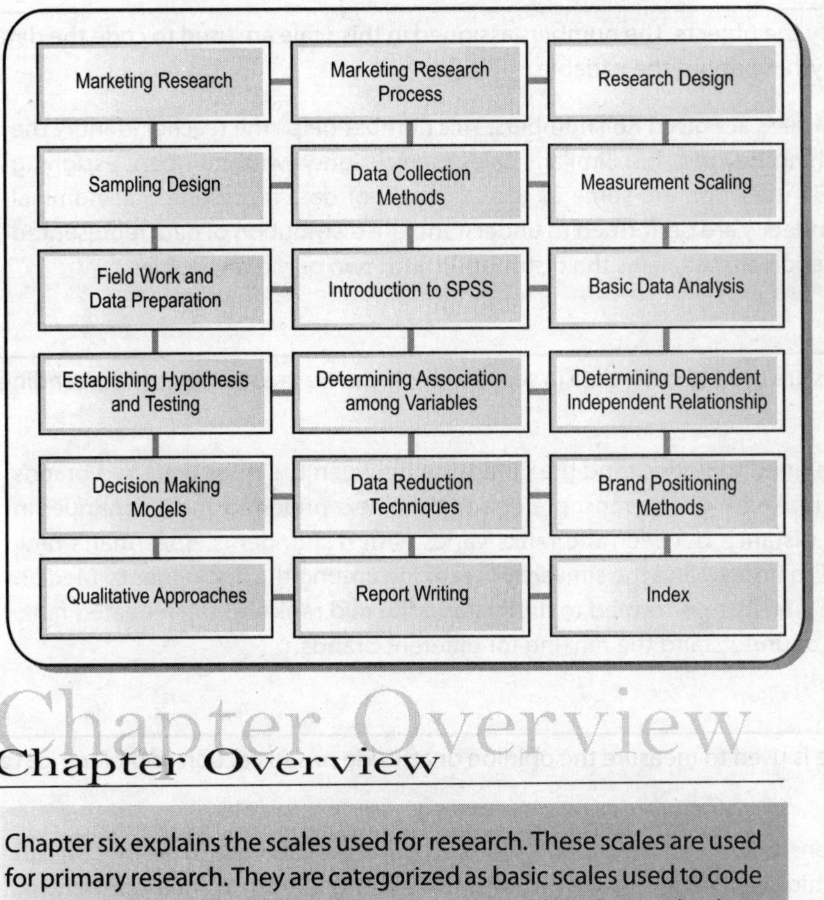

Outline

Chapter Structure

- Introduction
- Nominal Scale
- Ordinal Scale
- Interval Scale
- Ratio Scale
- Comparative Scales
- Non-comparative Scales
- Validity
- Reliability
- Review Questions

Chapter Overview

Chapter six explains the scales used for research. These scales are used for primary research. They are categorized as basic scales used to code data and comparative and non-comparative scales. The methods to ensure validity and reliability in using these scales are also discussed.

INTRODUCTION

Research in marketing deals with consumers, channel members and sales men. Dealing with human always has the risk in prediction. So the secondary data collected may not reveal the consumer opinion as on date. To overcome this problem, primary data appropriate for the research is collected. In collecting primary data using questionnaire, opinion, perception, satisfaction and attitude are measured in scale that converts them into numerical data. The variables and the extension of acceptance or rejection to the variable is measured in scales that are coded into numerical data. Primary scales used for measurement are: Nominal, Ordinal, Interval and Ratio.

NOMINAL SCALE

These scales are used to identify the objects. The numbers assigned in this scale are used to code the data collected. It doesn't explain anything about the variable.

For instance, the students in a class are given Roll numbers. This number helps the teacher identify the students but not reveal anything beyond this. Similarly sales men assigned with numbers, assigning numbers to the brands for identification are some of the examples of data represented as nominal scale. Measures are central tendency are performed to understand the distribution of data represented by nominal scale. Cross tabulation also explains the distribution with two or more variables.

ORDINAL SCALE

Ordinal scales or Ranking scales are used to code data in some order. It can be in ascending or descending order.

For example, ranks can be assigned to understand the difference between the most preferred brands to the least preferred. Brands ranked '1' will be most preferred, '2' the next preferred and it continues in the order of preference. The distance between the ranks varies with respondents. Spearman's rank correlation can be performed to understand the similarity in ranking among the respondents. Median and mode are the descriptive statistics performed to understand the mid rank and the repeated rank. Cross tabulation can be used to understand the ranking for different brands.

INTERVAL SCALE

Interval scale or the rating scale is used to measure the opinion or attitude or satisfaction or preference to its length or extent required.

For example, satisfaction of consumers with the product features, price, availability and promotion can be measured ranging from highly satisfied to highly dissatisfied. The extent of measurement of satisfaction depends on the requirement for the research. It may be 5 point or 7 point or 11 point scale. Average rating can be computed. Standard deviation from average ranks can also add meaning to the interpretation. Pearson correlation can be used to understand the relationship among the variables measured. Multivariate analysis like factor, cluster, discriminant and multiple regression can be computed for this scale. The distance between the scales 1 and 2 or 2 and 3 will be uniform.

RATIO SCALE

Some of the variables like age, weight, height, sales can be measured on a ratio scale. Zero point is fixed and the ratios of scale values are compared. The ratio of these variables explains the relationship measured between two points.

The measurement scales used can be broadly categorized as comparative and non-comparative. Comparative scales are: paired comparison, rank order, and constant sum. Non-comparative scales are: likert scale, semantic differential scale, and staple scales. Different types of measurement scales are presented in the Figure 6.1 below.

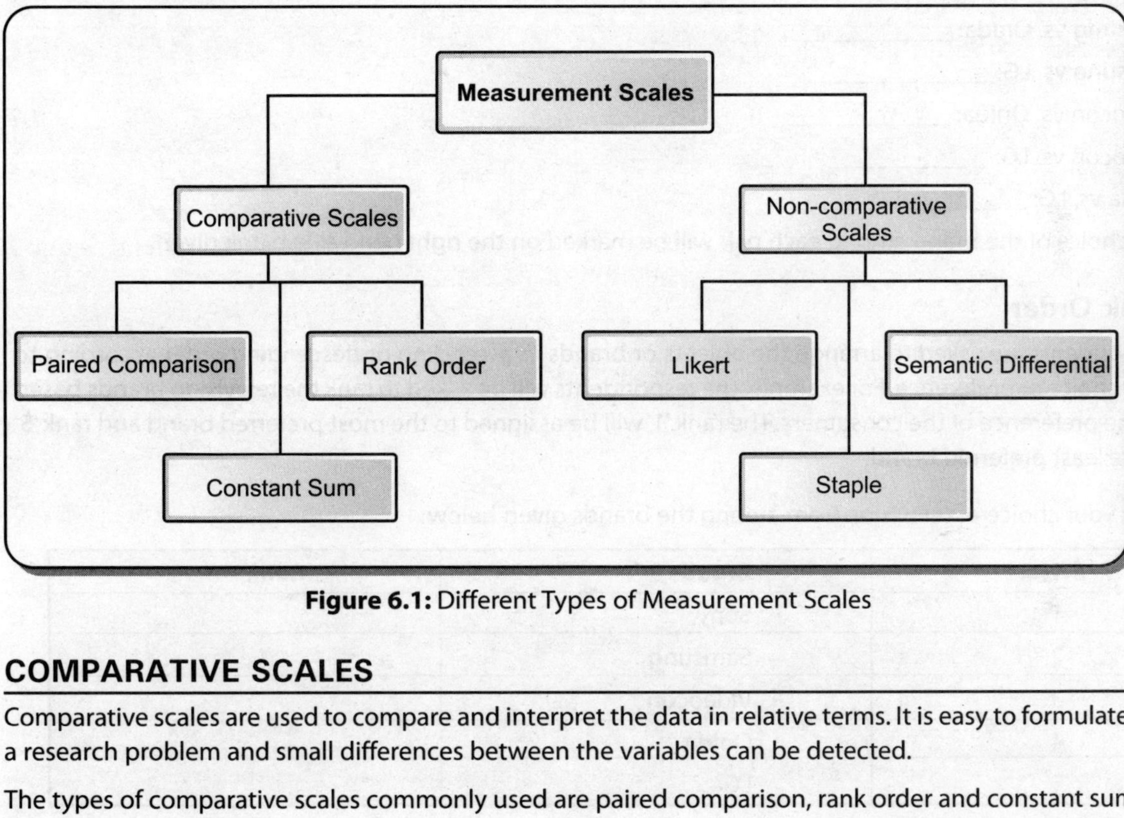

Figure 6.1: Different Types of Measurement Scales

COMPARATIVE SCALES

Comparative scales are used to compare and interpret the data in relative terms. It is easy to formulate for a research problem and small differences between the variables can be detected.

The types of comparative scales commonly used are paired comparison, rank order and constant sum.

Paired Comparison

Paired comparison scale is used to compare two different objects. For example, to compare brand A with brand B, paired comparison scales can be used. If there are more than two objects or brands to compare, each and every pair is compared. With 'n' number of brands,

[n (n-1) / 2] paired comparisons are made. For example to make a comparison among 5 different brands, 10 [i.e. 5 * (5-1)/2] possible paired comparisons are made. This brings out the choice of consumers among different pairs.

In order to make paired comparison to understand the preference of consumers in choosing a television among the brands - Sony, Samsung, Videocon, Onida, and LG, the scale will be as follows:

Give your choice of the television brands from among the pairs given below:

Sony vs. Samsung: ____________

Sony vs. Videocon: ____________

Sony vs. Onida: ____________

Sony vs. LG: ____________

Samsung vs. Videocon: ____________

Samsung vs. Onida: ____________

Samsung vs. LG: ____________

Videocon vs. Onida: ____________

Videocon vs. LG: ____________

Onida vs. LG: ____________

The choice of the brand among each pair will be marked on the right hand side blank given.

Rank Order

Respondents are asked to arrange the objects or brands in ascending or descending order according to their choice of preference. For example, the respondents will be asked to rank the television brands based on the preference of the consumers. The rank '1' will be assigned to the most preferred brand and rank '5' to the least preferred brand.

Rank your choice of television from among the brands given below:

S. No.	Brands	Rank
1	Sony	
2	Samsung	
3	Videocon	
4	Onida	
5	LG	

Rank order scaling results in ordinal data.

Constant Sum

Respondents are asked to assign a fixed sum of units to the attributes measured based on the importance. Every respondent distributes the fixed units among the attributes and the importance perceived is measured. More important attributes will receive more points and the vice versa. The fixed units may be 50 or 100 or 500. For example, among the five attributes in preferring bathing soap, allocate 50 points based on the relative importance attached to each attribute.

S. No.	Attributes	Points Assigned
1	Mildness	5
2	Fragrance	7
3	Price	8
4	moisturizing	20
5	Lather	10
	Total Sum	50

The above sample allocation of 50 points reveals that moisturizing is an important attribute in preferring a bathing soap as the points allocated by the respondent is high. The next important attribute is lather followed by price, fragrance and mildness.

NON-COMPARATIVE SCALES

Non comparative scale measures every variable independent from other variables considered for research. The resulting data is generally interval or ratio scales. Likert, semantic differential and staple are the major three types of non-comparative scales used in marketing research.

Likert Scale

Likert scale or the rating scale is used to measure the variables to its length. For instance, the agreement or satisfaction of the consumers with different factors can be measured on a 5 point or 7 point likert scale. The responses can be measured with the extent of agreement or disagreement; or the extent of satisfaction or dissatisfaction.

For example, among the five attributes in preferring a bathing soap, measure the preference on a five point scale where '1' refers to high level of preference, '2' prefer, '3' neutral, '4' not prefer and '5' don't prefer to a greater extent.

S. No.	Attributes	1	2	3	4	5
1	Mildness					
2	Fragrance					
3	Price					
4	Moisturizing					
5	Lather					

The respondents will give the extent of preference towards the variables studied by marking the respective column. If the number of variables is fewer, weighted average ranking can be used to understand the most important attribute to the least important attribute. If the number of variable is more, factor analysis can be performed to identify the important factors determining the preference in buying bathing soap.

Semantic Differential Scale

Semantic differential scale is a rating scale with bipolar adjectives on the two sides of the scales. It is otherwise called bipolar scales as it bears two adjectives on the two extreme points of the scale. For example, the service of a restaurant can be measured with semantic differential scale as,

Quality	|.....|.....|.....|.....|	Inferiority
Professional	|.....|.....|.....|.....|	Unprofessional
Expensive	|.....|.....|.....|.....|	Inexpensive
Welcoming	|.....|.....|.....|.....|	Unwelcoming
Hospitable	|.....|.....|.....|.....|	Inhospitable

The number of intermediate points in the scale can extend to 5 or 7 or 11 to the extent required.

Staple Scale

Respondents may give the preference in buying a product from one extreme to other extreme of the scale on equal distance. It is measured on a staple scale with positive to negative association with the variable. For example, the attributes of the product measured on features like price, quality, and availability can be represented in a staple scale as,

-4	-4	-4
-3	-3	-3
-2	-2	-2
-1	-1	-1
Quality	Price	Availability
+1	+1	+1
+2	+2	+2
+3	+3	+3
+4	+4	+4

The positive or negative association with the variables quality, price and availability can be measured with the extent of association.

VALIDITY

Validity determines the degree to which a measure assesses what it is meant to measure. Validity is ensured in the contents used in the research instrument, the extent to which it distinguishes the concept and measures the criteria. The validity of the instrument, questionnaire can be ensured at the time of pilot study.

Content Validity

Content Validity is established to substantiate that the questions used in the instrument will substantiate the objectives and it clearly explains to the respondent. This can be done by enquiring the sample considered for pilot study. Focus will give clarity on whether or not the respondents are able to understand the concept that is targeted in the questionnaire.

Construct Validity

Construct validity is established to ensure the arrangement or sequence of the questions in the instrument so that it brings out certain amount of convergence in the respondents opinion. If the construct of the questionnaire is unclear it will bring divergence in the data collected that may not help the researcher to draw conclusions.

Predictive Validity

The instruments are designed to have predictive validity. The research conducted brings out the respondents opinion toward a product or service and their expectations. This will ensure a pathway for the researcher to predict the behaviour based on the present behaviour and future expectations.

Criterion Validity

Criterion validity measures the sufficiency of the criterion used in the research. It ensures that the required dimensions are measured with scales of sufficient length and breadth.

RELIABILITY

Reliability refers to the consistency or repeatability of the instrument, questionnaire for further analysis. The reliability of the questions was empirically examined in order to understand the coherence in the responses made. Reliability of the scales was ensured with Cronbach's alpha coefficient. The coefficient varies between the values 0 to 1. If the score is closer to the value '1', the internal consistency in the questionnaire is perfect and if the score is closer to '0' there is poor internal consistency among the questions in the scale constructed.

Cronbach's alpha measures how well a set of items (or variables) measures a single unidimensional latent construct.

Cronbach's alpha can be written as a function of the number of test items and the average inter-correlation among the items. Cronbach's á is defined as

$$\alpha = \frac{N}{N-1}\left(1 - \frac{\sum_{i=1}^{N} \sigma_{Y_i}^2}{\sigma_X^2}\right)$$

where N is the number of components (items or testlets), σ_X^2 is the variance of the observed total test scores, and $\sigma_{Y_i}^2$ is the variance of component i.

Cronbach's alpha can be interpreted as the percent of variance the observed scale that would explain hypothetical true scale composed of all possible items in the universe. Alternatively, it can be interpreted as the correlation of the observed scale with all possible other scales measuring the same thing and using the same number of items.

The Chronbach alpha score can be calculated using SPSS. The commands to follow are:

ANALYSE → SCALE → RELLIABILITY ANALYSIS

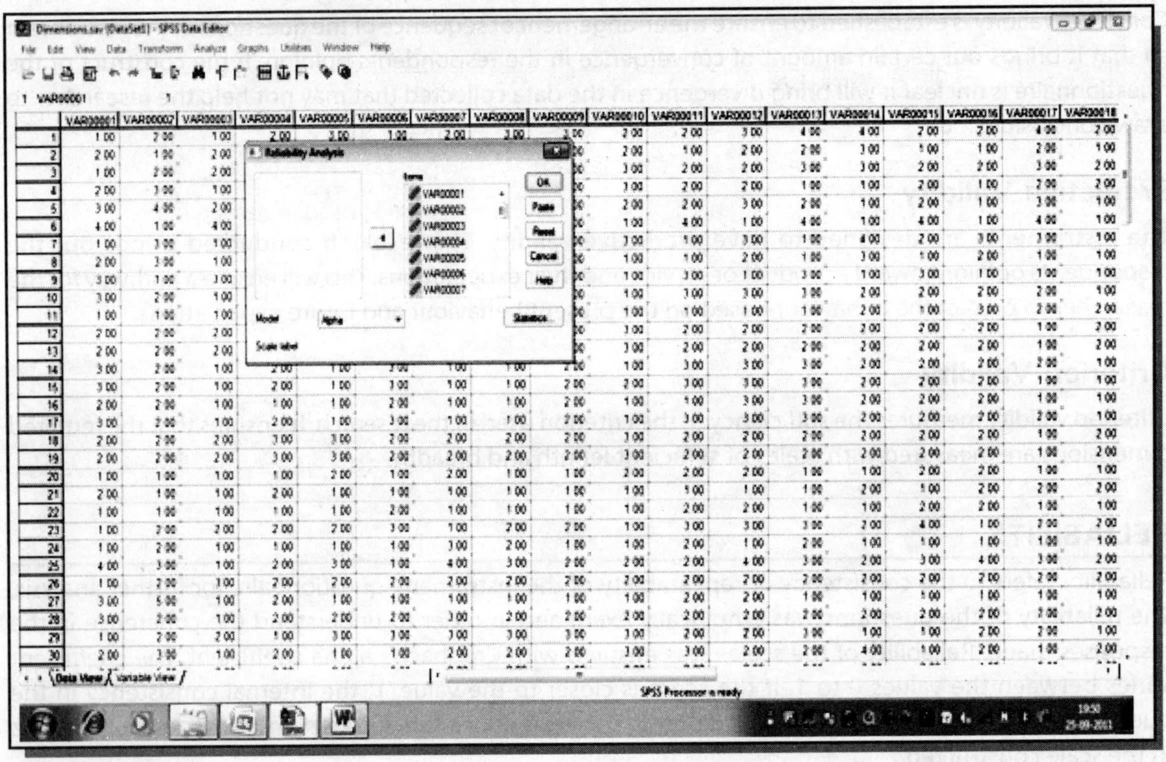

It opens the following drop down bod where all items of the scale are entered. Alpha model is selected and click OK.

The output table gives the reliability score.

Reliability Statistics

Cronbach's Alpha	No of Items
.863	21

Cronbach alpha score for the scale used is 0.863, value close to '1'. The internal consistency of the scale used in the questionnaire is good enough to proceed for further data collection and analysis. This ensures reliability of the scale used for research.

Qualitative research technique uses unstructured or open ended questions for collecting data. Measuring data quantitatively requiresa structured questionnaire with multiple alternatives in a closed ended form. To convert the opinion or preference expressed quantitatively, scales are to be established, comparative, rating or ranking. Scales make the measurement of the opinion of the respondents quantifiable. The scales can further be tested for validity and reliability to ensure generalization in prediction.

Review Questions

1. Explain the basic scales used in measuring data in research.
2. What are the major classifications of scales used to measure data?
3. Explain the types of comparative and non-comparative scales used in research.
4. Discuss the types of validity and reliability to be executed in research.

Chapter 7

Field Work and Data Preparation

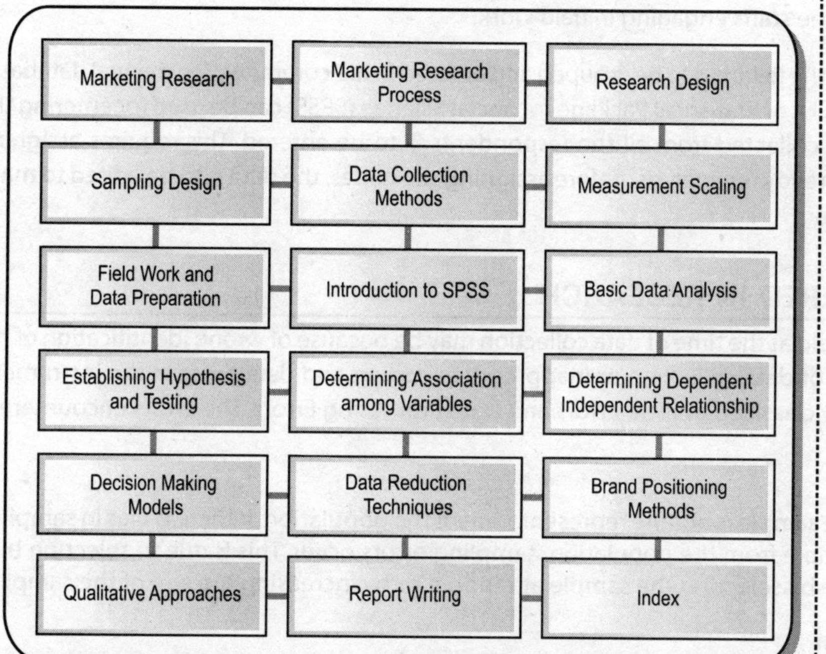

Outline

Chapter Structure

- Introduction
- Errors Encountered in Research
- Editing
- Coding and Adjusting the Data
- Review Questions

Chapter Overview

Chapter seven explains the basic work done in the field at the time of data collection and methods to prepare the data for analysis. It includes the work of editing, coding and adjusting the data for analysis.

INTRODUCTION

Field work includes collection of data through questionnaire or interview schedule. It requires clear choice of the sample with any of the sampling methods and the places where the field work or data collection is to be done. For example, if the research is on, 'Customer Satisfaction of Retail Service Quality in Cities', the researcher has to select the cities to conduct the field work. It may include cities like Mumbai, Delhi, Chennai and Kolkata or include cities like Hyderabad, Bangalore, Ahmedabad and Chandigarh. Sample size and characteristics of sample to be approached in each of these cities is to be determined. Based on the number and spread of the sample, manpower requirements for data collection will be decided.

Field work includes selection of field staff and research supervisor for each geographical area. Before the start of the field work, briefing work begins. It include explanation of the questionnaire and methods to approach the sample and discussion on contingency situation handling. There may be non-response due to non-availability of the respondent or non-cooperation of the respondent. Training to handle these situations will be given for the staffs engaging in field work.

Once the data is collected in the field, it is to be grouped and entered in the computer. The manual databases are less in use. Microsoft EXCEL or Statistical Package for Social Science (SPSS) can be used for entering the data collected. All the data collected from all the respondents is to be entered. This requires assigning codes and making the data ready for analysis. Before assigning the codes, the data is to be edited to make it ready for further processing.

ERRORS ENCOUNTERED IN RESEARCH

Errors encountered in the field at the time of data collection may be because of wrong identification of the sample or wrong methods of data collection or inappropriate coding and data entry in the instrument. These errors can be broadly classified as Field Errors and Data Processing Errors. The errors encountered

Errors in Sampling

Sampling errors occur if the sample is not the representation of the population. If there is bias in sampling method or selection of sample from the population, sampling errors occur. This is due to selection bias. This error can be overcome by selecting the sample at random or by increasing the size of the sample.

Errors in Observation

Errors occur with the biased observation. If there exist perception in the minds of the researcher towards the variables studied, it brings bias in the observations made and the data collected.

For instance, if the researcher believes that the service quality of a retail outlet will be good, the observations he makes with the respondents will be lopsided to prove his belief. This error can be overcome by the researcher by not jumping into any conclusion of the behaviour of the variables in advance.

Errors due to the Investigators Bias

Errors may occur due to wrong identification of sample, acquisition of data with inappropriate instruments or hooking up of the data by the field experts. For instance, to select every 7th member visiting a shopping mall in a mall intercept interview, the investigator may select the 4th member, 5th member, and 6th member continuously. If the number of customers walking in a mall is less and the time gap is good enough to interview every respondent, this type of selection may be executed that brings bias in the method of selection of the sample. The data revealed by the respondents sometimes may not fit into the existing choices in the questionnaire. In such cases there are chances that the field investigators will make them fall into any of the existing categories. This bias can be overcome by educating the field investigator to handle these situations.

Errors Due to Non-response

Errors occur if the respondent do not answer all the questions or do not respond to the research. This error can be overcome by motivating the respondents to participate and with limited number of questions required for the specific research.

Errors Due to the Respondents Bias

Errors occur if the respondent selects the wrong options, not revealing the actual data. This behaviour may be exerted to be socially desirable and prove themselves smart in front of the investigator. This error can be overcome by encouraging the respondents to give the actual responses and not the right response. The investigator can also bring in the realities by building confidence in the respondents.

Errors Due to Incorrect Recording

Errors occur due to incorrect recording of the data at the time of observation and interview. This error can be overcome with the usage of mechanical devices as supplementary in recording the data. Errors may also occur if the transcription of the primary data collected is not done correctly. This can be overcome by using trained or professional transcriptors.

EDITING

The process of editing helps to identify ambiguity, inconsistency, omissions and error due to lack of cooperation or identifying an incorrect sample, in the data collected from the sample respondents. If these problems are identified, the researcher can overcome by getting into contact with the respondent, or omitting the responses or the complete questionnaire.

For instance, if a respondent did not answer most of the questions, such questionnaire can be omitted completely. If the respondents did not answer certain questions like age, income or profession, the respondent's opinion on these variables can be omitted but his response to other questions can be considered. It is partial omission. If a wrong sample is considered, such responses can be completely omitted. For instance, if the data is to be collected from college going youth between 17 to 22 years of age, and one of the respondent is of 25 years of age, such responses can be completely omitted.

There are situations where the responses are not clear or legible. In such cases, the respondents can be called back to have clarity in the response.

For example, in selecting a category, the respondent might have given a tick between two categories. Such confusions and ambiguity can be overcome by call back option. Inconsistency in the response is another challenge in editing. For instance, the respondent who has selected the professional category in occupation might have selected the income category between rupees one lakh to two lakh per annum. This might be because of the confusion with per annum or per month salary or respondents easy attitude to fill the questionnaire. Such responses should be handled carefully by either eliminating or adjusting their salary with the industry norms. Respondents may not cooperate if the questionnaire is too long. In such cases, the field staff should continuously motivate the respondents.

CODING AND ADJUSTING THE DATA

Coding explains the ways to enter the data in the data sheet or the input file from the data collected through questionnaire. Coding makes the data quantifiable and helps in further data analysis. For instance, to create a 'Customer' data sheet, the data to be entered includes: the name of the customer, gender, age and income. Actual name will be entered in the name column. In case of age and income, if the questions are open ended, it to be categorized and then coded. It is easy to code the closed ended questions. If the gender of the respondents is Male then code as '1' and if it is female, code as '2'. Similarly if the age group has the categories of: less than 20 years, 20 years to 40 years, 40 years to 60 years, 60 years and above, then the coding can be 1, 2, 3, and 4 respectively for the four age categories. The income category will also be coded in the similar way.

In case of scaling data, from highly satisfied to highly dissatisfied, it can be coded from '1' to '5' in ascending or descending order. In case of dichotomous questions that have yes or no response, it can be coded as '1' and '2'. Thus opinion, satisfaction, level or agreement or any scaling data is coded to quantify and make it ready for further analysis.

Once the data is coded, the data is to be prepared for analysis. This requires adjusting the data and correcting it for similarity or standardization. This may be with the level of measurement or units of measurement. For instance, the price of the product may be expressed in rupees, dollars or any other unit of measurement. All these units should be adjusted to a single unit of measurement.

Review Questions

1. Explain the process of field work and data preparation for analysis.
2. What are the errors that can happen in the field during data collection?
3. What are the ways of data editing?
4. Explain the process of coding and adjusting the data for analysis.

Chapter 8

Introduction to SPSS

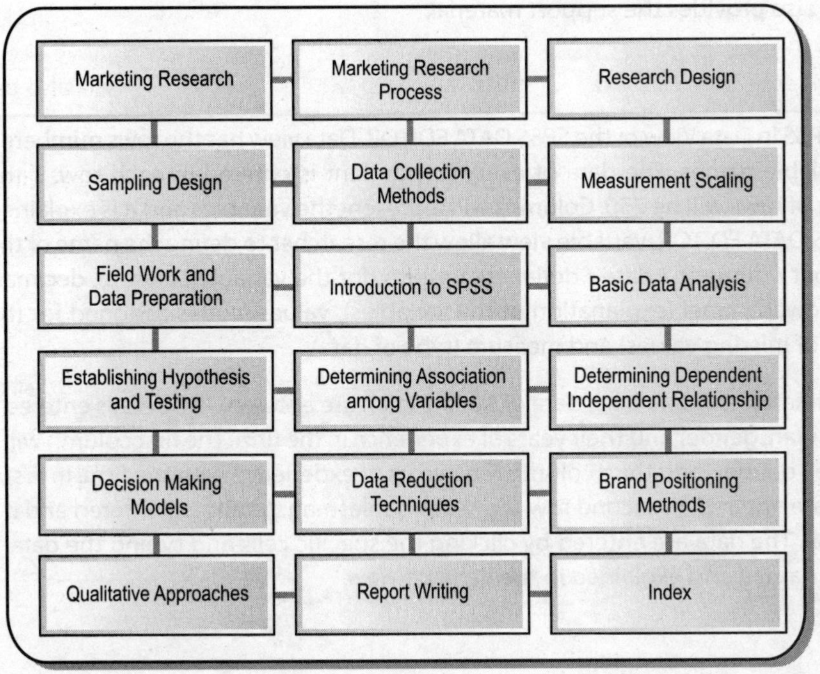

Outline

Chapter Structure

- Introduction
- Data Entry
- Case
- Data Readiness
- Case
- Sample Questionnaire
- Review Questions

Chapter Overview

Chapter eight explains the step by step process for entering the raw data into SPSS, from the questionnaire, assigning codes to the variables, naming of the variables, and the creation of input file in SPSS.

INTRODUCTION

Data collected through questionnaire is raw and it should be prepared for data analysis. The coded data is arranged by assigning the names of the variables. This requires entering the data in computer and getting it ready for analysis. For this purpose, SPSS (Statistical Package for Social Sciences) is used and data sheet or input file is created. SPSS is loaded with windows Operating system. If it is installed start button will list SPSS in programs list. Then click START → PROGRAMS →SPSS 16.0. This opens the SPSS DATA EDITOR. DATA EDITOR is the DATA FILE where the input data is entered. DATA EDITOR is similar to an EXCEL sheet with rows and columns. Rows represent the data collected from each respondent and columns represent the data of one variable. SPSS DATA EDITOR has two views – Data View and Variable View. Data to be analyzed will be entered in the Data View and the variables are named in the Variable View. Data analysis with SPSS can be performed from the menu or icon bars or with the help of Syntax Editor. The book explains the analysis using SPSS with the help of menus and icons. The menu driven SPSS helps the user to explore and use it accordingly. Help menu also provides the support material.

DATA ENTRY

Data for analysis is entered in SPSS in Data View of the SPSS DATA EDITOR. Data view has the rows numbered serially and columns with variable names. The data of every respondent is entered in each row. If the sample size is 250, the number of rows will be 250. Columns will represent the variables and it is explained in the Variable View of the SPSS DATA EDITOR. Variable view allow the researcher to define the name of the variables, type of data (alphabet / numeric / date / dollar etc.), width (for the variable column), decimals (number of decimals to be allowed), label (explanation of the variables), values (codes assigned for the variables), missing (treatment of missing values) and measure (type of data).

For example, to create a small salesman data base data of 10 salesmen are entered. The details entered include the name of the salesman, gender and their years of experience in the firm. The first column will have their names, second their gender -and third column their years of experience with the firm. In first row details of first salesman are entered, in second row the second salesman details are entered and it follows till the tenth salesman. The data are entered by clicking the specific cells and typing the data. The columns entered can be named and explained in the variable view.

In the Variable View:

1. Enter the name of the first variable in the first row in the variable view of the Data Editor. In the example discussed, it will be salesman.
2. Then select the variable type. Since it is a name with alphabets, select the option string. [Note: Numeric is the default data type selected. So change into string initially to enter names in data view]. Then click OK
3. In labels column, the name of the variable can be explained.

   For example: Name of the salesman. This column helps to define the variables elaborately.
4. By default width will be 8 characters this can be changed whenever needed.
5. By default measure column scale is nominal, and continue the same

Now the data view will have the first column name as salesman. To define the second column follows the same proofs.

Go to variable view

- Enter in the 'Name' column as 'Gender'
- Select the 'Type' as string as the data entered will be Male or Female
- Enter the 'Label' as 'Gender of the salesman'

Now the data view will have the second column named as Gender. In case Male is to the prefixed with 'M' and Female with 'F' in Data View, it can be defined in 'Values' column.

- Go to values. It opens a value label dialogue box as given.
- In values dialogue box type 'F' and in label box type Female. Then click 'Add'.
- Similarly in value box type 'M' and in label box type Male and click 'Add'.

This will code Male as 'M' and Female as 'F' in the data view.

To enter the name of third variable, Go to variable view.

- Enter the 'Name' as 'Experience'
- Type of data is 'Numeric' as the data entered will be the no of years of experience.
- Width and decimals can be default. Changes can be made if necessary.
- 'Label' can be explained as 'Years of experience of salesman'

Now the data view will have the third column named as 'Experience'.

To save this file, click File Menu, choose Save As. Then select the destination (here, select desktop or the drive to save). Then give the file name (in this example – salesman). Click Save. Thus data is entered in a Data Editor.

CASE

A retail outlet likes to create a data base of its ten loyal customers with their names, gender and date of birth. Create a 'CUSTOMER' data file for the retail outlet with the data given below.

CUSTOMER NAME	GENDER	DATE OF BIRTH
VIMAL	1	11. 07. 1975
KURANA	1	23. 05. 1988
SEEMA	2	02. 04. 1994
KARTHIK	1	09. 01. 2001
VARUN	1	18. 03. 2000

REEMA	2	16. 08. 1985
VAMSHI	1	13. 02. 1998
PADMA	2	12. 11. 2004
VISHNU	1	29. 12. 2003
RANI	2	20. 09. 1993

The first row is the data of Vimal, second row is of Kurana, third row is of Seema and it follows. The first column of the 'CUSTOMER' data file represent 'Customer Name', second column 'Gender' and third column 'Date of Birth'. The Data View of the input file is given below.

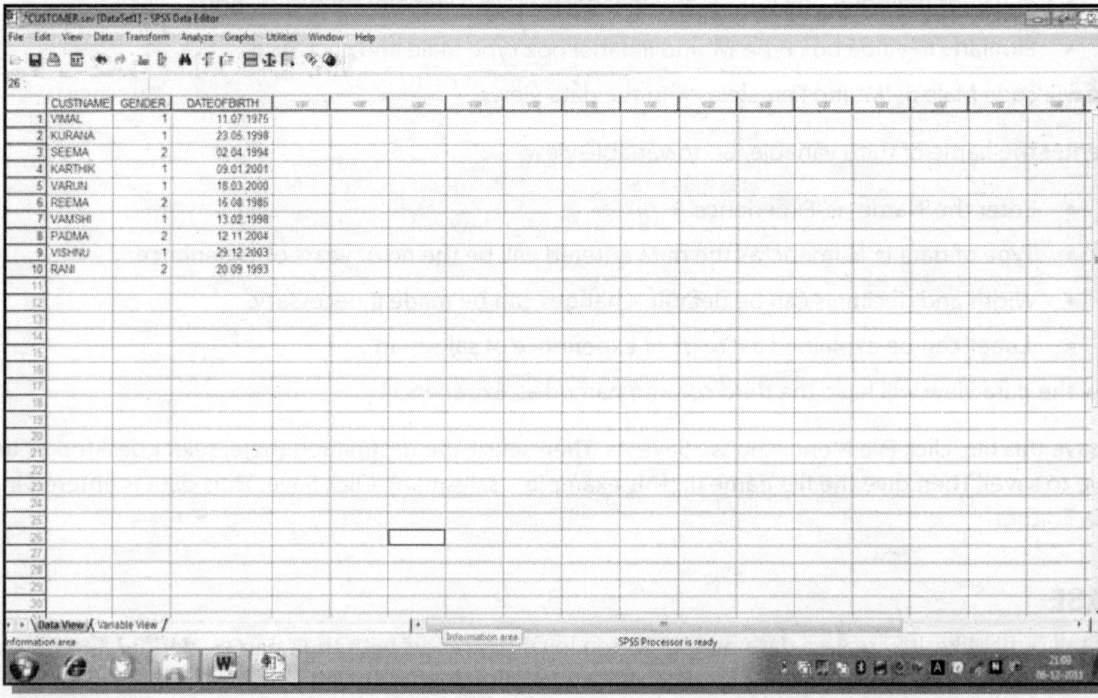

The variables can be named in the variable view of the SPSS DATA EDITOR. In the name column of the Variable view, names of the variables Customer Name, Gender and Date of Birth is entered. In the type column, type of the variable as String, Numeric, and Date is entered. In the width column, width of the variable column is default assigned as '8'. In the decimal column, if it required allowing decimals, it will be entered. Labels column gives the complete name of the variables for better understanding.

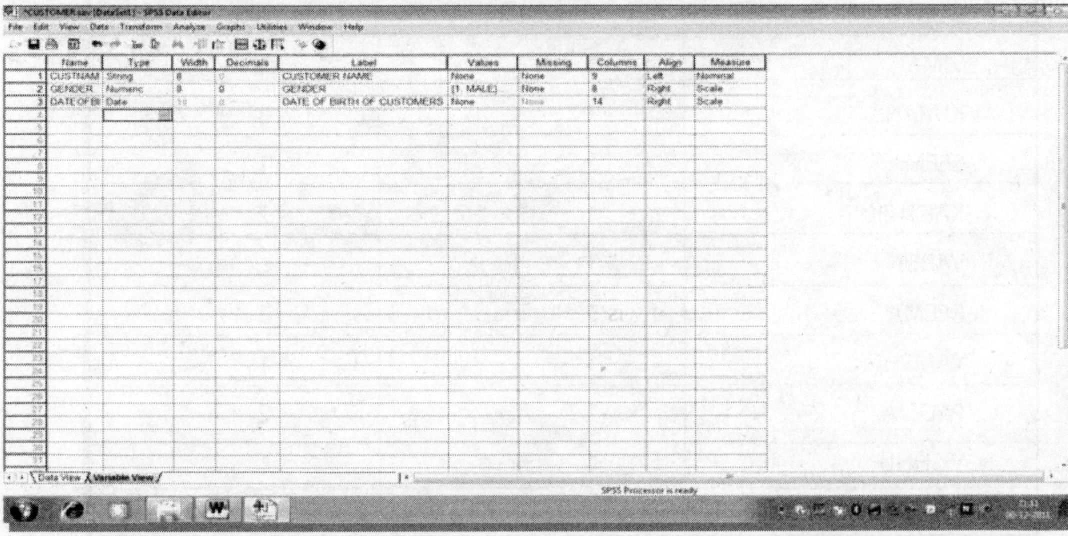

Values column gives the explanation of the coding done for the variables. For the variable Gender, Male is assigned as '1' and Female is assigned as '2'.

SPSS will give the output in a separate file called output viewer window or output file after performing the required analysis. The input and output files can be saved separately for future reference.

DATA READINESS

Once the data is coded and entered in SPSS, variables are named and data is ready for analysis. Then the data can be tabulated with Frequencies and the frequency distribution can be represented in histograms. In case of missing data, SPSS gives the option of treating missing values. The data ready for analysis can be represented in frequency table or cross tables. The representation of the data in frequencies and bar charts can be executed with the following commands in SPSS.

Enter the input data in the Data View and name the variables in the Variable View.

Select → ANALYSE → DESCRIPTIVE STATISTICS → FREQUENCEIS

In the FREQUENCIES dialog box, select the variables that require an understanding with frequency table and charts. Finally, select OK.

CASE

A retail outlet likes to create a data base of its ten customers with their names, gender and age group. Create a 'CUSTOMER' data file for the retail outlet with the data given below and present the frequency table and bar chart of the gender distribution and age group of the respondents.

CUSTOMER NAME	GENDER	AGE
VIMAL	1	1
KURANA	1	3
SEEMA	2	1
KARTHIK	1	2
VARUN	1	.
REEMA	2	3
VAMSHI	1	1
PADMA	2	2
VISHNU	1	1
RANI	2	4

On entering the data in data view, code Male as '1' and Female as '2' and age group less than 20 years as '1'; 20 to 40 years as '2'; 40 to 60 years as '3'; and 60 years and above as '4' in the variable view. The input file is given below. The age group of the 5th respondent Varun is not known. So it is considered as a missing data for calculation.

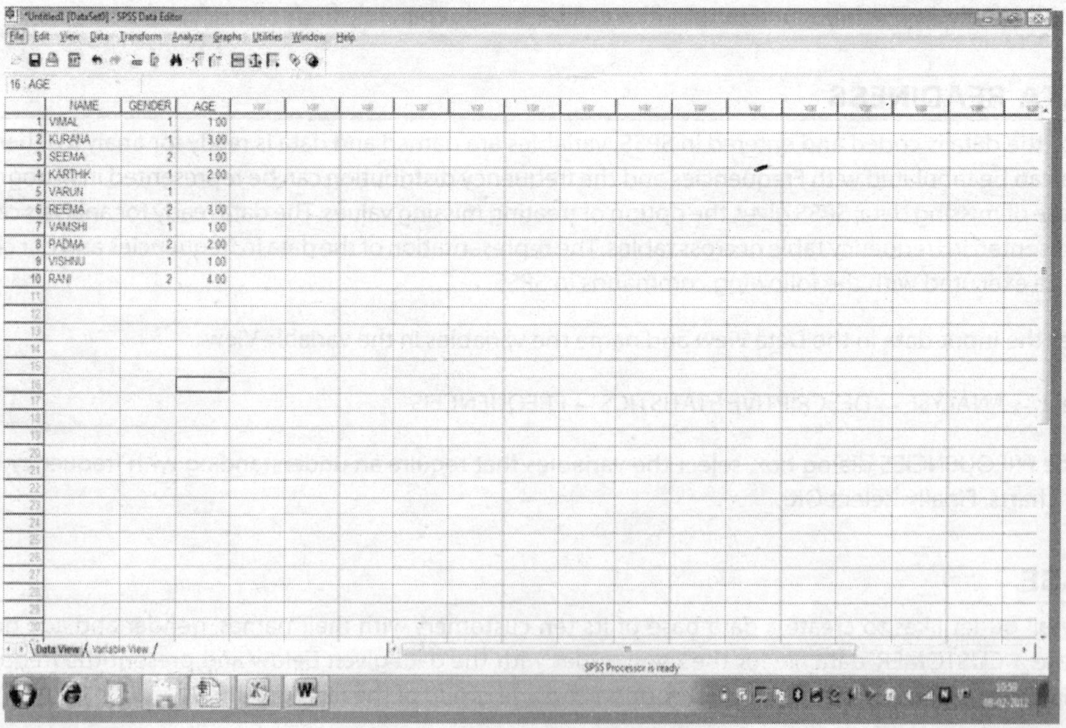

On clicking the FREQUENCIES from DESCRIPTIVE STATISTICS, the variables Gender and Age group are selected.

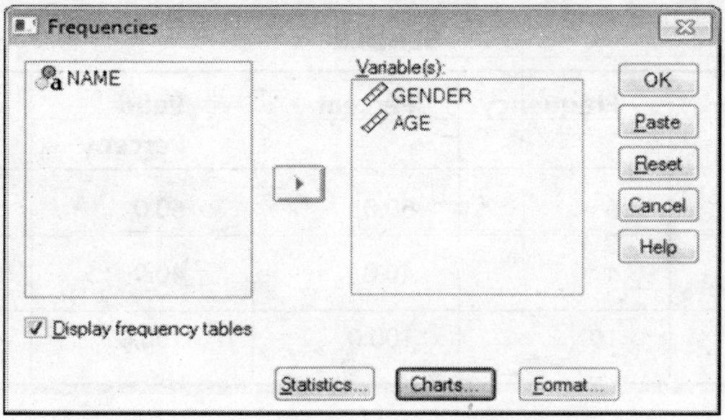

The chart type selected is Bar chart.

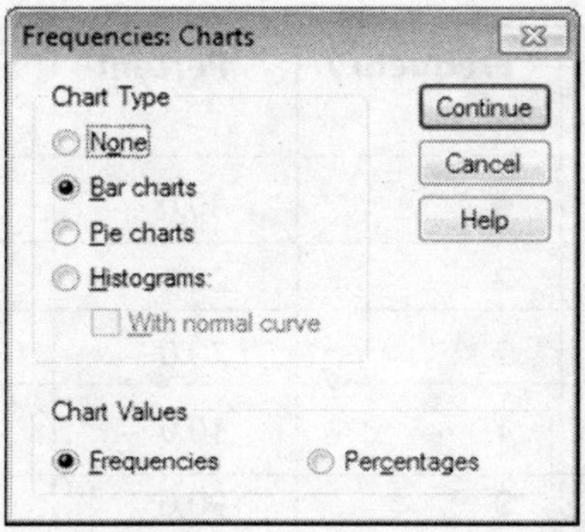

The statistics selected is Mean.

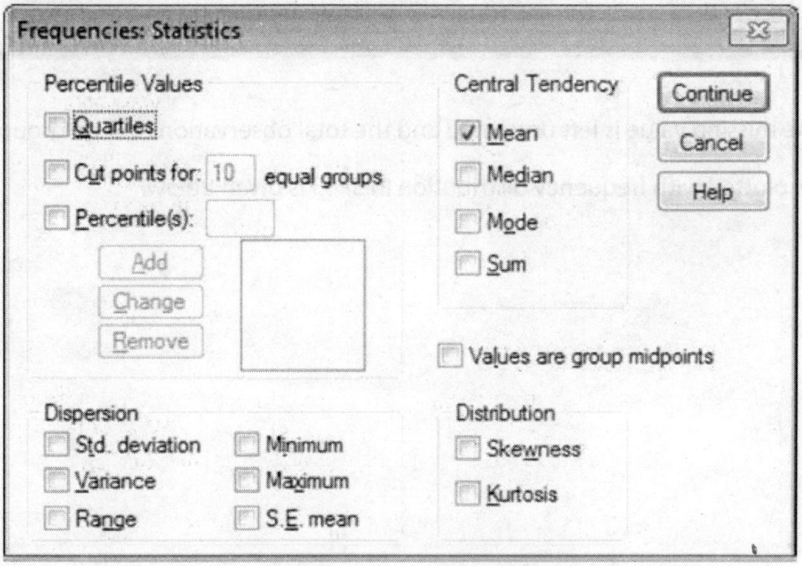

The output is given below:

GENDER

	Gender	Frequency	Percent	Valid Percent	Cumulative Percent
Valid	MALE	6	60.0	60.0	60.0
	FEMALE	4	40.0	40.0	100.0
	Total	10	100.0	100.0	

AGE

	Age Group	Frequency	Percent	Valid Percent	Cumulative Percent
Valid	LESS THAN 20 YEARS	4	40.0	44.4	44.4
	20 TO 40 YEARS	2	20.0	22.2	66.7
	40 TO 60 YEARS	2	20.0	22.2	88.9
	60 YEARS AND ABOVE	1	10.0	11.1	100.0
	Total	9	90.0	100.0	
Missing	System	1	10.0		
Total	10	100.0			

In this case, the missing value is left untreated and the total observations in Age group is 9.

The bar charts plotted with frequency distribution in SPSS is given below.

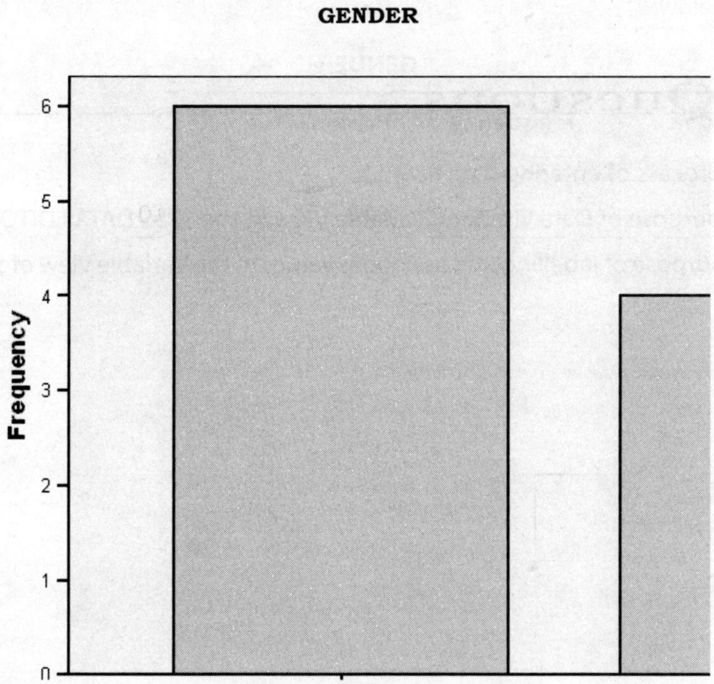
GENDER
Frequency
0
1
2
3
4
5
6

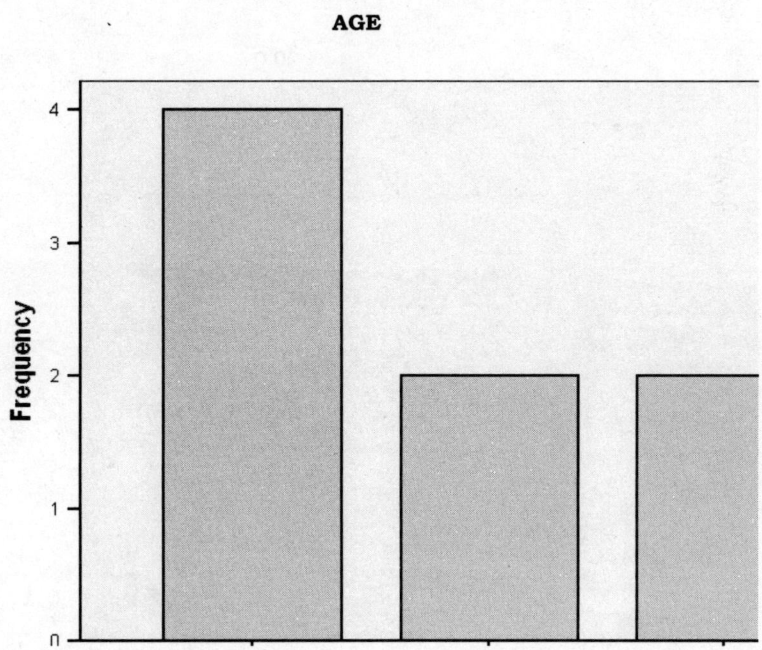
AGE
Frequency
0
1
2
3
4

Review Questions

1. Explain the process of entering data in SPSS.
2. What is the purpose of Data View and Variable View in the SPSS DATA EDITOR?
3. What is the purpose of labelling and assigning values in the Variable View of SPSS DATA EDITOR?

Chapter

9

Basic Data Analysis

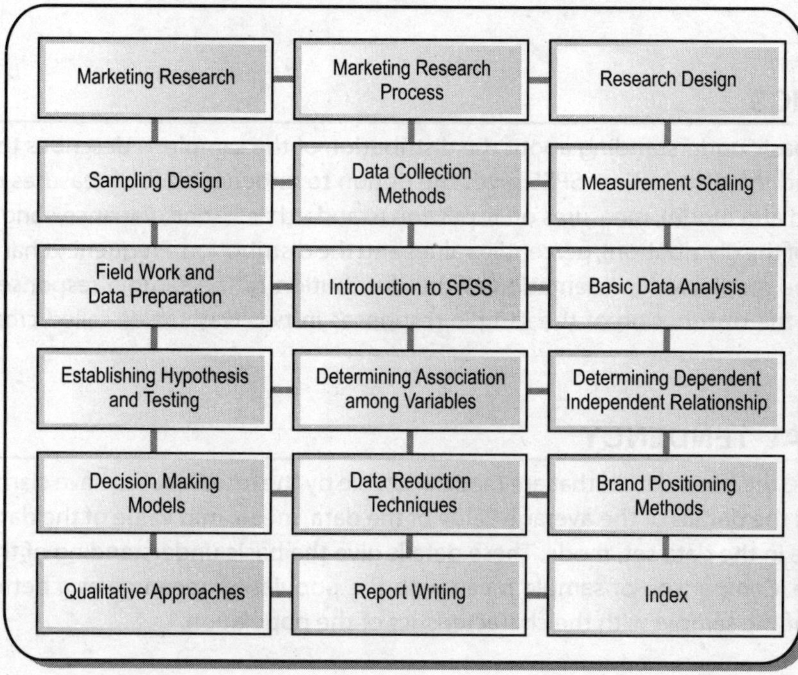

Outline

Chapter Structure

- Introduction
- Descriptive Statistics
- Measures of Central Tendency
- Case
- Sample Questionnaire
- Crosstabulation and Percentages
- Case
- Review Questions

Chapter Overview

Chapter nine discusses the methods of basic data analysis. It providesbetter understanding of the data for further processing and decision making. This chapter highlights the descriptive statistics or the measures of central tendency that includes mean, median and mode for understanding the sample characteristics. It also explains two way representation of the data with cross tabulation and the data distribution in percentages using SPSS.

INTRODUCTION

Data collected for research need to have better understanding with its distribution. This requires processing of the data into suitable information. It includes identifying the appropriate method to analyze the data for decision making. For this purpose it requires a better diagnosis of the variables. It is the first stage of data analysis. It helps the researcher to understand the distribution of the sample for different variables. Statistical methods like mean, median, mode, sum, percentages and variance give better understanding of the distribution of the sample. Once descriptive statistics is performed, inferential statistics gives better implication about the sample. Statistical inference is drawn with t-test, chi square and ANOVA. Further analytical statistics gives statistical significance to make decisions. It includes multiple regression, conjoint analysis, discriminant analysis, etc. This chapter deals with the descriptive statistics used in marketing research.

DESCRIPTIVE STATISTICS

Descriptive statistics gives the basic understanding about the distribution of the sample. It describes the characteristics of the sample and the distribution. SPSS gives the option to understand the measures of central tendency (mean, median and mode), measures of dispersion (standard deviation, variance, range, minimum and maximum value of the distribution), percentile values and the distribution. Frequency charts can also be made that gives the graphical representation of the distribution of the sample responses. Descriptive statistics also gives the distribution of the sample responses in two way tables called cross tabulation.

MEASURES OF CENTRAL TENDENCY

Measures of central tendency are the basic details that are made available by the researcher to have clarity in the data collected. It includes the details of the average value of the data, mean, mid value of the data, median, and the repeated value in the data set, mode. These details give the basic understanding of the data collected from the sample. Comparison of sample mean with the population mean gives a better idea about the representation of the sample with the characteristics of the population.

Measures of central tendency are:

- Mean – gives the average value of the data.
- Median – gives the mid value of the distribution.
- Mode – is the most frequently occurring value.

Measures of Variability

Measures of dispersion or variability explain the amount of deviation of the sample responses from the mean value or the mid value.

Measures of variability are:

- Variance and Standard Deviation – gives the deviation of the data from the mean value. Standard Deviation is the commonly used measure.

Measures of the Spread of Data

Measures of the data spread gives an understanding of the extent of distribution of the data.

Measures of the spread of data are:

- Maximum – gives the maximum value in the distribution.
- Minimum – gives the minimum value in the distribution.
- Range – gives the spread in the given data [i.e., difference between minimum and maximum values].
- Sum – gives the sum of the given data.

SPSS commands to execute the Descriptives
Open SPSS input file, enter the data.

In menu bar, click

ANALYSE → DESCRIPTIVES

A screen appears with the variables entered. Select the variable for which descriptive statistics is to be computed. Then click

OPTIONS → Select those statistics required. Eg. MEAN, SUM, SD, MIN, MAX, KURTOSIS, SKEWNESS, etc.

In display order select variable list that presents in the same order in the input file. Then click ok. The output file provides the output of the required descriptive statistics.

CASE

A manufacturing company collected data from 20 customers in the market regarding the performance of the sales force. The company wants to implement a training program in order to improve the efficiency of its sales force. Hence, the company wants to calculate the measures of central tendency and dispersion as it would enable the company to find out the current performance level of the sales force. As a part of the research, the customers were asked to rate the performance of the sales force on a 5 point scale. [Ratings are: 1-Poor, 2-Below Average, 3-Average, 4-Good, 5-Excellent]. Input data is shown in table.

Input Table:

SAMPLE	PERFROMANCE RATING
1	2
2	4
3	3
4	4
5	3

6	4
7	2
8	5
9	1
10	4
11	2
12	5
13	2
14	4
15	3
16	1
17	2
18	3
19	2
20	3

Output Tables:

Statistics - Performance

N	Valid	20
	Missing	79
Mean		2.9500
Median		3.0000
Mode		2.00
Std. Deviation		1.19097
Variance		1.418
Range		4.00
Minimum		1.00
Maximum		5.00
Sum		59.00

Performance

		Frequency	Percent	Valid Percent	Cumulative Percent
Valid	Poor	2	2.0	10.0	10.0
	Below Average	6	6.1	30.0	40.0
	Average	5	5.1	25.0	65.0
	Good	5	5.1	25.0	90.0
	Excellent	2	2.0	10.0	100.0
	Total	20	20.2	100.0	
Missing	System	79	79.8		
Total	99	100.0			

Interpretation

- Input data consists of responses from 20 customers. From the output table, we understand that the sum of the performance rating values, as given by the respondents, is 59.
- From the output table, we understand that the mean value of the performance rating, as given by the respondents, is 2.95. It means that the mean performance level of the sales force of the company is 2.95. On a 5 point scale, the customers opined that the mean performance level of the sales force is slightly less than the average performance level.
- The median value of the performance rating is 3, as shown in the output table. When arranged in ascending order, the data would be 1, 1, 2, 2, 2, 2, 2, 2, 3, 3, 3, 3, 3, 4, 4, 4, 4, 4, 5, 5. With the sample size of 20, the median values would be the average of 10th and 11th values of input data. Hence, median value would be (3 + 3) / 2, which is 3, as shown in the output table.
- Mode is the value that occurs most frequently in a given data set. In this example of sales force performance evaluation, performance rating value of 2 occurs most frequently. From the output table, we find that the value 1 occurs 2 times, 2 occurs 6 times, 3 occurs 5 times, 4 occurs 5 times and 5 occurs 2 times. Hence, mode of the performance rating of the sales force is 2, as shown in the output table..
- The maximum value in the data set is 5, as shown in the output table. The value 5 occurs twice in the data set. It means that 2 customers have rated the performance level of the sales force as 'Excellent'.
- The minimum value in the data set is 1, as shown in the output table. The value 1 occurs twice in the data set. It means that 2 customers have rated the performance level of the sales force as 'Poor'.

- Range is the difference between the maximum and the minimum values in a data set. In this example of sales force performance evaluation, the maximum value is 5 and the minimum value is 1. Hence, range is 4, as shown in the output table.
- From the output table, we understand that the standard deviation in this example is 1.19097.
- From the output table, we understand that the variance in this example is 1.418.

Navigation Guide

In order to enter data:

- Data must be entered in the 'Data View' page of the data sheet, as given by the respondents. (In this case, it is based on the response given by 20 customers, in the market regarding the performance of the sales force).

Data View

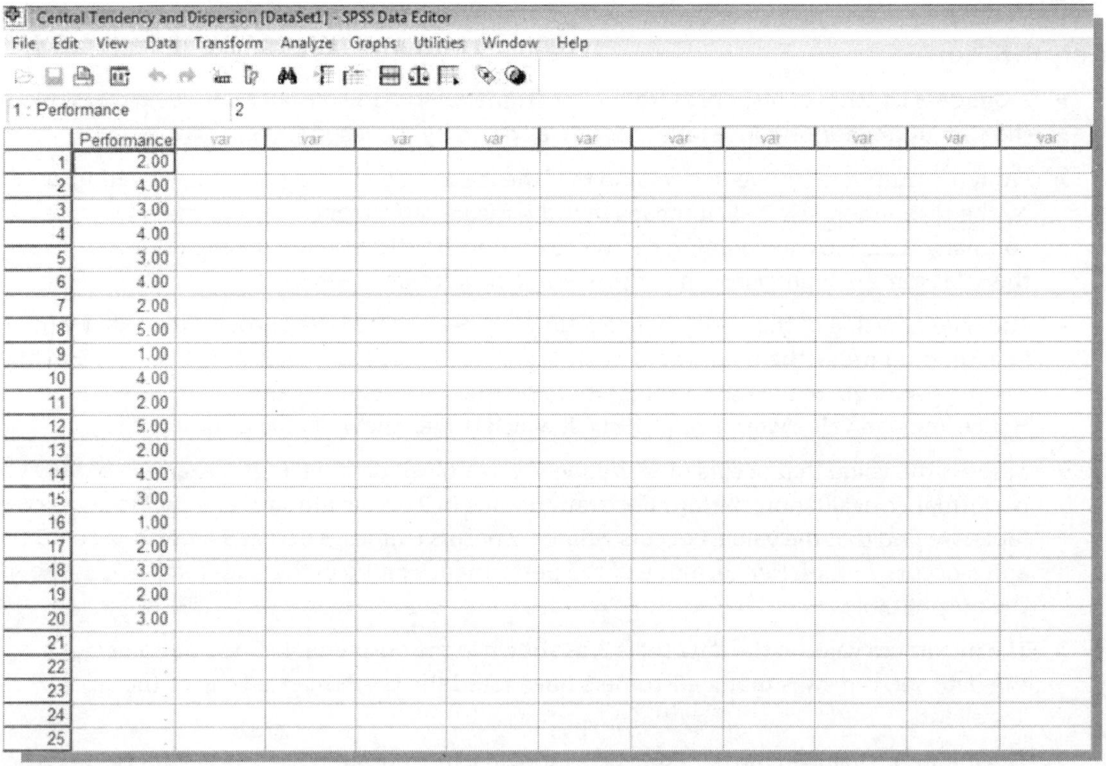

	Performance	var	var	var	var	var	var	var	var	var	var
1	2.00										
2	4.00										
3	3.00										
4	4.00										
5	3.00										
6	4.00										
7	2.00										
8	5.00										
9	1.00										
10	4.00										
11	2.00										
12	5.00										
13	2.00										
14	4.00										
15	3.00										
16	1.00										
17	2.00										
18	3.00										
19	2.00										
20	3.00										
21											
22											
23											
24											
25											

Variable View

- Open variable view and enter 'Performance' in Name column. It assigns by default, the type of data, width, decimals and measure.

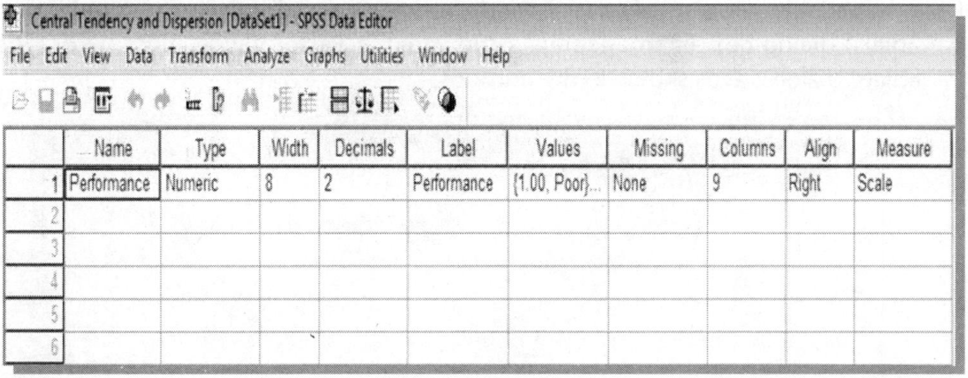

➢ In the 'Variable View' page, a suitable name and a label must be given for the variable. (In this example, the variable is: 'Performance'). The data is entered as collected through the questionnaire. The value is entered first, followed by the corresponding label. In this example, performance of the sales force is rated on a 5 point scale and the values assigned are: 1-Poor, 2-Below Average, 3-Average, 4-Good, 5-Excellent. Enter the values as:

Value: 1

Label: Poor

Click 'Add'

Similarly add the values for the scale

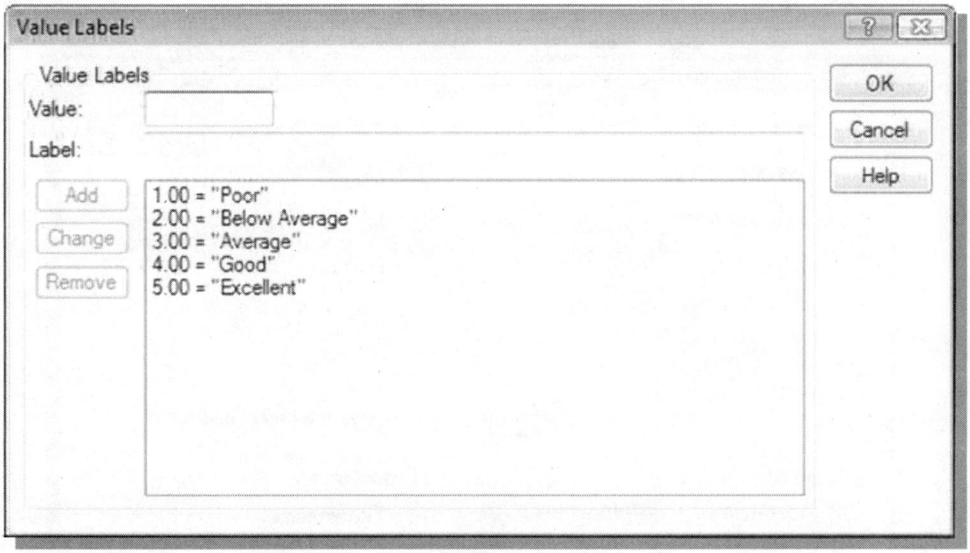

➢ Enter the values, click 'ok' and save the input file.

Then, the following procedure is followed to perform analysis:

- Select Analyze → Descriptive Statistics → Frequencies.

- Drag the variable, whose measures of central tendency and dispersion have to be found, to the Variable(s) dialog box. In this example, the variable 'Performance' must be dragged to the Variable(s) dialog box.

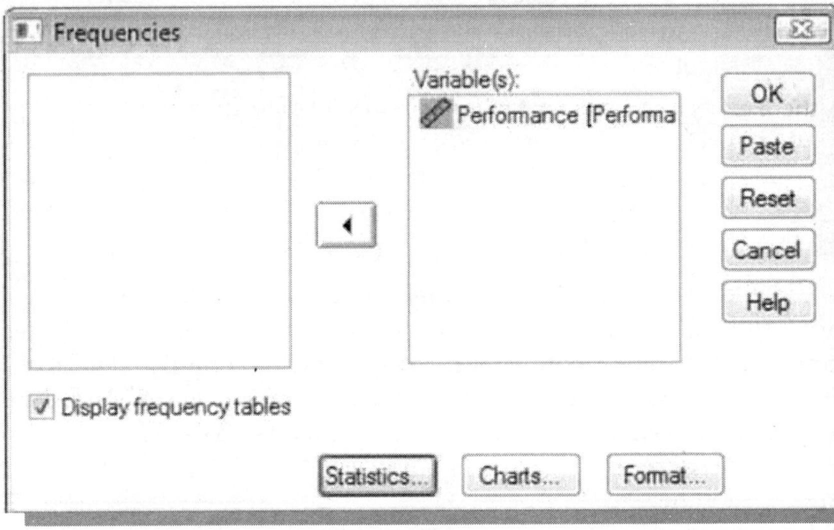

- Click 'Statistics' and select the measures, whose values have to be found out. In this case, click 'Statistics', select 'Mean', 'Median', 'Mode', 'Sum', 'Std. deviation', 'Variance', 'Range', 'Minimum' and 'Maximum' and then click 'Continue'.

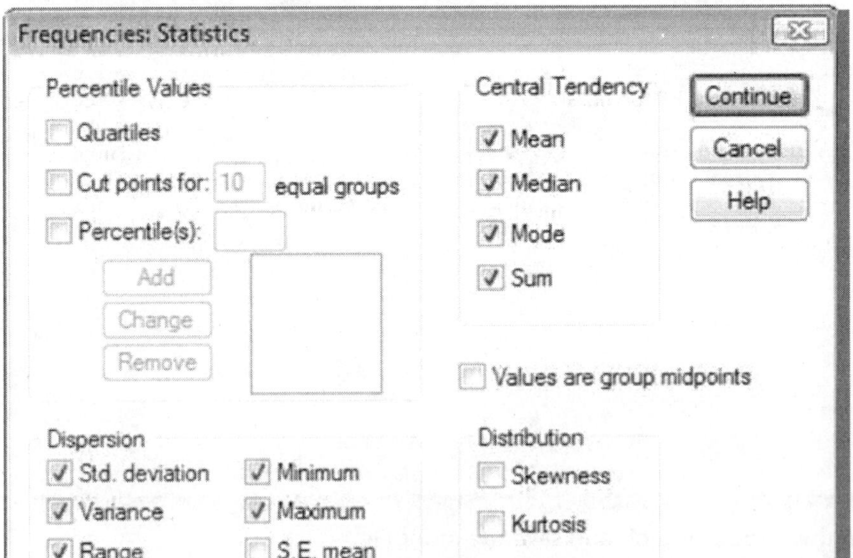

- Click 'OK' and the output file opens.

CROSSTABULATION AND PERCENTAGES

If there are two or more categories of variables, a better understanding of the spread under each category can be made with the help of cross tabulation. The amount of distribution of the variables to that of the row or column or overall total can be understood with percentages calculated for row total, column total and the overall total value. It gives clarity with the percentage of distribution to the row variable or column variable or to the overall total.

For example, there exists male and female population with different age groups of less than 20 years, 20 – 40 years, 40 – 60 years, 60 – 80 years, 80 years and above of age. To have a clear picture of men and women between different age categories, cross tabulation will be appropriate. In this case, there will be gender (2 categories) multiplied by age group (5 categories) cells ie.10 cells with respective value in each category. Each cell gives the frequency of occurrence in the respective category. This method of display can give better description of the respondents of different categories. Percentage to the row total (gender) gives the distribution of the sample responses among male and female in each category of age group to the respective row total.

CASE

A supermarket wants to identify the reasons for decline in its monthly sales in its chain of stores located across 4 different zones, namely, north, south, east and west. In order to identify the reasons, the supermarket conducted a survey among 100 customers and found that five factors caused dissatisfaction among the customers. The five factors are: [1-Poor Quality of Materials, 2-Poor Service, 3-Poor Ambience, 4-Higher Cost, 5-Billing Errors]. The 4 zones are coded as: [1-North, 2-South, 3-East, 4-West]. Input table is given below. Explain the reasons for dissatisfaction among the four zones. What are the zones that have major dissatisfaction among the five reasons that lead to dissatisfaction?

Sample	Reason for Dissatisfaction	Zone	Sample	Reason for Dissatisfaction	Zone
1	1	1	51	2	2
2	3	3	52	4	4
3	3	3	53	1	1
4	4	4	54	4	4
5	5	1	55	5	4
6	2	2	56	4	4
7	1	1	57	5	2
8	3	3	58	1	2
9	1	2	59	1	3
10	1	1	60	1	2
11	2	2	61	1	1

12	4	4	62	1	1
13	5	2	63	3	3
14	1	1	64	4	4
15	2	2	65	2	2
16	1	2	66	5	3
17	1	1	67	3	3
18	1	1	68	2	2
19	3	3	69	1	3
20	4	4	70	2	2
21	4	4	71	2	1
22	2	2	72	2	2
23	1	1	73	4	2
24	1	1	74	5	1
25	4	4	75	4	3
26	4	4	76	3	3
27	1	2	77	1	3
28	1	1	78	1	1
29	1	1	79	3	3
30	4	1	80	4	4
31	4	4	81	5	4
32	1	2	82	4	3
33	1	1	83	2	2
34	1	1	84	1	1
35	3	3	85	2	2
36	4	1	86	1	1
37	1	1	87	3	1
38	4	4	88	2	1
39	1	2	89	1	3
40	1	3	90	1	1

41	1	1	91	2	4
42	3	3	92	3	2
43	4	2	93	2	3
44	4	4	94	2	3
45	5	3	95	1	4
46	4	4	96	1	1
47	1	1	97	1	4
48	2	2	98	3	4
49	4	4	99	4	3
50	1	1	100	1	1

Zone of Location * Reasons for Dissatisfaction Crosstabulation

			Reasons for Dissatisfaction					Total
			Poor Quality of Materials	**Poor Service**	**Poor Ambience**	**Higher Cost**	**Billing Errors**	
Zone of Location	North Zone	Count	25	2	1	2	2	32
		% within Reasons for Dissatisfaction	64.1%	11.8%	7.7%	8.7%	25.0%	32.0%
	South Zone	Count	7	12	1	2	2	24
		% within Reasons for Dissatisfaction	17.9%	70.6%	7.7%	8.7%	25.0%	24.0%
	East Zone	Count	5	2	10	3	2	22
		% within Reasons for Dissatisfaction	12.8%	11.8%	76.9%	13.0%	25.0%	22.0%

West Zone	Count	2	1	1	16	2	22
	% within Reasons for Dissatisfa-ction	5.1%	5.9%	7.7%	69.6%	25.0%	22.0%
Total	Count	39	17	13	23	8	100
	% within Reasons for Dissatis-faction	100.0%	100.0%	100.0%	100.0%	100.0%	100.0%

Interpretation

From the tables, it can be inferred that the problem of poor quality of materials exists in the north zone. 64.1% of the respondents, who are dissatisfied due to poor quality of materials, are from north zone. Similarly, 70.6% of the respondents, who are dissatisfied due to poor service, are from south zone. 76.9% of the respondents, who are dissatisfied due to poor ambience of stores, are from east zone. 69.6% of the respondents, who are dissatisfied due to higher cost, are from west zone. Billing errors are prevalent throughout all the zones.

Navigation Guide

- Data must be entered in the 'Data View' page of the data sheet, as given by the respondents. (In this case, it is based on the response given by 100 customers of the supermarket regarding the factors that cause dissatisfaction for them. These customers are from all 4 zones, namely, north, south, east and west).
- In the 'Variable View' page, a suitable name and a label must be given for the variables. (In this example, the variables are named and labelled as 'Reasons for Dissatisfaction' and 'Zone of Location'). The values must be entered as mentioned in the questionnaire. The value must be entered first, followed by the corresponding label. (In this example, the reasons for dissatisfaction are coded as follows: 1-Poor Quality of Materials, 2-Poor Service, 3-Poor Ambience, 4-Higher Cost, 5-Billing Errors. Zones of location are coded as follows: 1-North, 2-South, 3-East, 4-West).
- Click 'OK' after entering the values and the corresponding labels.

Data View

*cross tabs [DataSet1] - SPSS Data Editor

File Edit View Data Transform Analyze Graphs Utilities Window Help

1 : Dissatisfaction 1

	Dissatisfaction	Zone	var	var	var	var	var	var	var	var	var
1	1.00	1.00									
2	3.00	3.00									
3	3.00	3.00									
4	4.00	4.00									
5	5.00	1.00									
6	2.00	2.00									
7	1.00	1.00									
8	3.00	3.00									
9	1.00	2.00									
10	1.00	1.00									
11	2.00	2.00									
12	4.00	4.00									
13	5.00	2.00									
14	1.00	1.00									
15	2.00	2.00									
16	1.00	2.00									
17	1.00	1.00									
18	1.00	1.00									
19	3.00	3.00									
20	4.00	4.00									
21	4.00	4.00									
22	2.00	2.00									
23	1.00	1.00									
24	1.00	1.00									
25	4.00	4.00									
26	4.00	4.00									
27	1.00	2.00									
28	1.00	1.00									
29	1.00	1.00									
30	4.00	1.00									
31	4.00	4.00									
32	1.00	2.00									
33	1.00	1.00									
34	1.00	1.00									
35	3.00	3.00									
36	4.00	1.00									
37	1.00	1.00									
38	4.00	4.00									
39	1.00	2.00									
40	1.00	3.00									
41	1.00	1.00									
42	3.00	3.00									
43	4.00	2.00									
44	4.00	4.00									
45	5.00	3.00									
46	4.00	4.00									
47	1.00	1.00									
48	2.00	2.00									
49	4.00	4.00									
50	1.00	1.00									
51	2.00	2.00									
52	4.00	4.00									
53	1.00	1.00									
54	4.00	4.00									
55	5.00	4.00									

56	4.00	4.00
57	5.00	2.00
58	1.00	2.00
59	1.00	3.00
60	1.00	2.00
61	1.00	1.00
62	1.00	1.00
63	3.00	3.00
64	4.00	4.00
65	2.00	2.00
66	5.00	3.00
67	3.00	3.00
68	2.00	2.00
69	1.00	3.00
70	2.00	2.00
71	2.00	1.00
72	2.00	2.00
73	4.00	2.00
74	5.00	1.00
75	4.00	3.00
76	3.00	3.00
77	1.00	3.00
78	1.00	1.00
79	3.00	3.00
80	4.00	4.00
81	5.00	4.00
82	4.00	3.00
83	2.00	2.00
84	1.00	1.00
85	2.00	2.00
86	1.00	1.00
87	3.00	1.00
88	2.00	1.00
89	1.00	3.00
90	1.00	1.00
91	2.00	4.00
92	3.00	2.00
93	2.00	3.00
94	2.00	3.00
95	1.00	4.00
96	1.00	1.00
97	1.00	4.00
98	3.00	4.00
99	4.00	3.00
100	1.00	1.00

Variable View

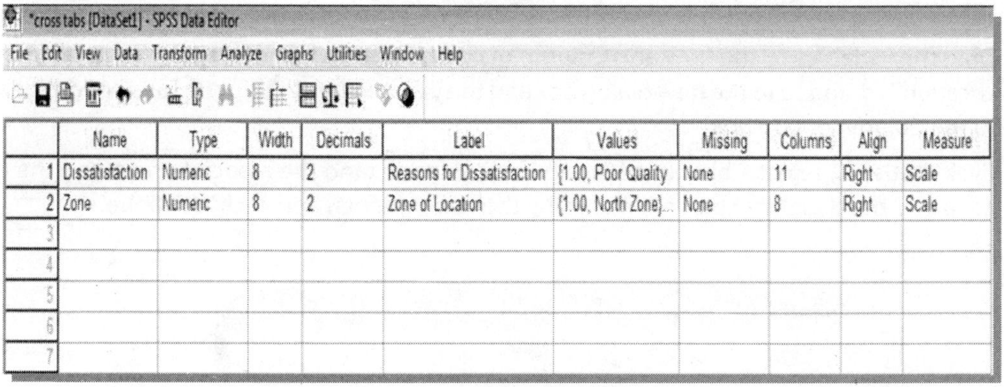

	Name	Type	Width	Decimals	Label	Values	Missing	Columns	Align	Measure
1	Dissatisfaction	Numeric	8	2	Reasons for Dissatisfaction	{1.00, Poor Quality	None	11	Right	Scale
2	Zone	Numeric	8	2	Zone of Location	{1.00, North Zone}...	None	8	Right	Scale
3										
4										
5										
6										
7										

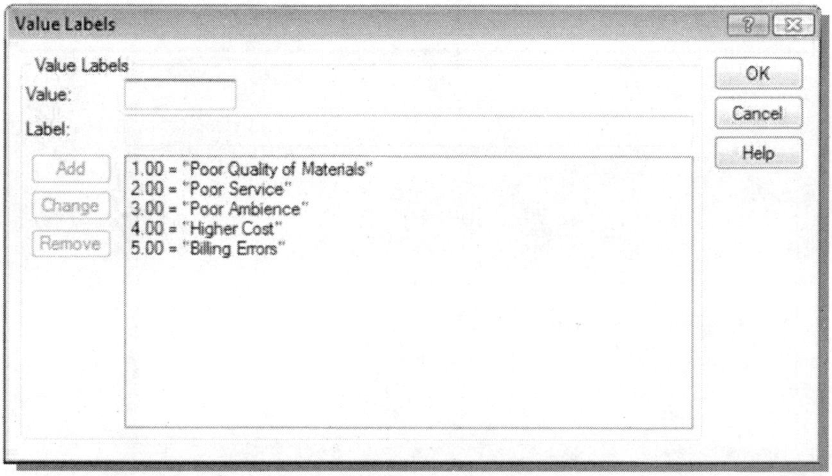

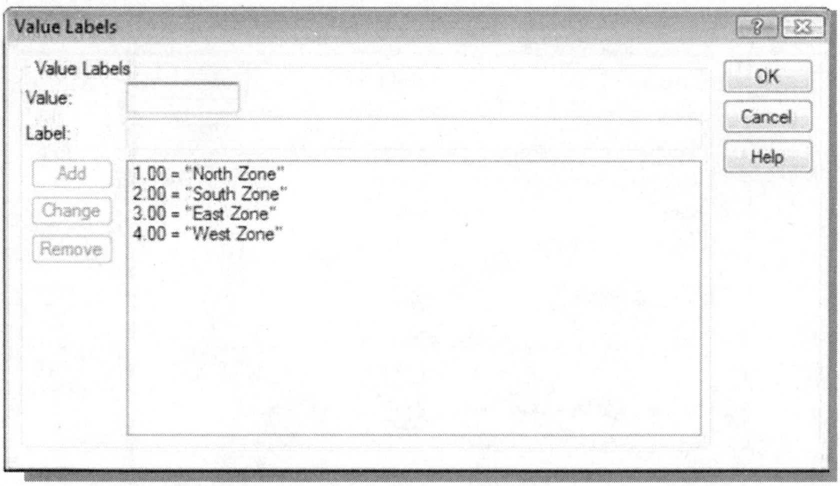

Then, the following steps are followed:

- Select Analyse → Descriptive Statistics →Crosstabs.
- Drag the variables to the Row and Column dialog blocks. (In this example, the variable 'Zone of Location' is dragged to the Row dialog box and the variable 'Reasons for Dissatisfaction' is dragged to the Column dialog box).
- Click 'Statistics', select 'Chi-square' (if required to understand the association among the type of zone and the dissatisfaction expressed by the respondents) and click 'Continue'.
- Click 'OK'.

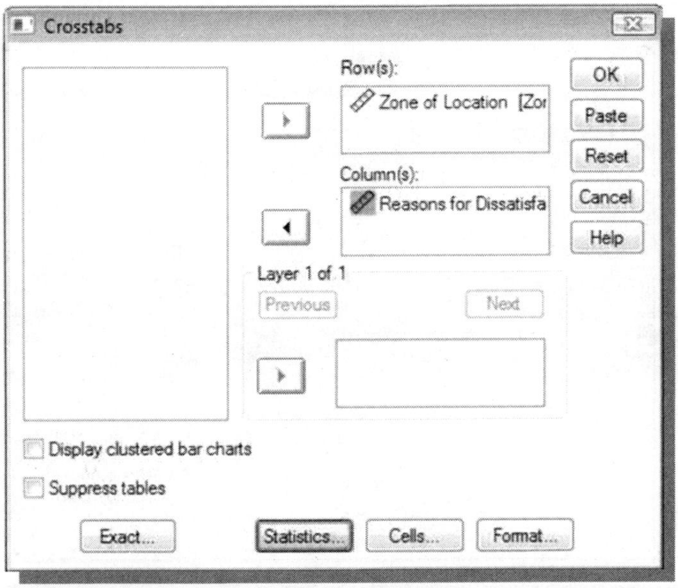

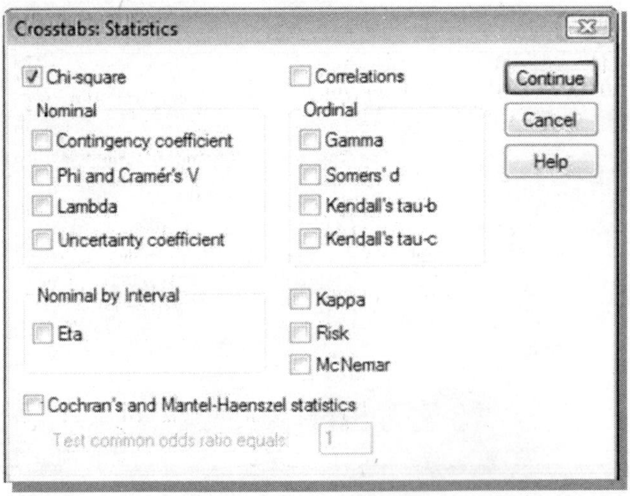

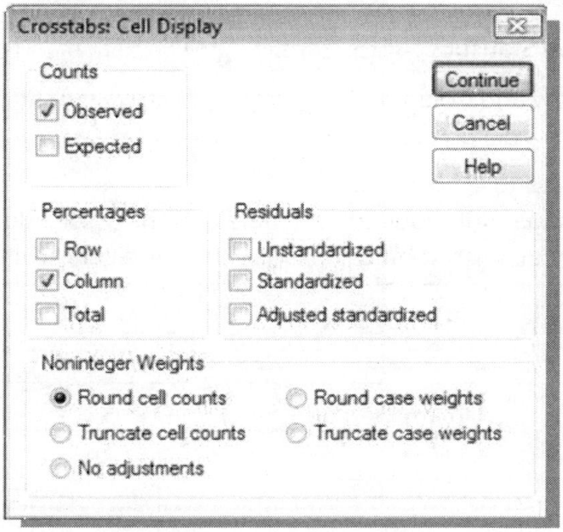

Descriptive statistics give clear understanding of the sample data and helps to understand the similarities or dissimilarities if exist from the population. This can be done by comparing the mean distribution of the sample and the population (mean) and the amount of variation that exists between the groups (standard deviation). Descriptive statistics will further lead to inferential and analytical statistics for making decisions in research.

Review Questions

1. Explain descriptive statics and its significance with examples.
2. Explain the application of cross tabulation and how it is executed using SPSS.
3. XYZ Ltd. manufactures electrical components that are used by the leading automobile manufacturers. The management of XYZ Ltd., had been receiving complaints that there is a large variation in the number of defectives from time to time. This made the company to gather data about the number of defectives present in three different work shifts. The work shifts are coded as [1-9:30 am to 11:30 am, 2-11:30 am to 1:30 pm, 3-2:30 pm to 4:30 pm]. The number of defectives are coded as [1-Less than 5 defectives, 2-5 defectives to 10 defectives, 3-More than 10 defectives]. Input data is given in table below:

Sample	Work Shift	Defectives	Sample	Work Shift	Defectives
1	1	2	31	1	2
2	2	2	32	2	2
3	3	3	33	3	2
4	1	1	34	1	1

5	2	2	35	2	2
6	3	3	36	3	3
7	1	2	37	1	1
8	2	2	38	2	2
9	3	3	39	3	2
10	1	2	40	1	2
11	2	2	41	2	2
12	3	2	42	3	3
13	1	1	43	1	1
14	2	1	44	2	1
15	3	3	45	3	3
16	1	1	46	1	2
17	2	2	47	2	2
18	3	2	48	3	2
19	1	2	49	1	1
20	2	3	50	2	2
21	3	3	51	3	3
22	1	2	52	1	1
23	2	2	53	2	2
24	3	3	54	3	2
25	1	2	55	1	2
26	2	2	56	2	2
27	3	3	57	3	3
28	1	1	58	1	1
29	2	1	59	2	1
30	3	2	60	3	3

Find out the percentage of defectives in different work shifts with a cross tabulation. Calculate the average amount of defectives and median and mode of the defectives.

4. Select any 4 telecom (mobile) service providers and conduct a survey among 50 respondents of each service provider to find out the reasons for dissatisfaction, if any. Understand the reasons for dissatisfaction among the four different telecom service providers with a cross tabulation.

Chapter 10

Establishing Hypothesis and Testing

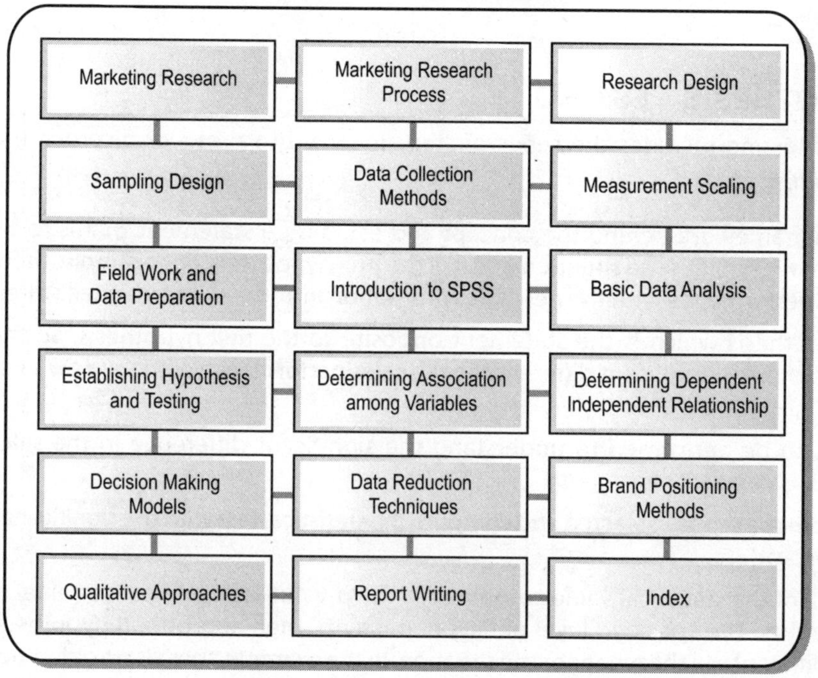

Outline

Chapter Structure

- Introduction
- Procedure for Hypothesis Testing
- T-test
- One sample T-test (Behaviour of an Individual Variable)
- Case
- Independent T-test (Difference in the Response among Two Set of Sample)
- Case
- Paired T-test (Impact of Test Variable)
- Case
- One-way Anova (Difference in the Sample Mean)
- Case
- Review Questions

Chapter Overview

Chapter ten explains the concept of establishing hypothesis and the statistical analysis done to prove or disprove them. In specific the chapter discusses the parametric tests used for hypothesis testing. The application of t-test and one way ANOVA is elaborated with examples and cases of application.

INTRODUCTION

Hypothesis is an unproven statement or proposition of a phenomenon or situation. It is an assumption set to have directions for research. For example, a sales manager may assume that new advertisement released will increase sales in the next quarter. These assumptions about future are hypothesis that is proved or disproved with statistical techniques. Null hypothesis (represented as H_0) nullifies the situation. For example, researches in the above case, assume hypothesis as there is no significant difference in the sales performance after the release of new advertisement. An alternate hypothesis (represented as H_A or H_1) is the statement or situation alternate or opposite of the null hypothesis. For the above case, the alternate hypothesis will be, there is significant difference in the sales performance after the release of new advertisement. Once the hypothesis are set, statistical procedures to prove or disprove it is decided. Statistical tests depend on the hypothesis and the results expected. Thus setting of the hypothesis gives clear direction as to the analysis to be performed, results to be achieved and decisions to be made. Hypothesis is established with a sequence or series of procedures.

PROCEDURE FOR HYPOTHESIS TESTING

The procedure for hypothesis testing includes the series of steps involved to prove or disprove the hypothesis established. It includes:

- Understand the theoretical framework behind the concept and establish a statement that is to be tested. The statement generally nullifies the situation and it is the null hypothesis. For example, there is no difference in the sales performance with the new sales promotion introduced in the retail stores.
- Establish the alternate hypothesis which is the statement opposite to the null hypothesis. So the alternate hypothesis will be there is significant difference in the sales performance with the new sales promotion.
- Finalise the statistical test to be performed to understand the significant difference in the sales performance.
- Collect the required data from the sample selected and compute the statistical test with the significance level decided (usually 5 percent).
- Check the significance level of the statistical value computed. If the p-value (or significance value) of the calculated test is more than the specified level of 0.05 (5 percent), then accept null hypothesis that there is no significant difference in the means or the situation. In the example, there is no difference in the sales promotion.
- If the significance level of the calculated test is less than the specified level of 0.05 (5 percent), then reject the null hypothesis and accept alternate hypothesis. So there is significant difference in the sales with the sales promotion introduced.

Hypothesis Tests

The statistical tests adopted for basic hypothesis testing are broadly classified as Parametric & Non-parametric. Parametric tests are used if measurement scale is interval & Non parametric tests are used for nominal or ordinary data.

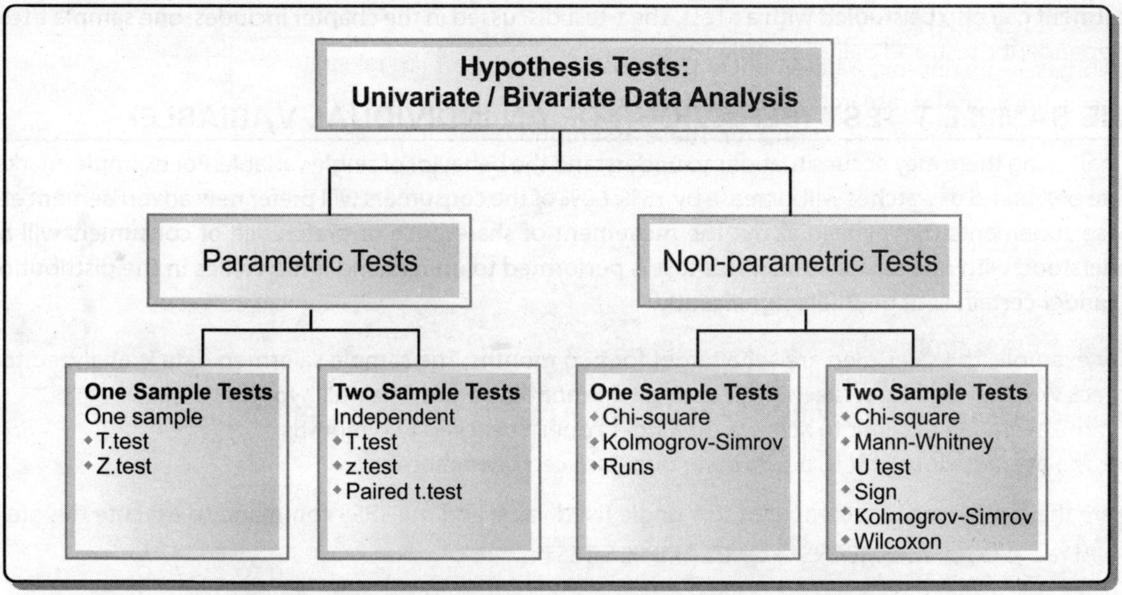

Figure 10.1: Hypothesis Test for Univariate Data Analysis

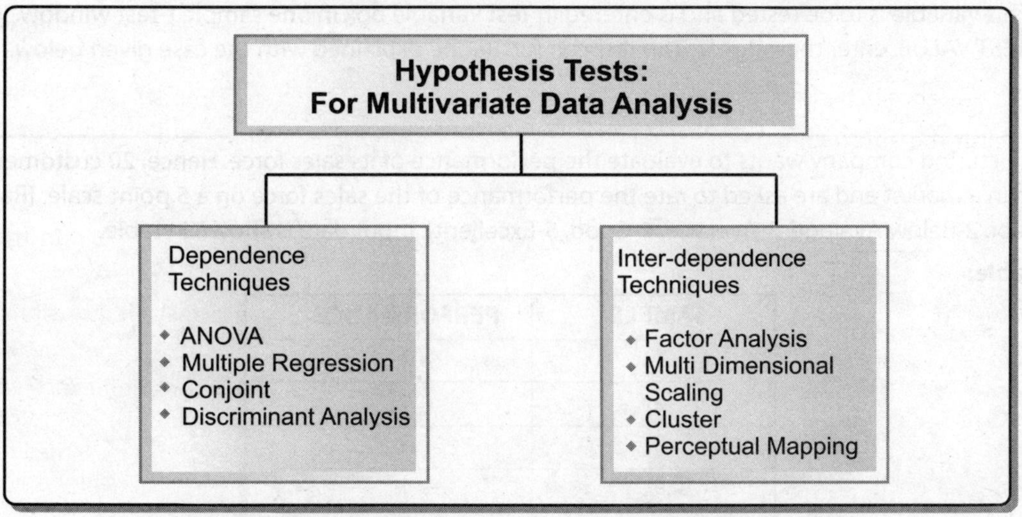

Figure 10.2: Hypothesis Test for Multivariate Data Analysis

This chapter discusses the parametric tests used for hypothesis testing.

T-TEST

T-test is used to study the similarity between the samples drawn from different population or to compare the mean of two different groups. It is also used to understand how different the mean of sample drawn from two different groups is. The difference in the behaviour of the same set of respondents with a specific treatment can also be studied with a t-test. The t-test discussed in the chapter includes: one sample t-test, independent t-test, and paired sample t-test.

ONE SAMPLE T-TEST (BEHAVIOUR OF AN INDIVIDUAL VARIABLE)

In marketing there may occur situations to understand the behavior of single variable. For example, market share of X brand of watches will increase by 15%; 60% of the consumers will prefer new advertisement etc. These statements that explain about the movement of share price or preference of consumers will be understood with one sample t-test. This test is performed to understand if the values in the distribution fall under certain limit or differs significantly.

For example, the sales men are set a target for two months. The sample salesmen data is analyzed to check whether his target is achieved during two months period. The null hypothesis is:
H_0: The average time limit to achieve the targets doesn't exceed two months
H_1: The average time limit to achieve the targets exceed two months

Here the sample mean is compared to a single fixed value and the SPSS command to execute this are:
ANALYSE → COMPARE MEANS → ONE SAMPLE T-TEST

The input file will have a variable 'Period' which explains the time taken by the respondents to achieve the target. This variable is to be tested and is entered in Test variable box in one sample t-test window. In the option TEST VALUE, enter the value '2'. The test can further be explained with the case given below.

CASE

A manufacturing company wants to evaluate the performance of its sales force. Hence, 20 customers are selected in a market and are asked to rate the performance of the sales force on a 5 point scale. [Ratings are: 1-Poor, 2-Below Average, 3-Average, 4-Good, 5-Excellent]. Input data is shown in table.

Input Table:

SAMPLE	PERFORMANCE
1	2
2	4
3	3
4	4
5	3
6	4
7	2
8	5
9	1
10	4
11	2

12	5
13	2
14	4
15	3
16	1
17	2
18	3
19	2
20	3

The company's expectation is that the performance of the sales force must be at least 4 and not less than that.

Null Hypothesis (H_0): There is no significant difference in the mean performance level of the sales force from the expected value of the company.

Alternate Hypothesis (H_1): There is significant difference in the mean performance level of the sales force from the expected value of the company.

Table presents the output from one-sample t-test.

Output Tables:

One-Sample Descriptive Statistics

	N	Mean	Std. Deviation	Std. Error Mean
Performance	20	2.9500	1.19097	.26631

One-Sample Test

	Test Value = 4					
Variable	t	df	Sig. (2-tailed)	Mean Difference	95% Confidence Interval of the Difference	
					Lower	Upper
Performance	-3.943	19	.001	-1.05000	-1.6074	-.4926

Interpretation

The t value is -3.943 and the p-value of this test is 0.001 at n-1 (20 – 1 = 19) degrees of freedom (df). The value of 'p' is less than the significance level of 0.05 (5 percent) and even less than 0.01 (1 percent). Hence, we reject the null hypothesis. It means that there is significant difference in the mean performance level of the sales force from the expected value of the company. From the tables, it can be inferred that the mean performance level is 2.95, which is less than the company's expected value of 4. The deviation is 1.19 that explains the variation from the mean value. The customers of the company are not satisfied with the performance of the sales force as it varies significantly from the company's expected mean performance.

Navigation Guide

In order to enter data:

- Data must be entered in the 'Data View' page of the data sheet, as given by the respondents. (In this case, it is based on the response given by 20 customers in the market regarding the performance of the sales force).

Data View

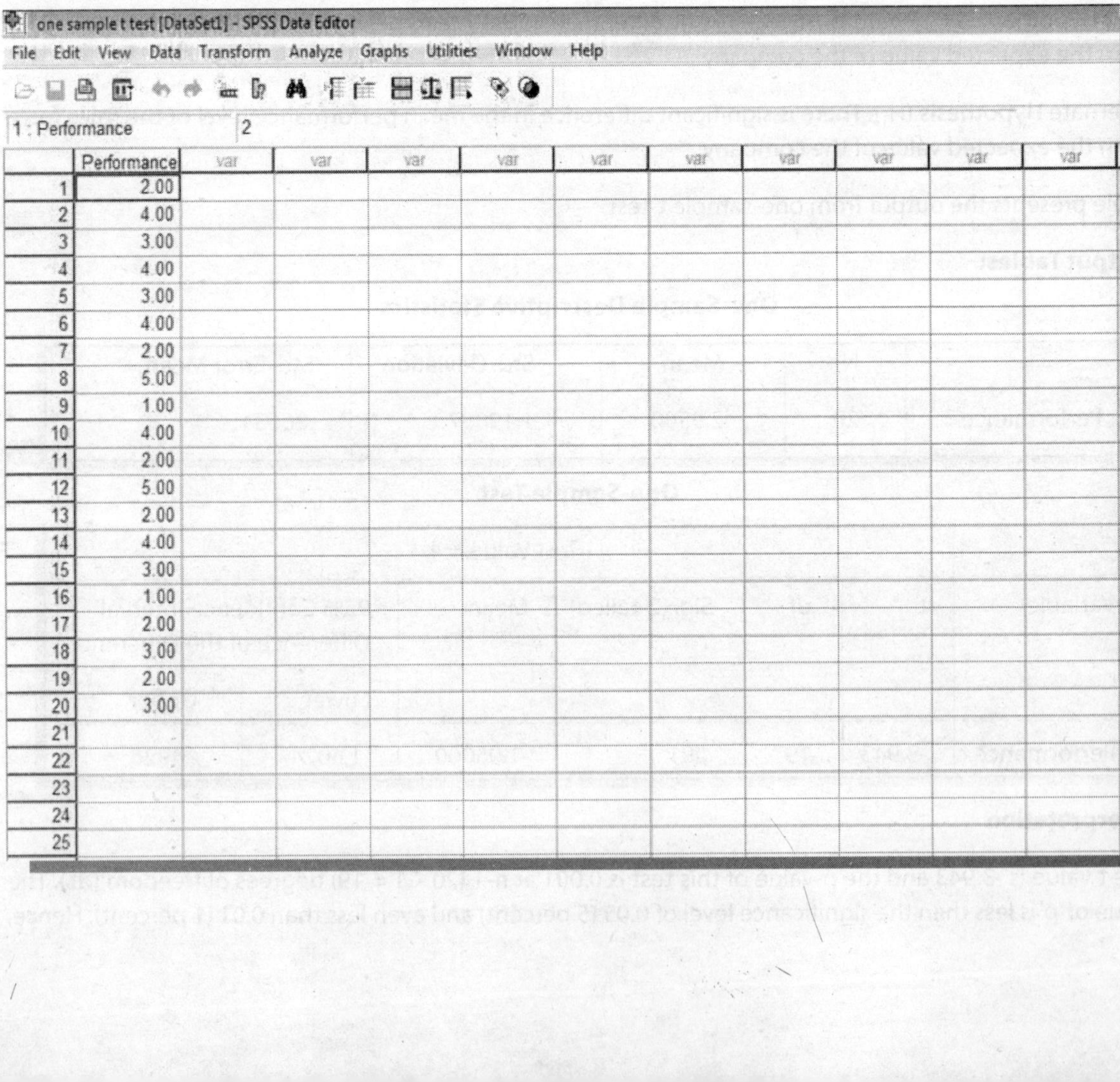

Variable View

- Open variable view and enter 'Performance' in the column Name. It assigns by default, the type of data, width, decimals and measure.

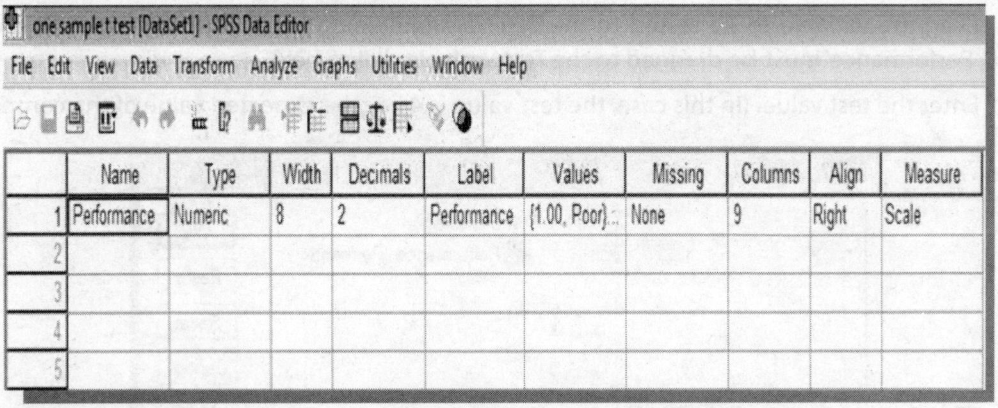

- In the 'Variable View' page, a suitable name and a label must be given for the variables entered. (In this example, the variable is: PERFORMANCE). The data must be entered as collected in the questionnaire. The value coded must be entered first, and then assign the corresponding labels. (In this example, performance of the sales force is rated on a 5 point scale and the values entered are: 1-Poor, 2-Below Average, 3-Average, 4-Good, 5-Excellent). In the pull down menu of Value, code the values as follows:

Value: 1

Label: Poor

Click 'Add'

Similarly add the values for the scale

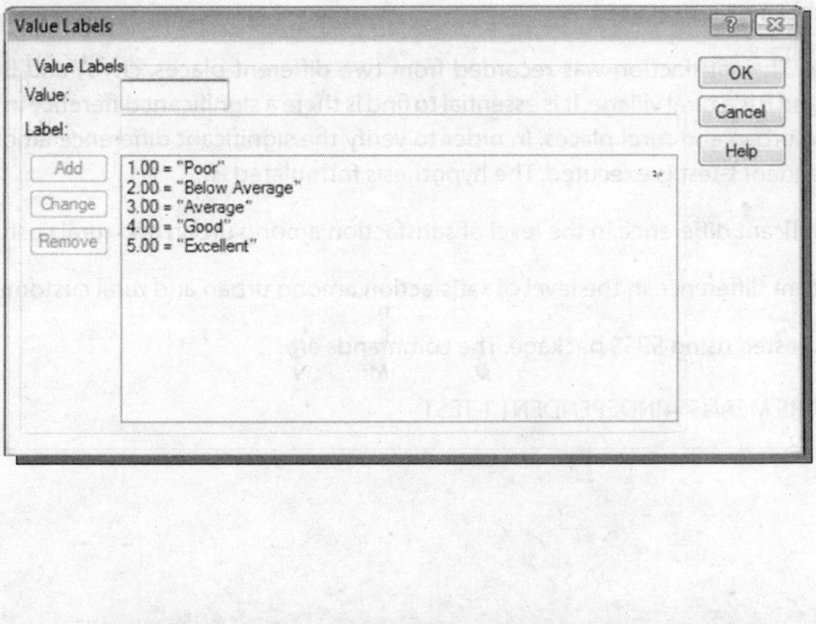

➢ Enter the values and click OK and save the input file.

Then, the following procedure must be followed to perform analysis:

- Select Analyse →Compare Means→ One-Sample T Test.
- Drag the variable to be tested to the Test Variable dialog box. (In this example, the variable 'Performance' must be dragged to the Test Variable dialog box).
- Enter the test value. (In this case, the test value is 4 i.e., the expected value of the company).

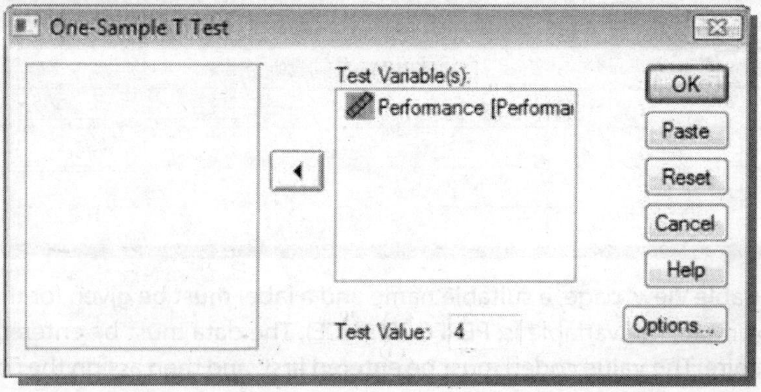

- Click 'OK'.

INDEPENDENT T-TEST (DIFFERENCE IN THE RESPONSE AMONG TWO SET OF SAMPLE)

The responses collected may be from two different populations, which may be of two cities, or two brands, or two distribution outlets. The responses from two different populations may be similar or different. In order to identify whether the responses collected from two different population has significant difference or not, independent t-test is executed.

schemes in a store. The satisfaction was recorded from two different places, city A and B where A is a metropolitan city and B is a rural village. It is essential to find is there a significant difference in the customer satisfaction among urban and rural places. In order to verify the significant difference among two set of customers, independent t-test is executed. The hypothesis formulated is:

H_0: There is no significant difference in the level of satisfaction among urban and rural customers

H_1: There is significant difference in the level of satisfaction among urban and rural customers

The significance is tested using SPSS package. The commands are:

ANALYSE →COMPARE MEANS →INDEPENDENT T-TEST

CASE

A manufacturing company wants to evaluate the performance of its sales force in two different markets. Hence, 20 customers from each market, A and B, are asked to rate the performance of the sales force of their respective market, on a 5 point scale. [Ratings are: 1-Poor, 2-Below Average, 3-Average, 4-Good, 5-Excellent]. Input data is shown in table.

Input Table:

SAMPLE	PERFORMANCE	SALES FORCE	SAMPLE	PERFORMANCE	SALES FORCE
1	2	1	21	5	2
2	4	1	22	4	2
3	3	1	23	4	2
4	4	1	24	4	2
5	3	1	25	5	2
6	4	1	26	4	2
7	2	1	27	4	2
8	5	1	28	4	2
9	1	1	29	5	2
10	4	1	30	3	2
11	2	1	31	4	2
12	5	1	32	5	2
13	2	1	33	3	2
14	4	1	34	4	2
15	3	1	35	5	2
16	1	1	36	2	2
17	2	1	37	5	2
18	3	1	38	5	2
19	2	1	39	4	2
20	3	1	40	4	2

Null Hypothesis (H_0): There is no significant difference in the mean performance level among the sales force from the markets A and B.

Alternate Hypothesis (H_1): There is significant difference in the mean performance level among the sales force from the markets A and B.

Table presents the output from independent sample t-test.

Output Tables:

Group Statistics

	Sales Force	N	Mean	Std. Deviation	Std. Error Mean
Performance	A	20	2.9500	1.19097	.26631
	B	20	4.1500	.81273	.18173

The descriptive statistics reveal that the respondents from each market A and B is 20 with a mean performance of 2.95 and 4.15 respectively. The deviation is 1.19 and 0.81 for the markets A and B from its mean performance level.

Independent Samples Test

	Levene's Test for Equality of Variances		t-test for Equality of Means						
Performance	F	Sig.	t	Df	Sig. (2-tailed)	Mean Difference	Std. Error Difference	95% Confidence Interval of the Difference	
								Lower	Upper
Equal variances assumed	3.619	.065	-3.722	38	.001	-1.20000	.32241	-1.85268	-.54732
Equal variances not assumed			-3.722	33.542	.001	-1.20000	.32241	-1.85554	-.54446

Interpretation

- Firstly, Levene's test for equality of variance is checked which is not significant as the significance value is 0.065, which is greater than 0.05. So "Equal Variances Assumed" test values are used. The significance of test substantiates the use of "Equal Variances Assumed" or "Equal Variances Not Assumed". If the Levene's test value is less than 0.05 then "Equal Variances Not Assumed" test values are used. In comparing groups, the similarity of the variances is checked.

- Secondly, the t-test value with equal variances assumed is -3.722. The p-value of this test is 0.001, which is less than the significance level of 0.01 (at 1 percent). Hence, we reject the null hypothesis. It means that there is significant difference in the mean performance level between the sales force in the markets of A and B.
- It is substantiated in the descriptive tables as the mean performance rating of sales force in market A is 2.95. It is less than the mean performance rating of the sales force in market B, whose mean performance rating is 4.15. It shows that the performance of sales force in market B is better than the performance of the sales force in market A.

Navigation Guide

In order to enter data:

➢ Data must be entered in the 'Data View' page of the data sheet, as given by the respondents. (In this case, it is based on the response given by 40 customers, of two different sales force, in the market).

Data View

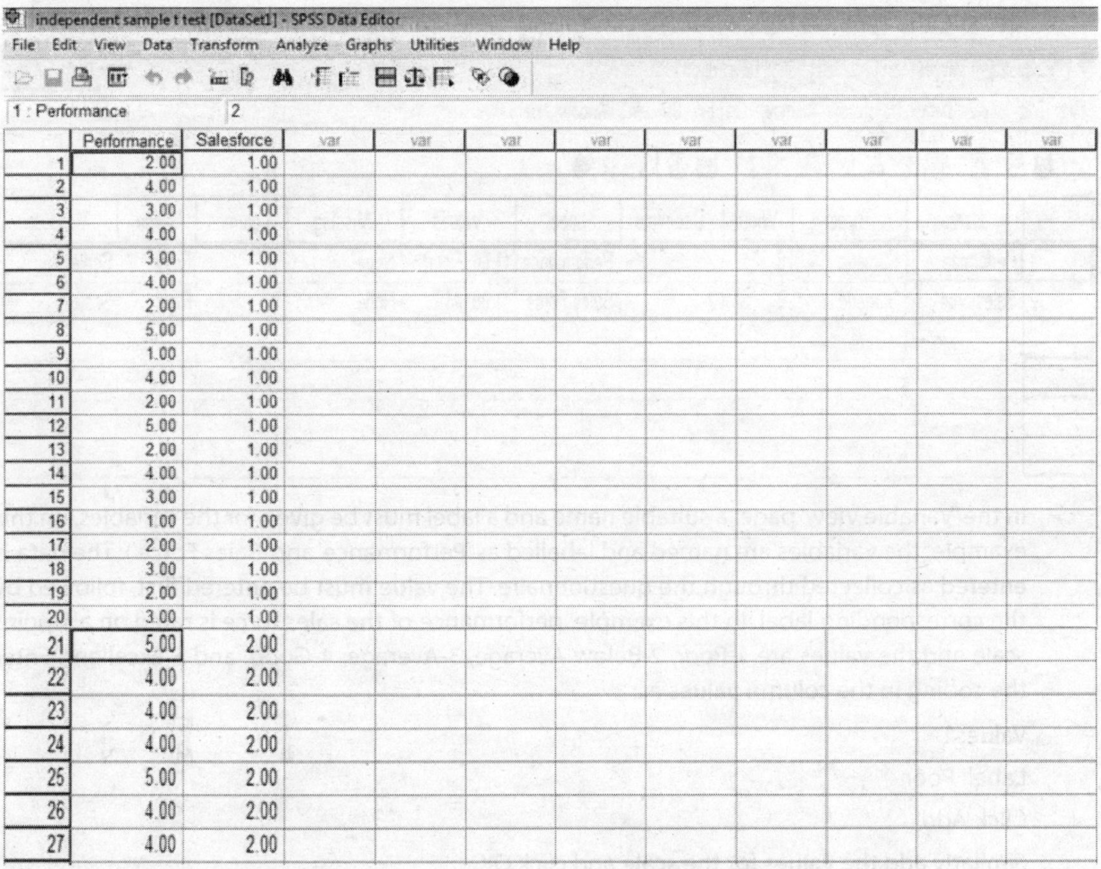

independent sample t test [DataSet1] - SPSS Data Editor

File Edit View Data Transform Analyze Graphs Utilities Window Help

1 : Performance | 2

	Performance	Salesforce	var	var	var	var	var	var	var	var	var
1	2.00	1.00									
2	4.00	1.00									
3	3.00	1.00									
4	4.00	1.00									
5	3.00	1.00									
6	4.00	1.00									
7	2.00	1.00									
8	5.00	1.00									
9	1.00	1.00									
10	4.00	1.00									
11	2.00	1.00									
12	5.00	1.00									
13	2.00	1.00									
14	4.00	1.00									
15	3.00	1.00									
16	1.00	1.00									
17	2.00	1.00									
18	3.00	1.00									
19	2.00	1.00									
20	3.00	1.00									
21	5.00	2.00									
22	4.00	2.00									
23	4.00	2.00									
24	4.00	2.00									
25	5.00	2.00									
26	4.00	2.00									
27	4.00	2.00									

28	4.00	2.00
29	5.00	2.00
30	3.00	2.00
31	4.00	2.00
32	5.00	2.00
33	3.00	2.00
34	4.00	2.00
35	5.00	2.00
36	2.00	2.00
37	5.00	2.00
38	5.00	2.00
39	4.00	2.00
40	4.00	2.00
41		
42		

Variable View

- Open variable view and enter 'Performance' and 'Salesforce' in the column Name. It assigns by default, the type of data, width, decimals and measure.

*independent sample t test [DataSet1] - SPSS Data Editor

File Edit View Data Transform Analyze Graphs Utilities Window Help

	Name	Type	Width	Decimals	Label	Values	Missing	Columns	Align	Measure
1	Performance	Numeric	8	2	Performance	{1.00, Poor}...	None	10	Right	Scale
2	Salesforce	Numeric	8	2	Sales Force	{1.00, A}...	None	9	Right	Scale
3										
4										
5										
6										

- In the 'Variable View' page, a suitable name and a label must be given for the variables. (In this example, the variables are named and labelled as 'Performance' and 'Sales Force'). The data is entered as collected through the questionnaire. The value must be entered first, followed by the corresponding label. In this example, performance of the sales force is rated on a 5 point scale and the values are 1-Poor, 2-Below Average, 3-Average, 4-Good, and 5-Excellent. Enter the coding in the column values as:

  Value: 1

  Label: Poor

  Click 'Add'

  Similarly add the values for the scale and click OK.

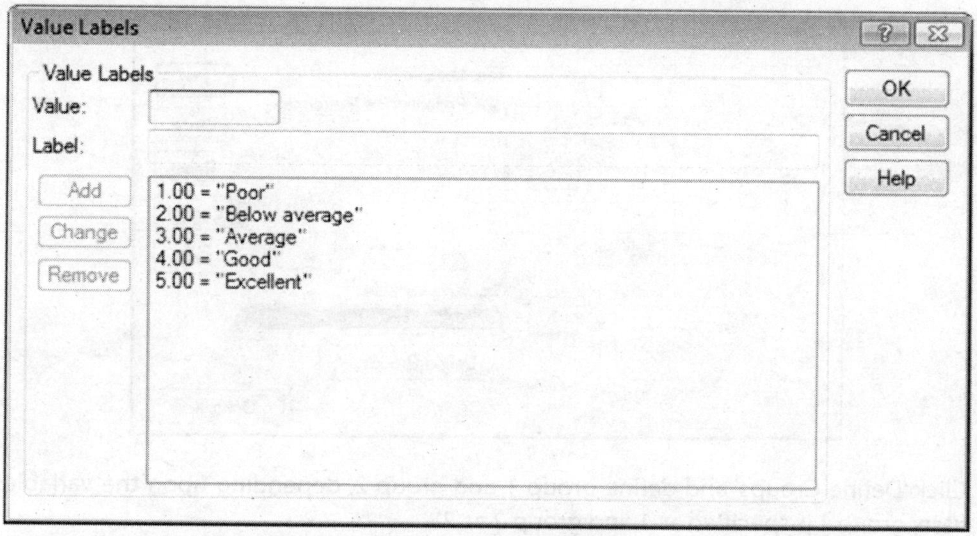

➢ Sales force considered for the study is from two markets: Market A and Market B. They sales force from Market A is coded with the value '1' and from Market B the value coded is '2'.

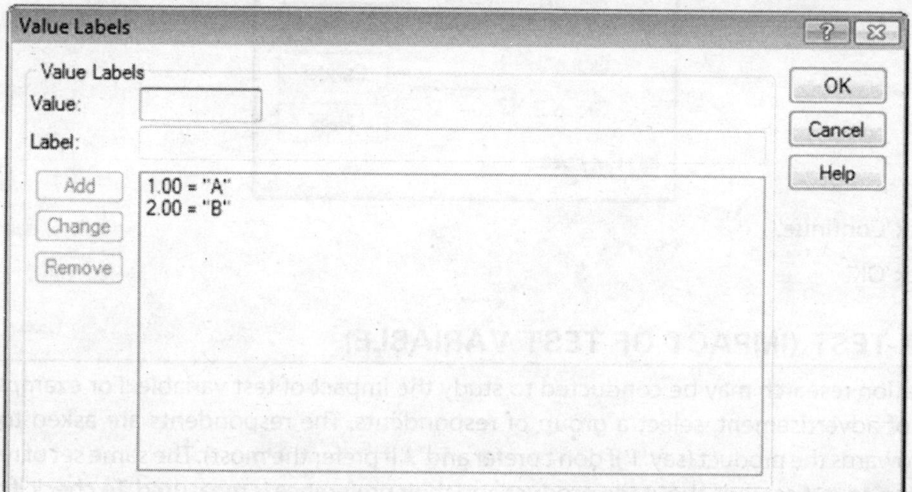

➢ Click ok and save the input file.

Then, the following procedure is followed to perform the analysis:

- Select Analyse→Compare Means →Independent Samples T Test.
- Drag the variable to be tested to the Test Variable dialog box. (In this example, the variable 'Performance' is dragged to the Test Variable dialog box).
- Drag the variable to be grouped to the Grouping Variable dialog box. (In this example, the variable 'Sales Force' is dragged to the Grouping Variable dialog box).

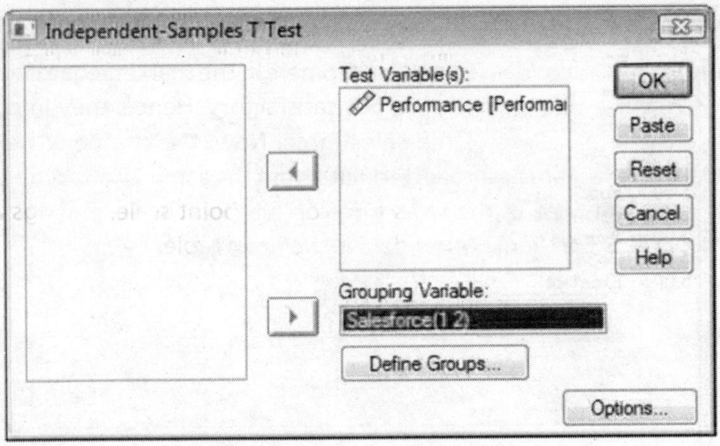

- Click 'Define Groups' and define group 1 and group 2, depending upon the variables. (In this case, group 1 is specified as 1 and group 2 as 2).

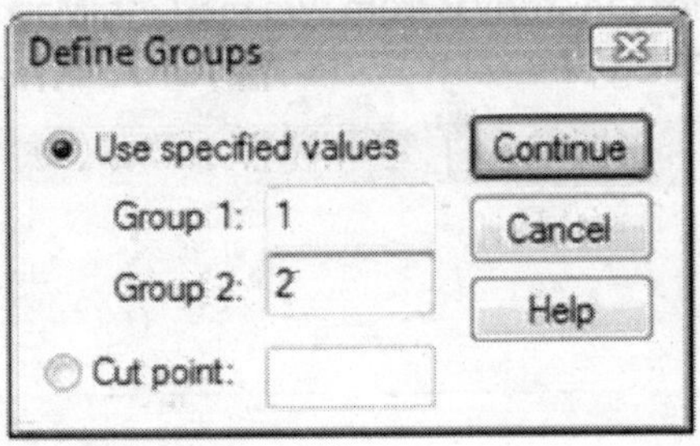

- Click 'Continue'.
- Click 'OK'.

PAIRED T-TEST (IMPACT OF TEST VARIABLE)

Experimentation research may be conducted to study the impact of test variable. For example, to study the impact of advertisement, select a group of respondents. The respondents are asked to give their preference towards the product (say '1' if don't prefer and '7' if prefer the most). The same set of respondents is shown in the advertisement about the product and their preference is measured. To check if there exists any significant difference in the preference because of advertisement, paired t-test can be performed.

The hypothesis formulated is:

H_0: There is no impact of advertisement in the preference for the product

H_1: There is impact of advertisement in the preference for the product

Is there exists an impact or not is tested statistically by paired t-test using SPSS package.

The commands used for executing the test are as follows:

ANALYSE →COMPARE MEANS → PAIRED T-TEST

CASE

A manufacturing company collected data from 20 customers in the market regarding the performance of the sales force and found that the performance not satisfactory. Hence, they implemented a training program to improve the performance of the sales force. Now, the company wants to evaluate the effectiveness of the training program and collected data from the same 20 customers in the market. They were asked to rate the performance of the sales force on a 5 point scale. [Ratings are: 1-Poor, 2-Below Average, 3-Average, 4-Good, 5-Excellent]. Input data is shown in table.

Input Table:

SAMPLE	PERFORMANCE BEFORE TRAINING	PERFORMANCE AFTER TRAINING
1	2	3
2	4	4
3	3	5
4	4	3
5	3	4
6	4	4
7	2	2
8	5	5
9	1	4
10	4	5
11	2	4
12	5	5
13	2	4
14	4	5
15	3	4
16	1	5
17	2	2
18	3	3
19	2	4
20	3	3

Null Hypothesis (H_0): There is no significant change in the mean performance level of the sales force before and after the implementation of the training program.

Alternate Hypothesis (H_1): There is significant change in the mean performance level of the sales force after the implementation of the training program.

Output Tables:

Paired Samples Statistics

		Mean	N	Std. Deviation	Std. Error Mean
Pair 1	Performance before training	2.9500	20	1.19097	.26631
	Performance after training	3.9000	20	.96791	.21643

The mean performance before training is 2.95 and after training is 3.9 for a sample of 20 respondents.

Paired Samples Test

		Paired Differences					t	df	Sig. (2-tailed)
		Mean	Std. Deviation	Std. Error Mean	95% Confidence Interval of the Difference				
					Lower	Upper			
Pair 1	Performance before training - Performance after training	-.95000	1.23438	.27601	-1.52771	-.37229	-3.442	19	.003

Interpretation

The paired t test values are -3.442 with a p-value of 0.003, which is less than the significance level of 0.01. Hence, we reject the null hypothesis and there is significant change in the mean performance level of the sales force after the training program from what it was before implementing it. From the tables, it can be inferred that the mean performance level of the sales force was 2.95, before the training program was implemented. But, after the training program, it has increased to 3.90. Thus, it can concluded that the training program was effective in improving the performance of the sales force.

Navigation Guide

In order to enter data:

➤ Data must be entered in the 'Data View' page of the data sheet, as given by the respondents. (In this case, it is based on the response given by 20 customers, in the market regarding the performance of the sales force before and after the implementation of a training program).

Data View

Paired sample t test [DataSet1] - SPSS Data Editor

File Edit View Data Transform Analyze Graphs Utilities Window Help

1 : Before 2

	Before	After	var	var	var	var	var	var	var	var	var
1	2.00	3.00									
2	4.00	4.00									
3	3.00	5.00									
4	4.00	3.00									
5	3.00	4.00									
6	4.00	4.00									
7	2.00	2.00									
8	5.00	5.00									
9	1.00	4.00									
10	4.00	5.00									
11	2.00	4.00									
12	5.00	5.00									
13	2.00	4.00									
14	4.00	5.00									
15	3.00	4.00									
16	1.00	5.00									
17	2.00	2.00									
18	3.00	3.00									
19	2.00	4.00									
20	3.00	3.00									
21	.	.									
22	.	.									
23	.	.									
24	.	.									
25	.	.									

Variable View

➤ Open variable view and enter 'Before' and 'After' in Name column. It assigns by default, the type of data, width, decimals and measure.

*Paired sample t test [DataSet1] - SPSS Data Editor

File Edit View Data Transform Analyze Graphs Utilities Window Help

	Name	Type	Width	Decimals	Label	Values	Missing	Columns	Align	Measure
1	Before	Numeric	8	2	Performance before training	{1.00, Poor}...	None	8	Right	Scale
2	After	Numeric	8	2	Performance after training	{1.00, Poor}...	None	8	Right	Scale
3										
4										
5										
6										

➢ In the 'Variable View' page, a suitable name and a label must be given for the variables. (In this example, the variables are: 'Performance before training' and 'Performance after training'). The data is entered as collected through the questionnaire. The value is entered first, followed by the corresponding label. In this example, performance of the sales force is rated on a 5 point scale and the values assigned are: 1-Poor, 2-Below Average, 3-Average, 4-Good, 5-Excellent. The labels remain the same for both the variables - 'Performance before training' and 'Performance after training'. Enter the values as:

Value: 1

Label: Poor

Click 'Add'

Similarly add the values for the scale

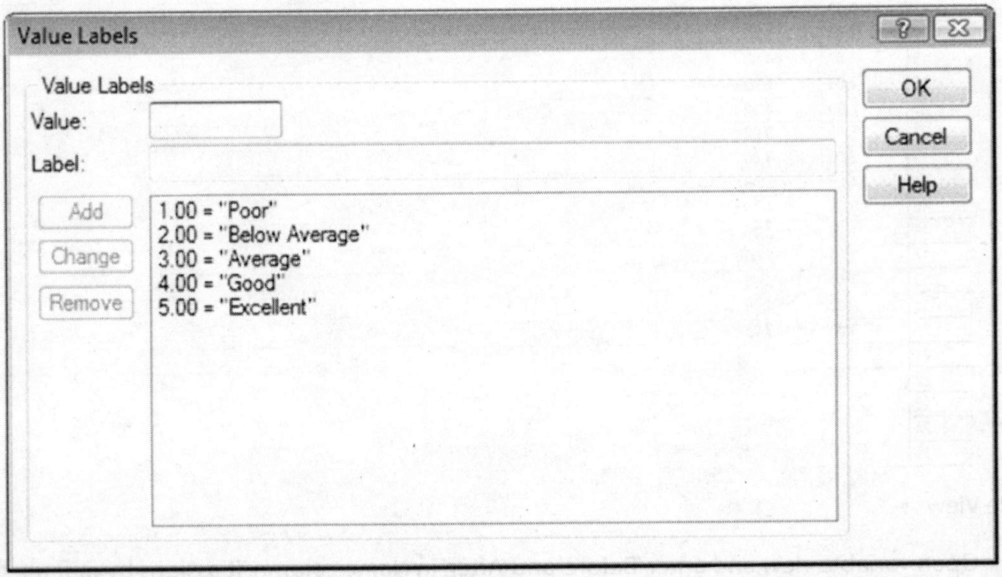

➢ Enter the values select ok and save the input file.

Then, the following procedure is followed to perform analysis:

- Select Analyse →Compare Means →Paired-Samples T Test.
- Drag the variables to be compared to the Paired Variables dialog box. In this example, the variables 'Performance before training' and 'Performance after training' must be dragged to the Paired Variables dialog box.
- Click 'OK' and the output file opens.

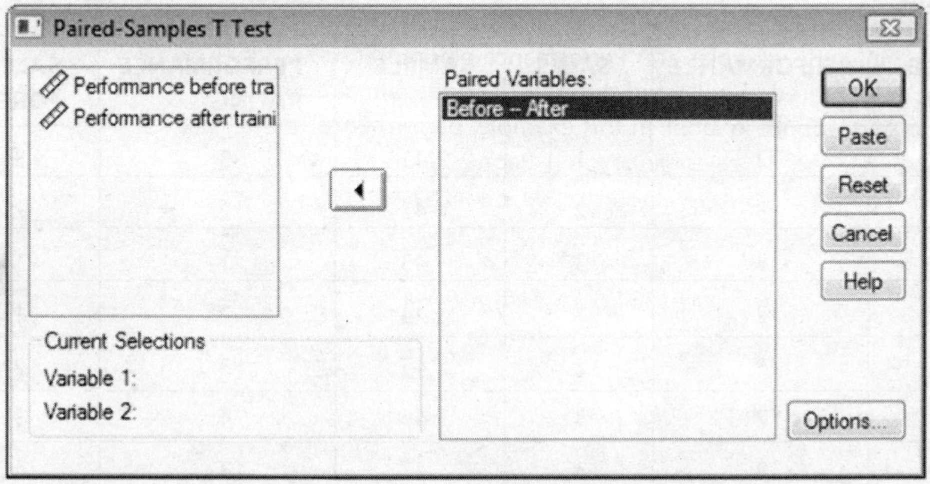

ONE-WAY ANOVA (DIFFERENCE IN THE SAMPLE MEAN)

Analysis of variance is used to compare whether the mean of the sample differs. Independent t-test compares the mean of the two distributions. For example, is there a difference in the opinion about the product or service among two different cities. If we want to check the opinion about the product among five different cities, one-way ANOVA is executed.

The hypothesis formulated is:

H_0: The mean response of the sample in five different cities is same

H_1: The mean response of the sample in five different cities is different

SPSS Command:

ANALYSE → COMPARE MEANS → ONE-WAY ANOVA

The screen on one way ANOVA has dependent list and factors to be entered. In our example, cities will be entered in FACTOR Box and opinion of the respondents in these cities will be entered in DEPENDENT LIST Box. This will compare the opinion of each of the five cities.

If descriptive statistics is required, select OPTIONS in the same window, which will give the option for descriptive. Press continues and ok.

CASE

A manufacturing company wants to evaluate the performance of its sales force in four different markets. Hence, 20 customers from each market, A, B, C and D, are asked to rate the performance of the sales force of their respective market, on a 5 point scale. [Ratings are: 1-Poor, 2-Below Average, 3-Average, 4-Good, 5-Excellent]. Input data is shown in table.

Input Table:

SAMPLE RATING	PERFORMANCE	SALES FORCE	SAMPLE	PERFORMANCE RATING	SALES FORCE
1	2	1	41	3	3
2	3	2	42	2	2
3	3	3	43	1	1
4	2	2	44	2	1
5	3	2	45	3	2
6	2	3	46	4	3
7	4	3	47	3	4
8	4	4	48	2	1
9	4	4	49	5	3
10	2	3	50	4	4
11	1	1	51	5	4
12	2	2	52	3	2
13	2	3	53	3	2
14	5	4	54	3	1
15	2	3	55	2	1
16	3	2	56	5	4
17	2	4	57	3	2
18	4	3	58	3	3
19	3	4	59	5	4
20	4	2	60	3	2
21	2	1	61	4	3
22	2	1	62	4	4
23	3	3	63	4	3
24	3	2	64	1	1
25	1	4	65	3	2

26	2	1	66	4	3
27	4	2	67	4	4
28	2	1	68	4	3
29	4	3	69	2	2
30	4	4	70	1	1
31	4	4	71	3	2
32	3	2	72	3	3
33	4	2	73	4	4
34	3	1	74	3	2
35	3	3	75	4	4
36	2	1	76	1	1
37	3	1	77	2	1
38	3	3	78	5	4
39	4	4	79	1	1
40	5	4	80	2	1

Null Hypothesis (H_0): There is no significant difference in the mean performance level between the sales forces in the markets A, B, C and D.

Alternate Hypothesis (H_1): There is significant difference in the mean performance level between the sales forces in the markets A, B, C and D.

Output Tables:

ANOVA

Performance

	Sum of Squares	Df	Mean Square	F	Sig.
Between Groups	46.338	3	15.446	23.176	.000
Within Groups	50.650	76	.666		
Total	96.988	79			

Descriptives

Performance

	N	Mean	Std. Deviation	Std. Error	95% Confidence Interval for Mean		Minimum	Maximum
					Lower Bound	Upper Bound		
A	20	1.8500	.67082	.15000	1.5360	2.1640	1.00	3.00
B	20	2.9500	.60481	.13524	2.6669	3.2331	2.00	4.00
C	20	3.3000	.86450	.19331	2.8954	3.7046	2.00	5.00
D	20	3.9500	1.05006	.23480	3.4586	4.4414	1.00	5.00
Total	80	3.0125	1.10801	.12388	2.7659	3.2591	1.00	5.00

Interpretation

The F test value of ANOVA is 23.176 with a p-value of 0.000, which is less than the significance level of 0.01 (at 1 percent). Hence, we reject the null hypothesis. So there is significant change or difference in the mean performance level of the sales forces in the markets A, B, C and D. From the tables, it can be inferred that the mean performance level of the sales force in market A is 1.85, B is 2.95 and that of C is 3.30. Sales Force in market D is the best of the four as it has earned a performance rating of 3.95, which is better than that of the other markets. It can concluded that the sales force in market D is the best among the four markets sales force.

Navigation Guide

- Data must be entered in the 'Data View' page of the data sheet, as given by the respondents. (In this case, it is based on the response given by 80 customers, in the market regarding the performance of 4 different markets sales force A, B, C and D).

Data View

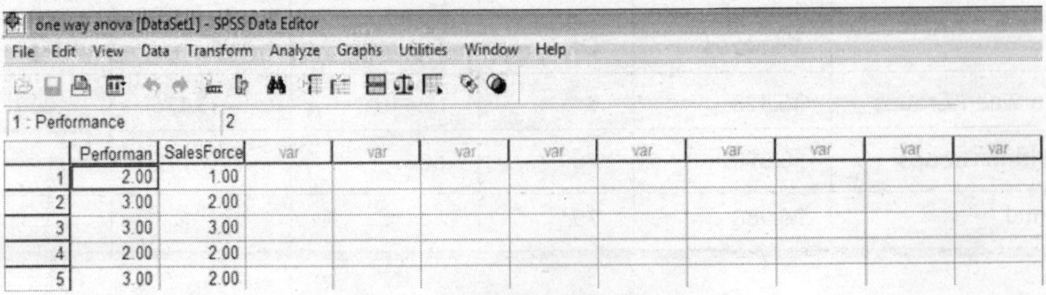

5	3.00	2.00
6	2.00	3.00
7	4.00	3.00
8	4.00	4.00
9	4.00	4.00
10	2.00	3.00
11	1.00	1.00
12	2.00	2.00
13	2.00	3.00
14	5.00	4.00
15	2.00	3.00
16	3.00	2.00
17	2.00	4.00
18	4.00	3.00
19	3.00	4.00
20	4.00	2.00
21	2.00	1.00
22	2.00	1.00
23	3.00	3.00
24	3.00	2.00
25	1.00	4.00
26	2.00	1.00
27	4.00	2.00
28	2.00	1.00
29	4.00	3.00
30	4.00	4.00
31	4.00	4.00
32	3.00	2.00
33	4.00	2.00
34	3.00	1.00
35	3.00	3.00
36	2.00	1.00
37	3.00	1.00
38	3.00	3.00
39	4.00	4.00
40	5.00	4.00
41	3.00	3.00
42	2.00	2.00
43	1.00	1.00
44	2.00	1.00
45	3.00	2.00
46	4.00	3.00
47	3.00	4.00
48	2.00	1.00
49	5.00	3.00
50	4.00	4.00
51	5.00	4.00
52	3.00	2.00
53	3.00	2.00
54	3.00	1.00
55	2.00	1.00
56	5.00	4.00
57	3.00	2.00
58	3.00	3.00
59	5.00	4.00
60	3.00	2.00

61	4.00	3.00
62	4.00	4.00
63	4.00	3.00
64	1.00	1.00
65	3.00	2.00
66	4.00	3.00
67	4.00	4.00
68	4.00	3.00
69	2.00	2.00
70	1.00	1.00
71	3.00	2.00
72	3.00	3.00
73	4.00	4.00
74	3.00	2.00
75	4.00	4.00
76	1.00	1.00
77	2.00	1.00
78	5.00	4.00
79	1.00	1.00
80	2.00	1.00
81		
82		

Variable View

➢ Open variable view and enter 'Performance' and 'SalesForce' in Name column. It assigns by default, the type of data, width, decimals and measure.

*one way anova [DataSet1] - SPSS Data Editor

File Edit View Data Transform Analyze Graphs Utilities Window Help

	Name	Type	Width	Decimals	Label	Values	Missing	Columns	Align	Measure
1	Performance	Numeric	8	2	Performance	{1.00, Poor}...	None	8	Right	Scale
2	SalesForce	Numeric	8	2	Sales Force	{1.00, A}...	None	8	Right	Scale
3										
4										
5										
6										

➢ In the 'Variable View' page, a suitable name and a label must be given for the variables. In this example, the variables are named as 'Performance' and 'Sales Force'. The data is entered as collected through the questionnaire. The value must be entered first, followed by the corresponding label. In this example, performance of the sales force is rated on a 5 point scale and the values coded are: 1-Poor, 2-Below Average, 3-Average, 4-Good, 5-Excellent. To enter these coded values, click values, enter the following data:

Value: 1

Label: Poor

Click add and perform the same for all the scales and click OK.

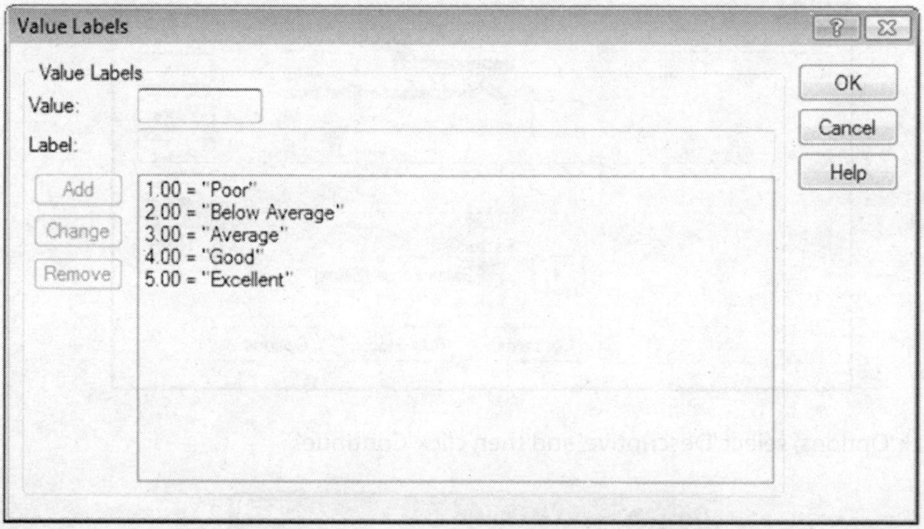

- In addition to this, the sales force is also given labels. 1 represents sales force in market A, 2 represents sales force in market B, 3 represents sales force in market C and 4 represents sales force in market D). The coding is entered in the variable view in the same format and it looks as follows:

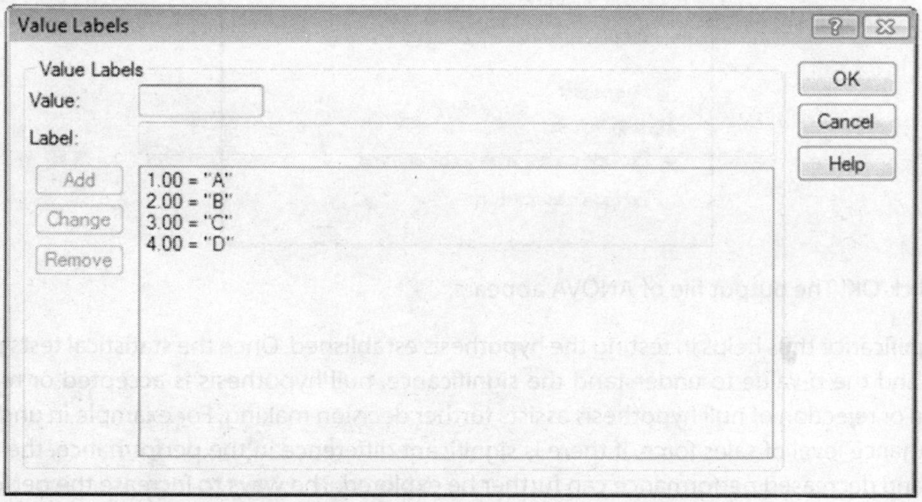

- Enter the values and save the input file.

Then, the following procedure must be followed:

- Select Analyse→Compare Means →One Way ANOVA.

- Select and drag the respective variables to the Dependent List and the Factor dialog blocks. (In this example, the variable 'Performance Rating' must be dragged to the Dependent List dialog box and the variable 'Sales Force' must be dragged to the Factor dialog block).

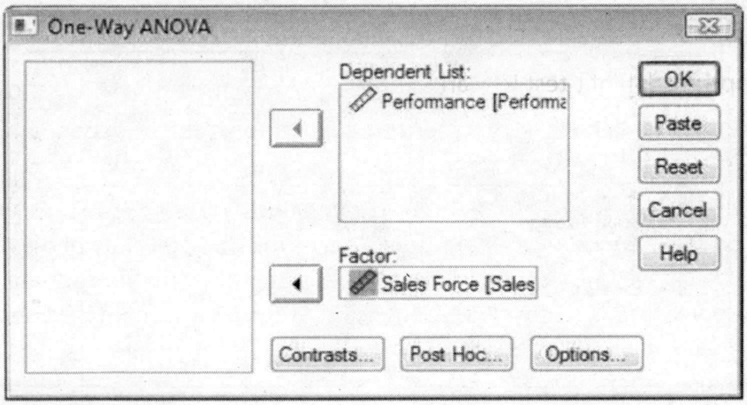

- Click 'Options', select 'Descriptive' and then click 'Continue'.

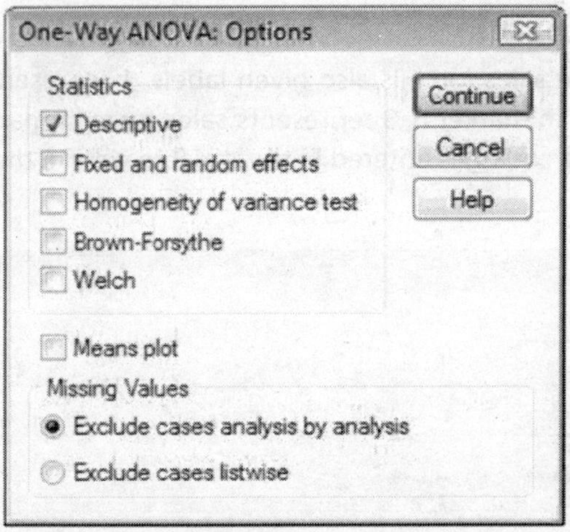

- Click 'OK'. The output file of ANOVA appears.

Tests of significance thus helps in testing the hypothesis established. Once the statistical tests provide the test value and the p-value to understand the significance, null hypothesis is accepted or rejected. The acceptance or rejection of null hypothesis assists further decision making. For example in understanding the performance level of sales force, if there is significant difference in the performance, the reasons for increased and decreased performance can further be explored. The ways to increase the performance of the sales force further can also be thought out by the management. Hypothesis testing thus results in future actions and decisions made by the managers.

Review Questions

1. Explain hypothesis testing and the process involved in it.
2. Explain the application of t-test in marketing.
3. What are the steps involved in SPSS to perform one sample t-test, independent t-test and paired t-test?
4. An advertising manager has devised three ad campaigns. He wanted to check the effectiveness of the ad campaign and test whether it varies across cities. Sample data of the respondents from three cities is given below. Develop the hypothesis and perform appropriate statistical test in SPSS to test the hypothesis. Effectiveness of the ad campaign is measured on a five point scale from highly effective (5) to least effective (1).

Sample Respondents	City	Effectiveness of the Ad Campaign
1	1	4
2	1	3
3	1	4
4	1	2
5	1	1
6	2	4
7	2	5
8	2	5
9	2	4
10	2	3
11	3	3
12	3	2
13	3	1
14	3	1
15	3	2

Chapter 11

Determining Association among Variables

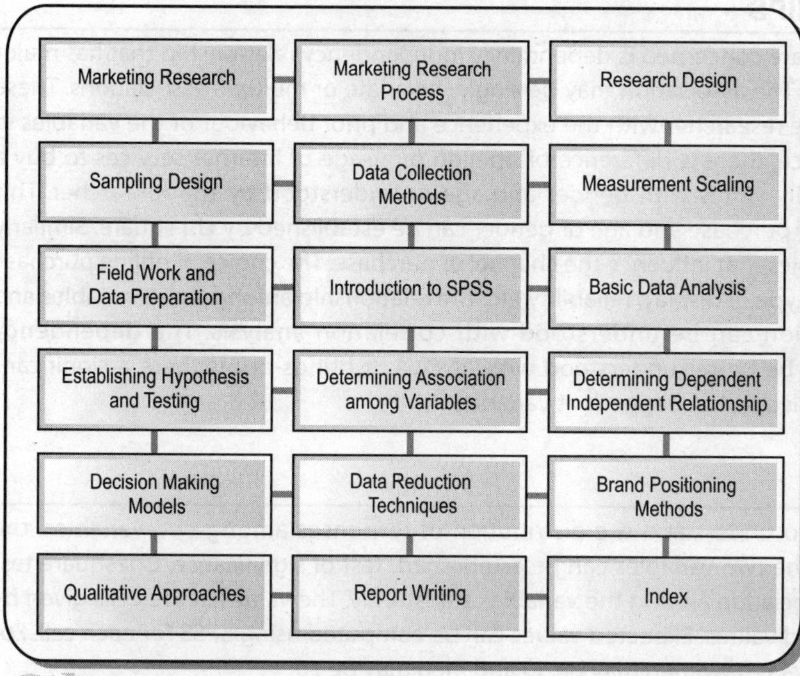

Outline

Chapter Structure

- Introduction
- Types of Relationships
- Chisquare
- Case
- Correlation
- Case
- Two-way Anova
- Case
- Review Questions

Chapter Overview

Chapter eleven explains the types of relationships and the statistical analysis performed to establish them. In specific the chapter discusses the application of chi-square, correlation and ANOVA to understand the associations that exist among variables and testing of hypothesis to establish the relationship significantly. The application of chi-square, correlation and two way ANOVA is elaborated with examples and cases of application.

INTRODUCTION

Data collected for research is first understood with its type and nature with descriptive statistics. Descriptive statistics gives the distribution of the data and it will not further lead to decision making. In market scenario, decision making depends on the influence of different variables. It is better understood by establishing the relationship or association among variables. It may include the association of the study variable, e.g. Preference towards a retail stores, with demographic variable e.g. Age or gender of the respondent. Association may also exist among different independent variables. The independent variables may have an influence on dependent variable. These associations are studied with chi-square, correlation and ANOVA. These statistical methods of test of independence and interdependence, bring out the strength of the association.

TYPES OF RELATIONSHIPS

The relationship that marketers are concerned is dependency independency relationship that has major implication on decision making. The association may be single, bivariate or multiple associations. These associations are identified by the researcher with the experience and prior behaviour of the variables in the universe studied. For instance, there is difference of opinion on usage of internet services to buy a product. The difference primarily varies with gender and age as understood by the researcher. This association among the choice of purchase and age or gender can be established by chi-square. Similarly there may exist numerous variables that influence the channel of purchase. The choice of online purchase may be influenced by the price, type of display, reliability etc. The relationship among these variables and the strength of their association can be understood with correlation analysis. The dependency independency relationship can be better understood with ANOVA. It brings out is there a significant influence of independent variables on the dependent variables.

CHI-SQUARE

In preparing cross tabulation, to understand the distribution of responses among two variables, the relationship that exists among the two variables can be established. Test of significance, Chi-square test will establish the significant association among the variables statistically. The values in the cells given by cross tabulation are the observed values. Expected values can be computed using SPSS for each cell. For example, of the 100 people, expected women may be 30 and men may be 70.

Chi-square test explains is there a significant difference between the observed and expected values. If the difference is large, then the chi-square value is also large. To ensure the statistical significance, p-value is considered. If $p < 0.05$ then we conclude that there is significant difference between the expected values and the observed value at 5 percent level of significance.

SPSS command to perform Chi-square test:

In menu bar, ANALYSE → DESCRIPTIVE STATISTICS → CROSS TABS

Select the variable for Row [e.g. Gender] and variable for column [e.g. Age group]

In cells the observed count is considered by default.

In the CROSS TABS window, select STATISTICS

In this dialogue box, select chi-square. If correlation is required, select the option for correlation. Then select continue and click ok. It will bring the chi-square value and its significance that explains the association between row and column variable.

CASE

A supermarket prefers to identify the reasons for decline in its monthly sales. In order to identify the reasons, the supermarket conducted a survey among 100 customers and found that five factors caused dissatisfaction among the customers. The five factors are: [1-Poor Quality of Materials, 2-Poor Service, 3-Poor Ambience, 4-Higher Cost, 5-Billing Errors]. Input table is shown below:

Sample	Reason for Dissatis-faction	Sample	Reason for Dissatis-faction	Sample	Reason for Dissatis-faction	Sample	Reason for Dissatis-faction
1	1	26	4	51	2	76	3
2	3	27	1	52	4	77	1
3	3	28	1	53	1	78	1
4	4	29	1	54	4	79	3
5	5	30	4	55	5	80	4
6	2	31	4	56	4	81	5
7	1	32	1	57	5	82	4
8	3	33	1	58	1	83	2
9	1	34	1	59	1	84	1
10	1	35	3	60	1	85	2
11	2	36	4	61	1	86	1
12	4	37	1	62	1	87	3
13	5	38	4	63	3	88	2
14	1	39	1	64	4	89	1
15	2	40	1	65	2	90	1
16	1	41	1	66	5	91	2
17	1	42	3	67	3	92	3
18	1	43	4	68	2	93	2
19	3	44	4	69	1	94	2
20	4	45	5	70	2	95	1

21	4	46	4	71	2	96	1
22	2	47	1	72	2	97	1
23	1	48	2	73	4	98	3
24	1	49	4	74	5	99	4
25	4	50	1	75	4	100	1

Null Hypothesis (H_0): The reasons that cause dissatisfaction among customers are equally important (i.e. the theoretical distribution is a uniform distribution).

Alternate Hypothesis (H_1): The reasons that cause dissatisfaction among customers are not equally important.

The table presents the output of Chi-Square Test for goodness-of-fit.

Test Statistics

	Reasons for Dissatisfaction
Chi-Square(a)	28.600
Df	4
Asymp. Sig.	.000

A 0 cells (.0%) have expected frequencies less than 5. The minimum expected cell frequency is 20.0.

Reasons for Dissatisfaction

	Observed N	**Expected N**	**Residual**
Poor Quality of Materials	39	20.0	19.0
Poor Service	17	20.0	-3.0
Poor Ambience	13	20.0	-7.0
Higher Cost	23	20.0	3.0
Billing Errors	8	20.0	-12.0
Total	100	100	

Interpretation

The p-value of this test is 0.000, which is less than the significance level of 0.05. Hence, we reject the null hypothesis. It means that the various reasons that cause dissatisfaction among the customers are not equally important and the distribution is not a uniform distribution. From the tables, it can be inferred that poor quality of materials caused dissatisfaction among 39 out of 100 respondents and hence it is the primary cause of dissatisfaction. It is followed by higher cost of materials (23 out of 100 respondents), poor service (17 respondents) and poor ambience (13 respondents). Billing errors are of least importance as only 8 respondents are dissatisfied by the billing errors caused.

Navigation Guide

- Data must be entered in the 'Data View' page of the data sheet, as given by the respondents. (In this case, it is based on the response given by 100 customers of the supermarket regarding the factors that dissatisfy them).
- In the 'Variable View' page, a suitable name and a label must be given for the variable. (In this example, the variable is named and labelled as 'Reasons for Dissatisfaction'). The values must be entered as mentioned in the questionnaire. The value must be entered first, followed by the corresponding label. (In this example, the reasons for dissatisfaction are codedas follows: 1-Poor Quality of Materials, 2-Poor Service, 3-Poor Ambience, 4-Higher Cost, 5-Billing Errors).
- Click 'OK' after entering the values and the corresponding labels.

Data View

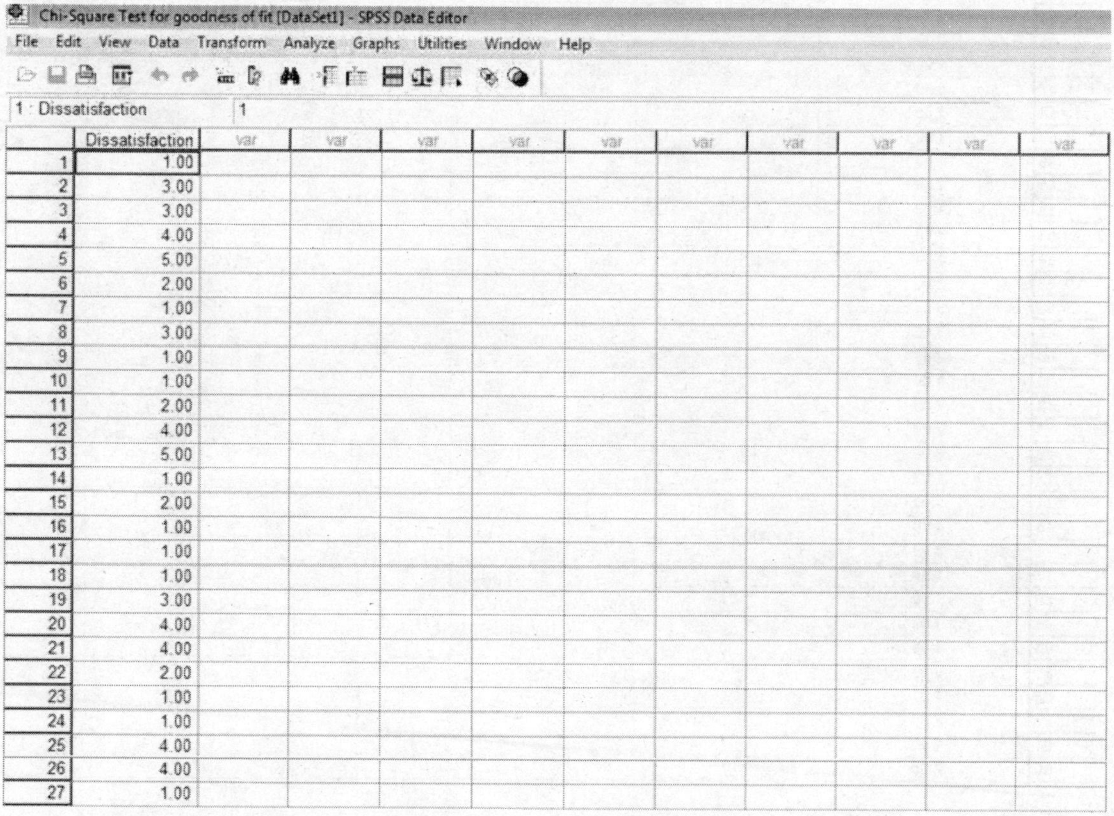

	Dissatisfaction	var	var	var	var	var	var	var	var	var	var
1	1.00										
2	3.00										
3	3.00										
4	4.00										
5	5.00										
6	2.00										
7	1.00										
8	3.00										
9	1.00										
10	1.00										
11	2.00										
12	4.00										
13	5.00										
14	1.00										
15	2.00										
16	1.00										
17	1.00										
18	1.00										
19	3.00										
20	4.00										
21	4.00										
22	2.00										
23	1.00										
24	1.00										
25	4.00										
26	4.00										
27	1.00										

28	1.00
29	1.00
30	4.00
31	4.00
32	1.00
33	1.00
34	1.00
35	3.00
36	4.00
37	1.00
38	4.00
39	1.00
40	1.00
41	1.00
42	3.00
43	4.00
44	4.00
45	5.00
46	4.00
47	1.00
48	2.00
49	4.00
50	1.00
51	2.00
52	4.00
53	1.00
54	4.00
55	5.00
56	4.00
57	5.00
58	1.00
59	1.00
60	1.00
61	1.00
62	1.00
63	3.00
64	4.00
65	2.00
66	5.00
67	3.00
68	2.00
69	1.00
70	2.00
71	2.00
72	2.00
73	4.00
74	5.00
75	4.00
76	3.00
77	1.00
78	1.00
79	3.00
80	4.00
81	5.00
82	4.00
83	2.00
84	1.00
85	2.00

86	1.00
87	3.00
88	2.00
89	1.00
90	1.00
91	2.00
92	3.00
93	2.00
94	2.00
95	1.00
96	1.00
97	1.00
98	3.00
99	4.00
100	1.00

Variable View

*Chi-Square Test for goodness of fit [DataSet1] - SPSS Data Editor

File Edit View Data Transform Analyze Graphs Utilities Window Help

	Name	Type	Width	Decimals	Label	Values	Missing	Columns	Align	Measure
1	Dissatisfaction	Numeric	8	2	Reasons for Dissatisfaction	{1.00, Poor Quality	None	11	Right	Scale
2										
3										
4										
5										
6										

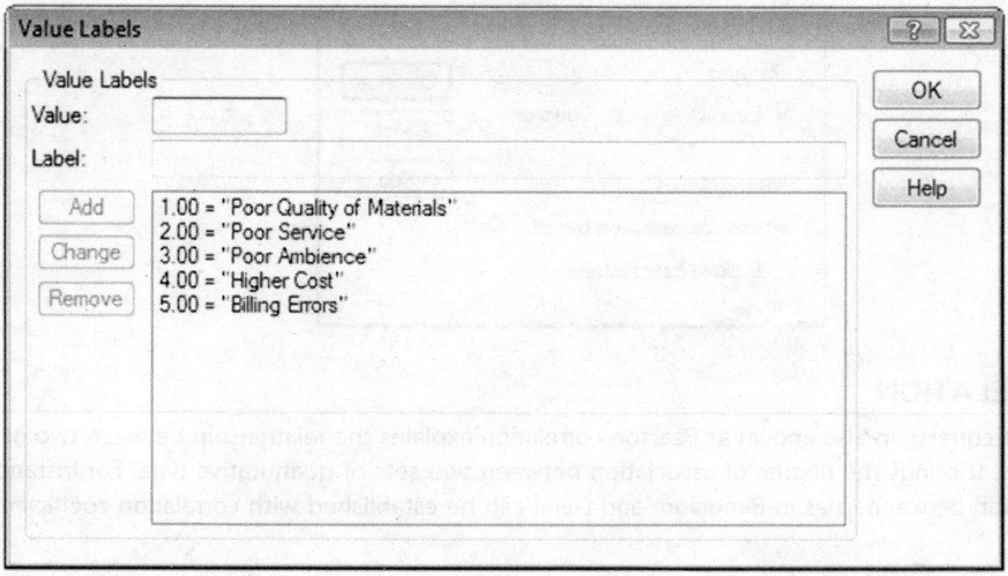

Then, the following procedure is followed:

- Select Analyse → Nonparametric Tests →Chi-Square.
- Drag the variable to be tested to the Test Variable List dialog box. (In this example, the variable 'Reasons for Dissatisfaction' must be dragged to the Test Variable List dialog box).
- Click 'Options', select 'Descriptive' and click 'Continue'.
- Click 'OK'.

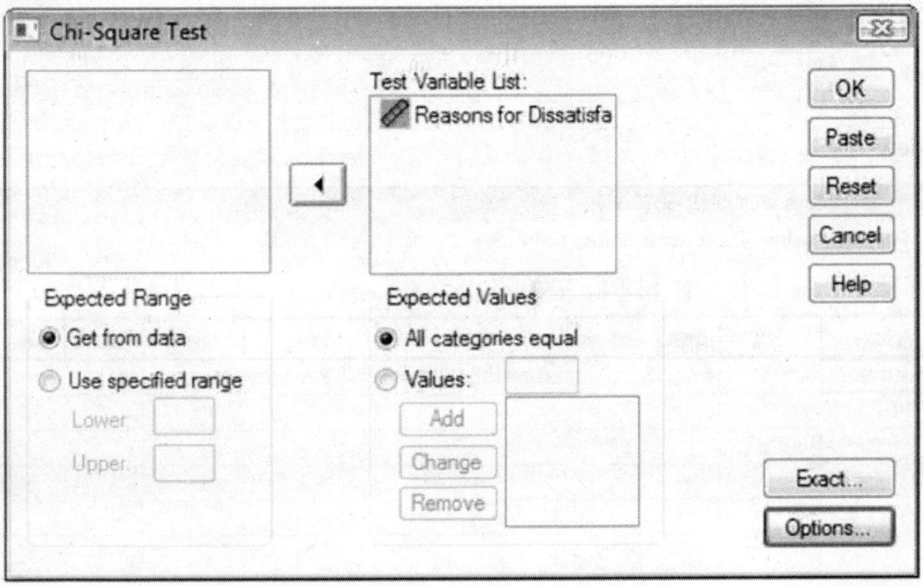

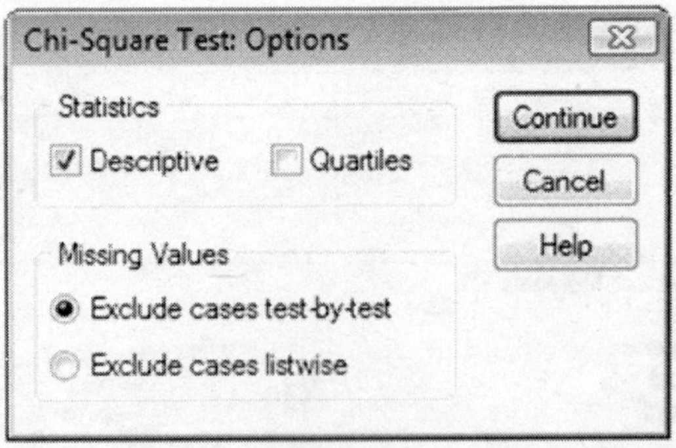

CORRELATION

Bivariate correlation also known as Pearson correlation explains the relationship between two or more variables. It brings the degree of association between two sets of quantitative data. For instance the association between sales in Bangalore and Delhi can be established with correlation coefficient. The existence of relation is established by correlation and the extent of dependency independency relation is brought out by regression. Pearson's correlation is executed if the data is normally distributed. If normality doesn't exist, given values are ranked and Spearman's rank correlation is executed on the ranks.

Correlation varies between +1 to – 1. If the correlation is positive, it reveals positive correlation between variables ie., increase in one variable will cause an increase in another. On the other hand, if the correlation is negative, there exists inverse relationship. In case of negative correlation, increase in one variable, will decrease the other variable. If correlation values are +1 or – 1, it reveals perfect positive or negative correlation and represented by 'r'. If the value of 'r' tends to '0' then there exists no relation between the two variables. The relationship is stronger ie., there exists correlation among variables only if the values of 'r' are closer to +1 or – 1. As in the other statistical tests, significance is also computed to determine there exists significant relationship or not. Generally two tailed significance is considered as we may not know the direction of the relation [ie. either increase or decrease]. If it is sure that there exists only positive relation [or negative relation] then one-tailed significance can be considered. At 95 percent confidence level, there exists relation between variables if p-value is less than 0.05.

SPSS Commands:

In menu bar, ANALYSE → CORRELATE → BIVARIATE

Bivariate window opens listing all the variables. Select those variables for which correlation is to be executed. In correlation coefficient window, select PEARSON. In test of significance, select two-tailed. Also select FLAG SIGNIFICANT CORRELATION. This gives asterisk [**] symbol for variables which have significant correlation.

CASE

A is a manufacturing company that sells its products in a market. The company does not have a permanent sales force. Instead, the company has outsourced its marketing and sales activities to another company, B. Now, the management of company A has an idea of carrying out the marketing and sales activities on its own, instead of outsourcing it to B. Hence, the company A gathered data from the market regarding the past 20 weeks in order to make a decision on outsourcing. The company collected data such as sales (in Rs. Lakhs per week), market demand (in Rs. Lakhs per week), number of sales representatives, competition index (on a 5 point scale, where 1 represents very low, 2 represents low, 3 represents neither high nor low, 4 represents high and 5 represents very high) and promotional expenditure (in Rs. Lakhs per annum) over the past 20 weeks. The company A carried out a correlation analysis to find out the relationship between the variables. Input data is shown in table.

Input Table:

Sample Week	Sales (in Rs. Lakhs per Week)	Market Demand (in Rs. Lakhs per Week)	Number of Salesmen	Promotional Expenditure (in Rs. Lakhs per Week)	Competition Index
1	20	31	20	8	2
2	6	14	39	6	4
3	35	52	12	5	5
4	39	60	30	7	3
5	16	40	12	6	1
6	32	51	26	8	1
7	11	20	14	10	3
8	23	34	19	13	4
9	7	25	19	6	2
10	4	18	17	8	3
11	6	19	15	9	2
12	31	43	26	14	2
13	46	60	32	8	4
14	52	61	40	6	2
15	12	24	30	9	2
16	5	17	31	10	4
17	42	58	32	12	4
18	47	61	33	6	2
19	39	52	27	7	2
20	42	56	37	5	3

Null Hypotheses (H_0):

- There is no significant association between the variables 'sales of the company' and 'market demand'.
- There is no significant association between the variables 'sales of the company' and 'number of sales men'.
- There is no significant association between the variables 'sales of the company' and 'promotional expenditure'.
- There is no significant association between the variables 'sales of the company' and 'competition index'.

Alternate Hypotheses (H_1):

- There is significant association between the variables 'sales of the company' and 'market demand'.
- There is significant association between the variables 'sales of the company' and 'number of sales men'.
- There is significant association between the variables 'sales of the company' and 'promotional expenditure'.
- There is significant association between the variables 'sales of the company' and 'competition index'.

Table presents the output from correlation analysis.

Output Table:

Correlations

		Sales (in Rs. Lakhs per week)	Market Demand (in Rs. Lakhs per week)	Number of Salesmen	Promotional Expenditure (in Rs. Lakhs per week)	Competition Index
Sales (in Rs. Lakhs per week)	Pearson Correlation	1	.972(**)	.479(*)	-.153	.031
	Sig. (2-tailed)		.000	.033	.521	.898
	N	20	20	20	20	20
Market Demand (in Rs. Lakhs per week)	Pearson Correlation	972(**)	1	.375	-.210	-.032
	Sig. (2-tailed)	.000		.103	.373	.892
	N	20	20	20	20	20
Number of Sales Men	Pearson Correlation	.479(*)	.375	1	-.120	.098
	Sig. (2-tailed)	.033	.103		.616	.680
	N	20	20	20	20	20
Promotional Expenditure (in Rs. Lakhs per week)	Pearson Correlation	-.153	-.210	-.120	1	.123
	Sig. (2-tailed)	.521	.373	.616		.605
	N	20	20	20	20	20

Competition Index	Pearson Correlation	.031	-.032	.098	.123	1
	Sig. (2-tailed)	.898	.892	.680	.605	
	N	20	20	20	20	20

** Correlation is significant at the 0.01 level (2-tailed).

* Correlation is significant at the 0.05 level (2-tailed).

Interpretation:

- The p-value of this test is 0.000 between the variables 'sales of the company' and 'market demand', which is less than the significance level of 0.05. Hence, we reject the null hypothesis as the relationship among these variables is statistically significant. It explains that there is significant association between the variables 'sales of the company' and 'market demand'. The Pearson Correlation coefficient between these variables is 0.972, which is very closer to 1. Hence, the variables 'sales of the company' and 'market demand' are positively correlated and the correlation is very strong as the Pearson Correlation coefficient is closer to 1.
- The p-value of this test is 0.033 between the variables 'sales of the company' and 'number of sales men', which is less than the significance level of 0.05. Hence, we reject the null hypothesis as the relationship among these variables is statistically significant. It describes that there is significant association between the variables 'sales of the company' and 'number of sales men'. The Pearson Correlation coefficient between these variables is 0.479, which means the variables 'sales of the company' and 'number of sales men' are positively correlated.
- The p-value of this test is 0.521 between the variables 'sales of the company' and 'promotional expenditure', which is greater than the significance level of 0.05. Hence, we accept the null hypothesis as the relationship among these variables is statistically not significant. It explains that there is no significant association between the variables 'sales of the company' and 'promotional expenditure'. The Pearson Correlation coefficient between these variables is -0.153.
- The p-value of this test is 0.898 between the variables 'sales of the company' and 'competition index', which is greater than the significance level of 0.05. Hence, we accept the null hypothesis as the relationship among these variables is statistically not significant. It clarifies that there is no significant association between the variables 'sales of the company' and 'competition index'. The Pearson Correlation coefficient between these variables is 0.031.

Navigation Guide

In order to enter data:

- Data must be entered in the 'Data View' page of the data sheet, as obtained. (In this case, it is based on the data collected for the past 20 weeks regarding the sales, market demand, number of sales men, promotional expenditure and the competition index).

Data View:

correlation [DataSet1] - SPSS Data Editor

File Edit View Data Transform Analyze Graphs Utilities Window Help

1 : Sales 20

	Sales	Demand	Salesmen	Promotions	Competitors	var	var	var	var	var	var
1	20.00	31.00	20.00	8.00	2.00						
2	6.00	14.00	39.00	6.00	4.00						
3	35.00	52.00	12.00	5.00	5.00						
4	39.00	60.00	30.00	7.00	3.00						
5	16.00	40.00	12.00	6.00	1.00						
6	32.00	51.00	26.00	8.00	1.00						
7	11.00	20.00	14.00	10.00	3.00						
8	23.00	34.00	19.00	13.00	4.00						
9	7.00	25.00	19.00	6.00	2.00						
10	4.00	18.00	17.00	8.00	3.00						
11	6.00	19.00	15.00	9.00	2.00						
12	31.00	43.00	26.00	14.00	2.00						
13	46.00	60.00	32.00	8.00	4.00						
14	52.00	61.00	40.00	6.00	2.00						
15	12.00	24.00	30.00	9.00	2.00						
16	5.00	17.00	31.00	10.00	4.00						
17	42.00	58.00	32.00	12.00	4.00						
18	47.00	61.00	33.00	6.00	2.00						
19	39.00	52.00	27.00	7.00	2.00						
20	42.00	56.00	37.00	5.00	3.00						
21											
22											
23											

- Open variable view and enter 'Sales, Demand, Salesmen, Promotions and Competitors' in the column Name. It assigns by default, the type of data, width, decimals and measure.

correlation [DataSet1] - SPSS Data Editor

File Edit View Data Transform Analyze Graphs Utilities Window Help

	Name	Type	Width	Decimals	Label	Values	Missing	Columns	Align	Measure
1	Sales	Numeric	8	2	Sales (in Rs. Lakhs per week)	None	None	8	Right	Scale
2	Demand	Numeric	8	2	Market Demand (in Rs. Lakhs per week)	None	None	9	Right	Scale
3	Salesmen	Numeric	8	2	Number of Sales Men	None	None	10	Right	Scale
4	Promotions	Numeric	8	2	Promotional Expenditure (in Rs. Lakhs per week)	None	None	10	Right	Scale
5	Competitors	Numeric	8	2	Competition Index	{1.00, Very Low}...	None	11	Right	Scale
6										
7										
8										
9										
10										

- In the 'Variable View' page, a suitable name and a label must be given for the variables entered. (In this example, the variables are: SALES (in Rs. Lakhs per week), MARKET DEMAND (in Rs. Lakhs per week), NUMBER OF SALES MEN, PROMOTIONAL EXPENDITURE (in Rs. Lakhs per week) and COMPETITION INDEX). The value coded must be entered first, and then assign the corresponding labels. (In this example, Competition Index is coded as 1-Very Low, 2-Low, 3-Neither High or Low, 4-High, 5-Very High). In the pull down menu of Value, code the values as follows:

  Value: 1

Label: Very Low

Click 'Add'

Similarly add the values for the scale

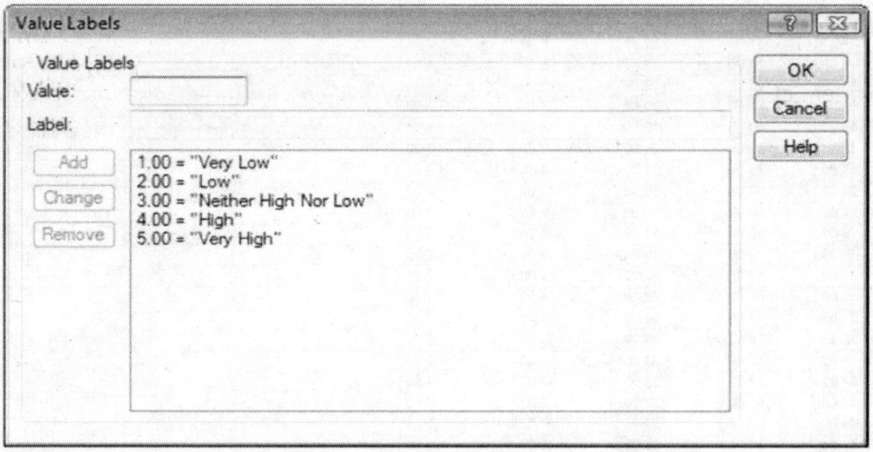

➢ Enter the values and click 'OK' and save the input file.

Then, the following procedure is followed to perform analysis:

- Select Analyse→ Correlate→Bivariate Correlations.
- Drag the variables to be tested to the 'Variables' dialog box. (In this example, the variables 'Sales (in Rs. Lakhs per week), Market Demand (in Rs. Lakhs per week), Number of Sales Men, Promotional Expenditure (in Rs. Lakhs per week) and Competition Index' must be dragged to the 'Variables' dialog box. 'Pearson', 'Two-tailed' and 'Flag significant correlations' are the default selections).

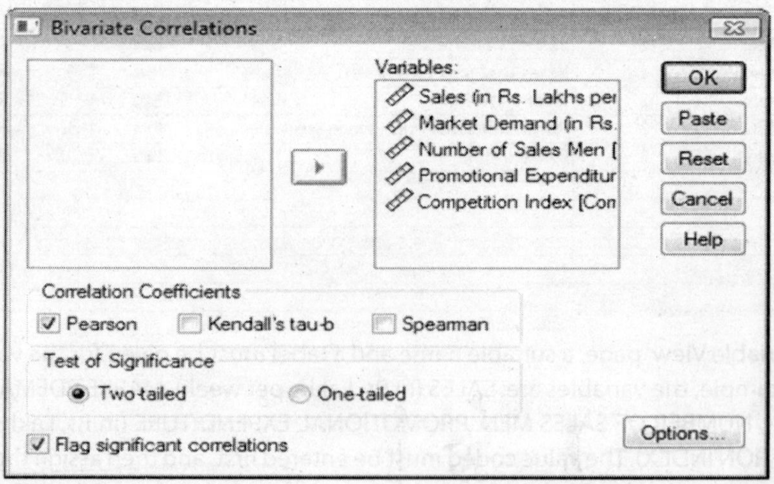

- Click 'OK' and the output file opens.

TWO-WAY ANOVA

In one way ANOVA, significant difference between groups by comparing the means of those groups is studied. In the example, the significant difference in the opinion about the product offered is studied. Tounderstand the opinion across cities with gender differences then two-way ANOVA is performed. Two-way ANOVA helps us to understand is there impact of cities on the opinion about the product, impact of gender and combined effect of city and gender on the opinion about the product. The main effect and the interaction effect are better understood in two way ANOVA. Moreover the impact of independent variable on dependent with a block variable can be explained. In the example, opinion about the product depends on gender. Type of city is the block that may have an impact on the dependent variable.

SPSS Command:

In MENU Bar: ANALYSE → GENERAL LINEAR MODEL → UNIVARIATE

The Univariate screen opens with a column for dependent variable, fixed factors, random factors, covariance and WLS weight.

- Select the dependent variable in dependent variable box. In our example, opinion about the product is the dependent variable
- Fixed factors box include the independent variables. In our example, the variables will be cities and gender.
- Random factors and WLS weight options are rarely used.

If descriptive statistics is required, it is available in OPTIONS in the same window. Two way ANOVA output will be given that helps to understand the association among the variables studied.

CASE

A manufacturing company sells its products in different markets. The company collected data on sales (in Rs. Lakhs per week) and market demand (in Rs. Lakhs per week) for the three different markets. Do sales depend on market demand and does that vary with the type of market?

Input data is shown in table.

Sales (in Rs. Lakhs per month)	Market Demand (in Rs. Lakhs per month)	Type of Market
20	31	1
6	14	2
35	52	3
39	60	1

16	40	2
32	51	3
11	20	1
23	34	2
7	25	3
4	18	1
6	19	2
31	43	3
46	60	1
52	61	2
12	24	3
5	17	1
42	58	2
47	61	3

Null Hypothesis (H_0): There is no significant difference in the sales performance with market demand in the three types of markets

Alternate Hypothesis (H_1): There is significant difference in the sales performance with market demand in the three different types of markets.

The table presents the output of Two way ANOVA

Tests of Between-Subjects Effects

Dependent Variable: SALES

Source	Type III Sum of Squares	df	Mean Square	F	Sig.
Corrected Model	4647.278(a)	16	290.455	11.855	.225
Intercept	8240.855	1	8240.855	336.361	.035
MARKETDEMAND	4520.500	14	322.893	13.179	.213
TYPEOFMARKET	12.500	1	12.500	.510	.605

MARKETDEMAND * TYPEOFMARKET	.000	0	.	.	.
Error	24.500	1	24.500		
Total	15136.000	18			
Corrected Total	4671.778	17			

a R Squared = .995 (Adjusted R Squared = .911)

Interpretation

- ANOVA value for the overall model is 11.855 with the significance of 0.225. The significance value is greater than 0.05 at 5 percent level. Hence the null hypothesis is accepted as there is no significant difference in the sales performance with market demand in the three types of markets.
- Impact of market demand on the sales performance is individually given with its F (ANOVA) value and significance. Significance of market demand is less than 0.05. Hence there exist a significant association between market demand and sales performance. Sales performance is influenced by the market demand that exists
- But the type of market doesn't have an associate as the significance of F is 0.605 which is greater than 0.05.
- Hence sales performance of the manufacturing company depends on market demand individually but market demand and type of market combined together doesn't influence the sales performance.

Navigation Guide

In order to enter data:

- Data must be entered in the 'Data View' page of the data sheet, as obtained. (In this case, it is based on the data collected for the sales, market demand, and type of market).

Data View

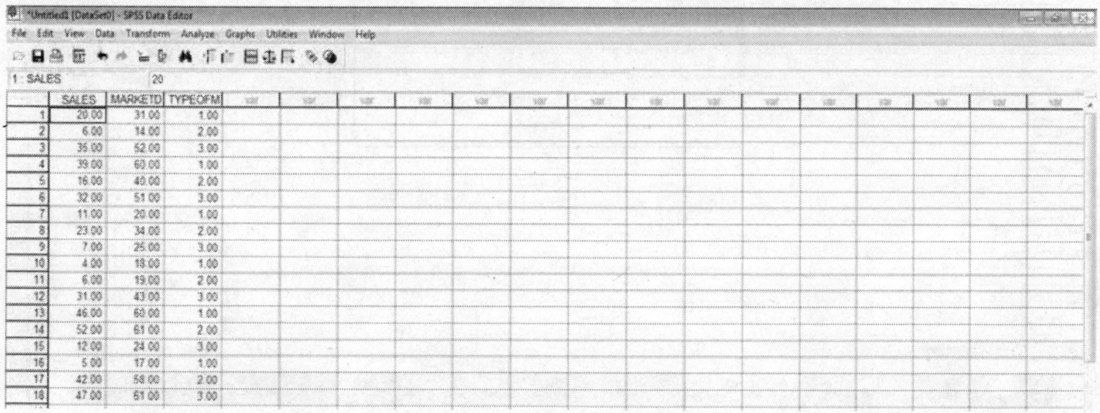

	SALES	MARKETD	TYPEOFM
1	20.00	31.00	1.00
2	6.00	14.00	2.00
3	35.00	52.00	3.00
4	39.00	60.00	1.00
5	16.00	40.00	2.00
6	32.00	51.00	3.00
7	11.00	20.00	1.00
8	23.00	34.00	2.00
9	7.00	25.00	3.00
10	4.00	18.00	1.00
11	6.00	19.00	2.00
12	31.00	43.00	3.00
13	46.00	60.00	1.00
14	52.00	61.00	2.00
15	12.00	24.00	3.00
16	5.00	17.00	1.00
17	42.00	58.00	2.00
18	47.00	61.00	3.00

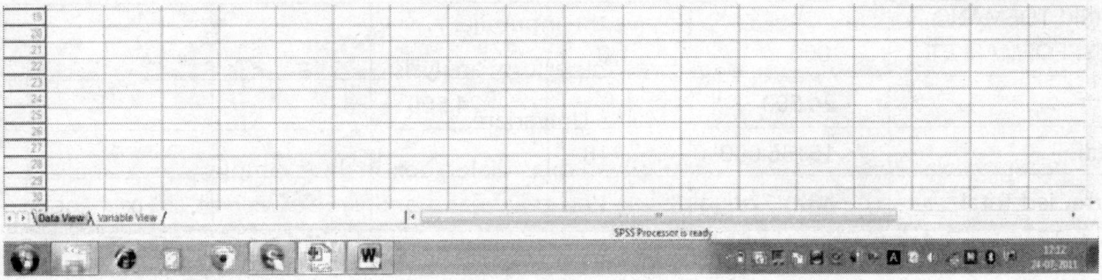

- Open variable view and enter 'Sales, Market Demand, and Type of Market' in the column Name. It assigns by default, the type of data, width, decimals and measure.
- In the 'Variable View' page, values must be assigned for the variables coded. In this example, the variables are: SALES (in Rs. Lakhs per month), MARKET DEMAND (in Rs. Lakhs per month), and TYPE OF MARKET (Market1, Market2, and Market3). The value coded must be entered first, and then assign the corresponding labels.

Value: 1

Label: Market1

Click 'Add'

Similarly add the values for the three types of Markets

Variable View

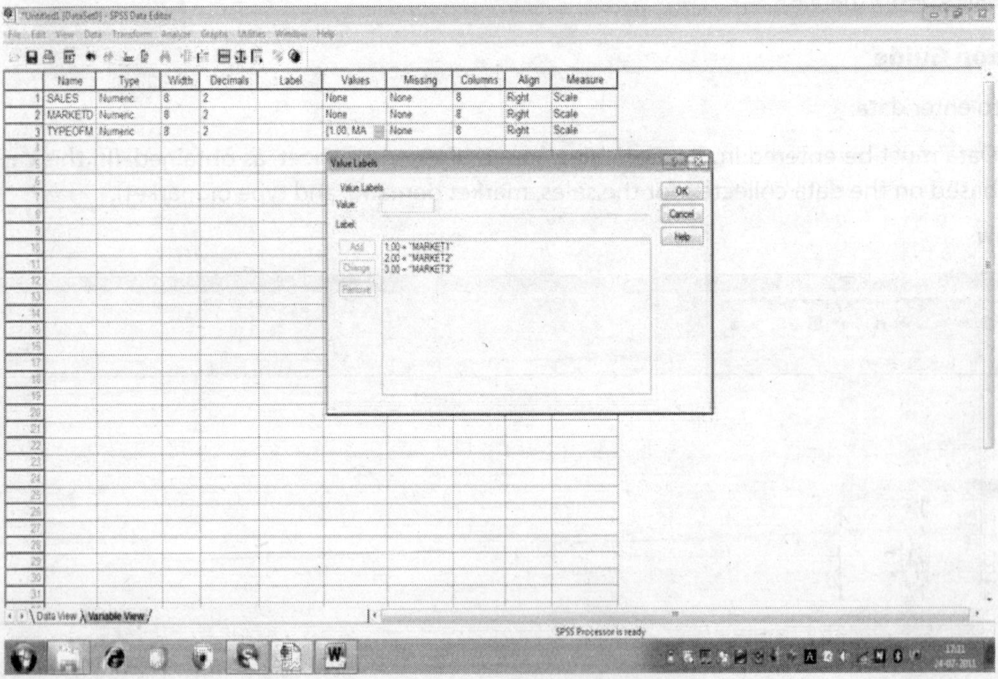

➢ Enter the values and click 'OK' and save the input file.

Then, the following procedure is followed to perform analysis:

- Select Analyse →General Linear→ Model Univariate.
- Drag the variables to be tested to the 'Variables' dialog box. In this example, the variables 'Sales' is entered as Dependent Variable and 'Market Demand' and 'Type of Market' as Fixed Factors.

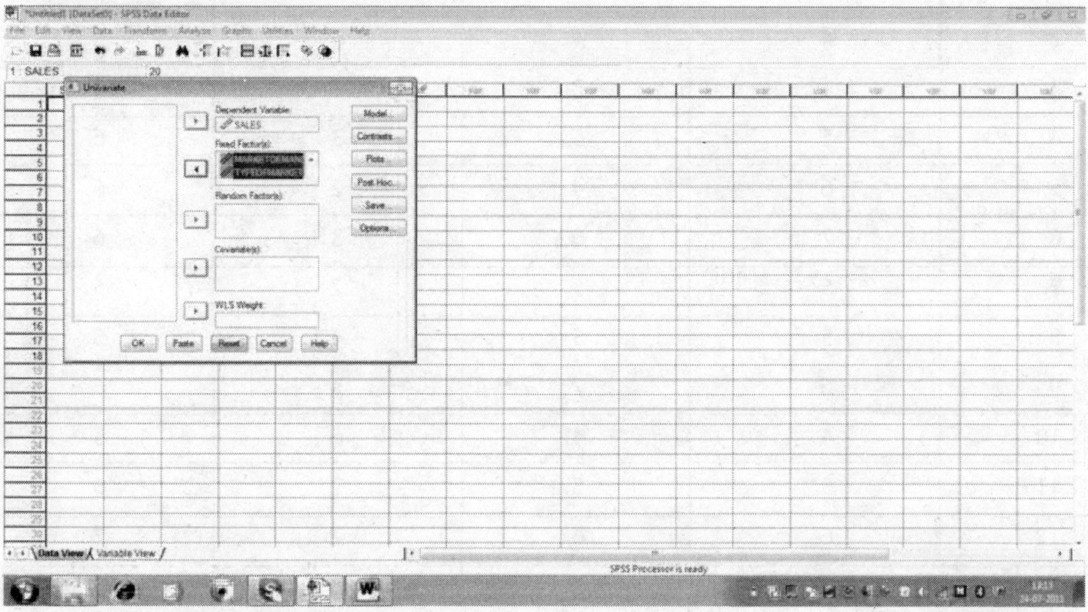

- Click 'OK' and the output file opens.

The associative analysis thus brings out the relationships that exist among independent variables and between dependent and independent variables. Establishment of association is the stage next to descriptive analysis. The significant relationship established further helps to formulate the predictive model.

Review Questions

1. Explain hypothesis testing with example and the process involved in establishing association among variables with chi-square.
2. Explain the application of correlation.
3. Explain the situation to perform ANOVA.
4. What are the steps involved in SPSS to perform Chi-square, Correlation and ANOVA?
5. The store manager of a departmental store wants to identify the primary reasons of its customer

satisfaction. This would help the store manager to concentrate on those specific satisfiers and may result in customer delight. Hence, the store manager collected data from 25 customers, who regularly purchase from that store. The data collected is shown in the table below:

Sample	Customer Satisfaction	Product Quality	Ambience of the Store	Discounts
1	2	2	5	5
2	4	4	4	6
3	1	3	3	3
4	5	5	3	6
5	6	4	2	6
6	7	6	3	6
7	5	5	2	5
8	5	5	4	5
9	6	7	3	6
10	4	4	6	5
11	5	5	2	6
12	6	6	2	7
13	3	5	3	3
14	2	2	6	2
15	3	2	4	4
16	4	3	3	4
17	3	3	4	3
18	5	6	5	5
19	6	5	2	6
20	4	4	3	5
21	3	4	4	3
22	5	6	1	6
23	6	7	4	5
24	5	5	1	6
25	4	4	1	4

Perform correlation to identify the variables that has significant association with customer satisfaction.

6. Twenty respondents of different age groups were selected to study the impact of age on the choice of drink. Check whether there is relationship between the Age of the respondents and Type of Drink Preferred. Study was conducted in a retail outlet and the input data is given below.

Input Data

Serial No	Age (In Years)	Drink Preferred
1	Less than 15	Fruit Juice
2	Less than 15	Sprite
3	Less than 15	Mirinda
4	Less than 15	Pepsi
5	Less than 15	Coke
6	15 – 20	7 up
7	15 – 20	Maza
8	15 – 20	Fruit Juice
9	15 – 20	Sprite
10	15 – 20	Mirinda
11	20 – 25	Pepsi
12	20 – 25	Coke
13	20 – 25	7 up
14	20 – 25	Maza
15	20 – 25	Coke
16	25 and Above	7 up
17	25 and Above	Maza
18	25 and Above	Coke
19	25 and Above	7 up
20	25 and Above	Maza

7. A survey conducted with a sample set gives their ratings toward the ad copy on a10 point scale. Rating of '1' represent 'highly disliked' and '10' represents 'highly liked', with other ratings falling in between the scale. The ad copy is coded 1, 2, and 3 respectively indicating three different

versions of the ad. Price of the ad copy varies with the version and the ratings. Six responded have rated each ad. Is there a difference on the ratings given for the three ads with different price ranges?

S. No	Rating	Ad Copy	Price
1	7	1	1
2	3	1	2
3	3	1	3
4	4	1	1
5	1	1	2
6	4	1	3
7	8	2	1
8	5	2	2
9	3	2	3
10	4	2	1
11	9	2	2
12	4	2	3
13	10	3	1
14	3	3	2
15	4	3	3
16	6	3	1
17	4	3	2
18	5	3	3

Chapter 12

Determining Dependent Independent Relationship

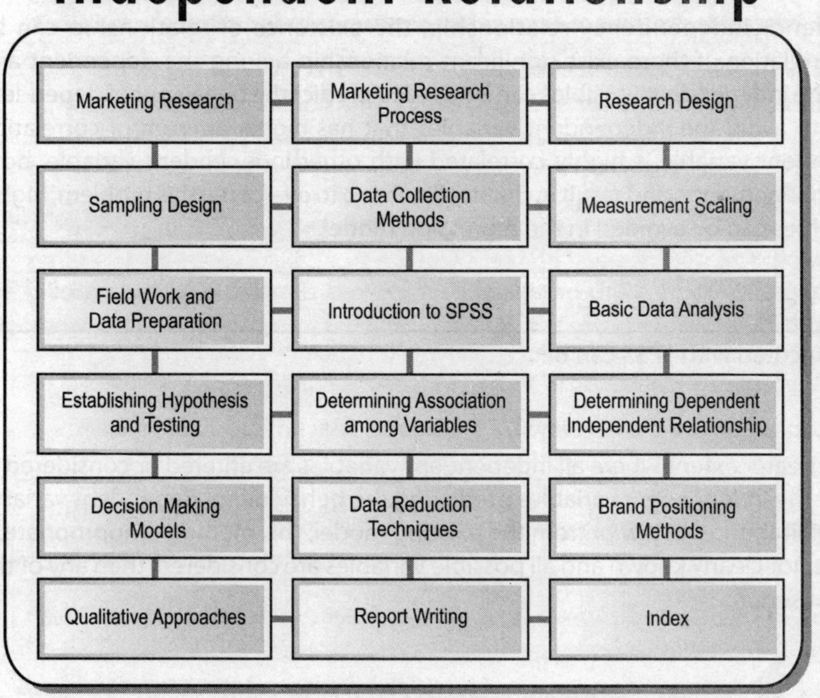

Outline

Chapter Structure

- Introduction
- Regression with SPSS
- Linear Regression
- Case
- Multiple Regression
- Case
- Logistic Regression
- Case
- Review Questions

Chapter Overview

Chapter twelve explains the methods of regression used in marketing for prediction. It includes the linear, multiple and logistic regression that brings out the relationship between dependent and independent variables. The extent of prediction of the behaviour of dependent variables with the influence of independent variables is discussed with the cases.

INTRODUCTION

Behaviour of human is influenced by various variables. Similarly, consumer behaviour is not an individual entity. It is the resultant behaviour of various other elements called as variables. These variables that affect the resultant variable consumer behaviour are called independent variables. Every variable is dependent on various other variables. They are dependent variable, in the example, consumer behaviour is the dependent variable. In other words, the variables in the universe revolve around relationship among each other. These relationship if exist among two variables, it is simple linear relationship. If the relationship between dependent and more than one independent variable exists, it explains multiple regression. In understanding this relationship, the independent and dependent variables are interval or ratio scaled or metric data. Ordinary Least Square (OLS) method of estimation is used in estimating a regression equation. The assumptions of regression can also be tested before execution of regression.

In determining the dependency independency relationship, the existence of relationship can be understood by executing correlation. If there exist significant relationship among the dependent and independent variables, then the independent variables can be used to predict the behaviour of dependent variable. Care is to be taken to avoid the independent variables that has higher amount of correlation among them. If one independent variable is highly correlated with other independent variable, both variables may reveal a similar phenomenon and result in multicollinearity. To overcome this problem, highly correlated independent variables can be avoided in the regression model.

REGRESSION WITH SPSS

The methods of regression executed with SPSS can be:

Enter Method

This is the method used to a greater extent where all independent variables are entered or considered in stabling a regression mode. If the independent variables predicting the behaviour of dependent variable are explained with the help of literature review or from the existing model, this method is appropriate. If the independent variables are not clearly known and all possible variables are considered, then any of the methods given below can be used.

Stepwise Method

Independent variables are added to the model if significant and removed if not. Variables already in the regression equation are removed if their probability of F becomes sufficiently large. The first variable considered for entry into the equation is the one with the largest positive or negative correlation with the dependent variable. This variable is entered into the equation only if it satisfies the criterion for entry. If the first variable is entered, the independent variable not in the equation that has the largest partial correlation is considered next.

Forward Method

It is a stepwise method where independent variables are sequentially entered into the model if considered significant.

Backward Method

This method is backward elimination where the variables are entered in the equation and sequentially removed. The removal is done with that independent variable that has no or less significant impact on dependent variable.

Remove

All independent variables that are not significant in predicting the dependent variable are removed in single step.

LINEAR REGRESSION

The relationship that exists between one dependent and one independent variable can be statistically expressed as simple linear regression. For example, Consumer spending power depends on the income earned. This can be statistically expressed as:

$$Y = \beta_0 + \beta_1 X_1$$

Consumer spending power is the dependent variable and this income is the independent variable. The coefficients of the dependent and independent variables can be derived using excel or SPSS package. The method of establishing simple linear relationship in SPSS is explained below.

Open SPSS data file, input data then, execute the following command:

ANALYSE → REGRESSION → LINEAR

In the Window that opens, enter consumer spending power as → Dependent and Income as → Independent. In method box, select Enter. Then, click OK. The output files opens and provide the model summary table of co efficient and ANOVA table.

Regression, with the least square method of estimates gives the best fit lines "Goodness' of fit" is tested with the hypothesis established. In the example discussed the Null hypothesis (H_0) will be: there is no relationship between income and consumer spending power. The first stage of interpretation is to check whether the null hypothesis or the alternative holds good. If the null hypothesis holds good. If the null hypothesis holds good, there is relation between casual spending power and income. Therefore there is nonexistence of linear relationship. The significance value of 'f' given in the ANOVA Table explains the relationship between dependent and independent variables. At 95% confidence level (or 5% level of significance) if 'f' significance is less than 0.05 then, there exists relationship among dependent and independent variables. If "f" significance is less than 0.01 then, the relationship between variables is at 99% confidence level. Then we reject null hypothesis (H_0) & state that alternative holds good. Then we proceed to understand the explanatory power of the equation. Model summary table has the values of R Square and adjusted R Square. If there is only one independent variable considers the value of R square and if more than one independent variable considers the value of adjusted R square. R Square gives the co-efficient of correlation that gives the explanatory power of the regression established. The extent to which the relationship holds good is given by the values of R Square.

The next stage, consider the coefficient table that gives both standardized & unstandardized coefficient are the intercept (β_0) & slope (β_1) of the regression equation. The slope explains the extent to which the independent variable (Here, incases) increases/decreases dependent variable Consumer spending power. The intercept value explains consumer spending power where the income is '0'. The 't' statistics column with significance level explains whether each and every independent variable significantly influences the dependent variables. The example is explained with the input & output tables in SPSS.

The regression equation also called as regression model, can fit in any paired values (X & Y) & estimate the goodness of fit line. The estimated equation by least square method the least fit time should satisfy certain assumptions[1] to be unbiased, consistent & efficient. Any regression equation established, may deviate from the actual/observed values of Y. It is captured as the error term and expressed as,

$Y = \beta_0 + \beta_1 X_i + e_i$

Y = dependent Variable

β_0 = Intercept

β_1 = Scope of Independent variable

e_i = Error term/Random disturbance

CASE

A is a manufacturing company that sells its products in a market. The company does not have a permanent sales force. Instead, the company has outsourced its marketing and sales activities to another company, B. Now, the management of company A has an idea of carrying out the marketing and sales activities on its own, instead of outsourcing it to B. Hence, the company A gathered data from the market regarding their sales performance during previous ten years in order to predict the future performance.

Input data is shown in table.

Years	SALES (per annum of one territory in Crores rupees)
2001	12.00
2002	14.00
2003	16.00
2004	18.00
2005	19.00
2006	22.00
2007	45.00
2008	66.00
2009	77.00
2010	89.00

Dependent Variable: Sales (in Rs. crores per annum)

Independent Variables: Years in which it occurred

Null Hypothesis (H_0): There is no significant trend that exists in predicting the behaviour of sales.

Alternate Hypothesis (H_1): There exists significant trend in predicting the behaviour of sales.

Table presents the output from regression analysis.

ANOVA(b)

Model	Sum of Squares	Df	Mean Square	F	Sig.
Regression	6530.376	1	6530.376	44.378	.000(a)
Residual	1177.224	8	147.153		
Total	7707.600	9			

a Predictors: (Constant), Sales per annum of one territory in Crore Rupees

b Dependent Variable: Year

Model Summary

Model	R	R Square	Adjusted R Square	Std. Error of the Estimate
1	.920	.847	.828	12.13066

Predictors: (Constant), Sales per annum of one territory in Crore Rupees

Coefficients (a)

Model	Unstandardized Coefficients		Standardized Coefficients	t	Sig.
	B	Std. Error	Beta		
(Constant)	-11.133	8.287		-1.343	.216
Sales per year of one territory in Crore Rupees	8.897	1.336	.920	6.662	.000

a Dependent Variable: Year

Interpretation

The p-value of F-test is 0.000, which is less than the significance level of 0.05. Hence, we reject the null hypothesis and the model is statistically significant for prediction. It explains the existence trend in the sales of the company.

The R^2 (R Square) value is 0.847 that describes that 84.7 % of the total variance in the dependent variable, sales of the company, is explained by the trend in the sales. The regression model that establishes the relationship is:

$$Y = \beta_0 + \beta_1 X$$

From the output tables of the regression analysis, the relationship can be established in the form of the following equation.

Sales = -11.133 + 8.897 (Years)

The coefficients table indicates the significance of individual independent variables (with p-value of 0.000) in this model as their p-values are less than the significance level of 0.05. Hence, the regression model can be used to predict the trend in the sales. For instance, the sales of the 11th and 12th years will be predicted using the regression model as given in the table.

Years	SALES (per annum of one territory in Crores rupees)
2011	-11.133 + (8.897 * 11) = 86.73
2012	-11.133 + (8.897 * 12) = 95.63

Navigation Guide

- Data must be entered in the 'Data View' page of the data sheet, as collected from the past data. (In this case, the data of sales performance collected for the past 20 years).
- In the 'Variable View' page, a suitable name and a label must be given for the variables. (In this example, the variables are named and labelled as 'Sales' (Sales per annum of one territory in Crore Rupees) and 'Year'.
- Click 'OK' after entering the values and the corresponding labels.

Data View

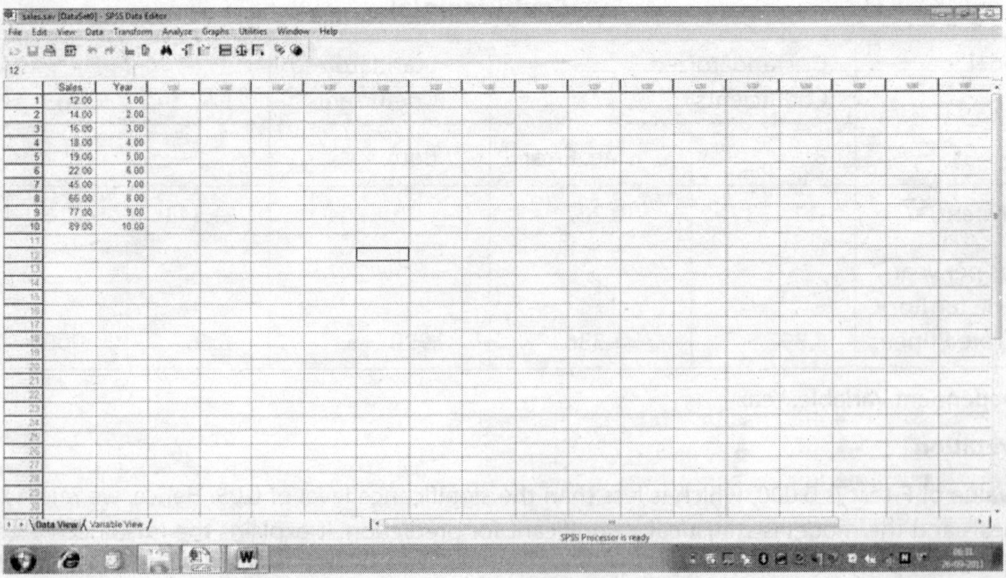

Variable View

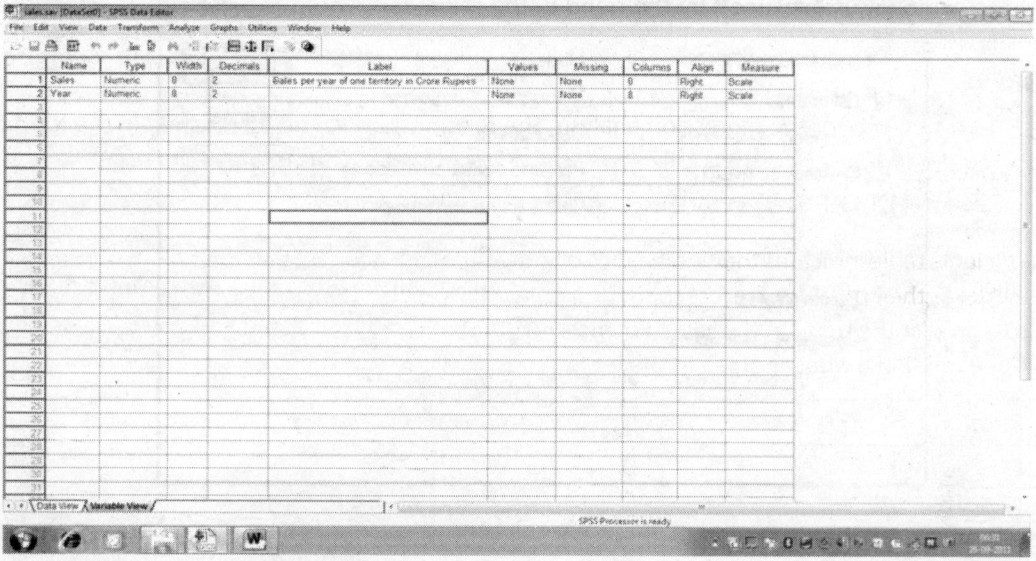

Then, the following procedure is followed:

- Select Analyse ⟶ Regression ⟶ Linear.
- ➢ Drag the dependent variable to the Dependent dialog block and the independent variables to the Independent(s) dialog block. In this example the dependent variable is 'Sales' (Sales per annum of one territory in Crore Rupees) and independent variable is 'Year'.
- Click 'Statistics', select 'Estimates', select 'Model Fit' and click 'Continue'.
- Click 'OK'.

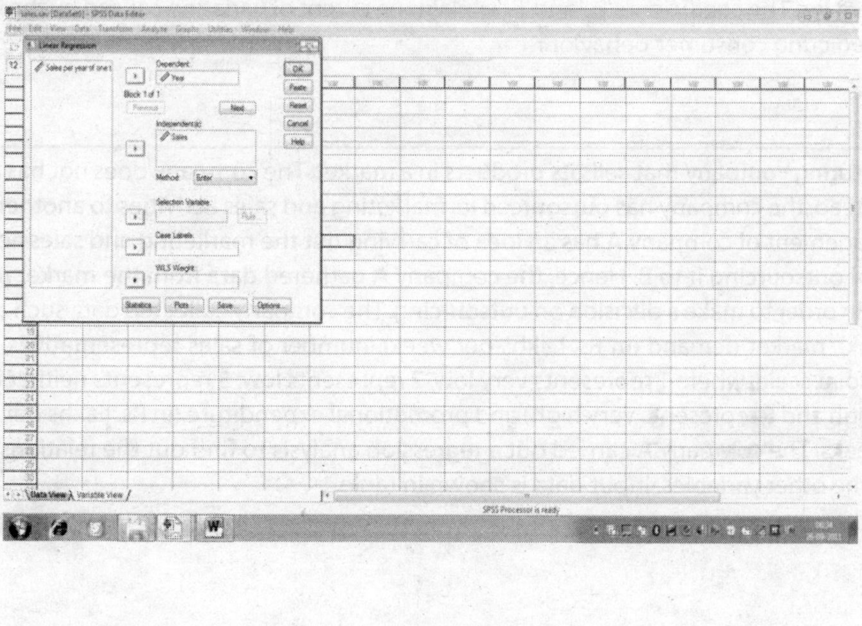

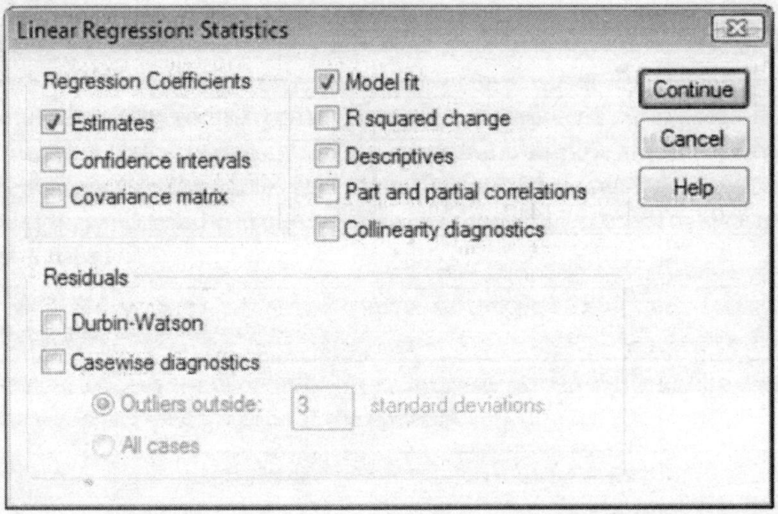

MULTIPLE REGRESSION

The relationship that exists between one dependent and two or more independent variables can be statistically expressed as multiple regression. For example, Consumer spending power depends on the income earned and stage in the family lifecycle. This can be statistically expressed as:

$$Y = \beta_0 + \beta_1 X_1 + \beta_2 X_2$$

The method of establishing multiple regression using SPSS is similar to that explained in LINEAR REGRESSION. In the dependent list, consumer behaviour will be entered and in the independent list, income earned and stage in the family lifecycle are entered. Both independent variables are entered together in the independent list. The coefficients 'β_1' and 'β_2' explain the extent of variation caused by the independent variables in predicting consumer behaviour.

CASE

A is a manufacturing company that sells its products in a market. The company does not has a permanent sales force. Instead, the company has outsourced its marketing and sales activities to another company, B. Now, the management of company A has an idea of carrying out the marketing and sales activities on its own, instead of outsourcing it to B. Hence, the company A gathered data from the market regarding the past 20 weeks in order to make a decision on outsourcing. The company collected data such as sales (in Rs. Lakhs per week), market demand (in Rs. Lakhs per week), number of sales representatives, competition index (on a 5 point scale, where 1 represents very low, 2 represents low, 3 represents neither high nor low, 4 represents high and 5 represents very high) and promotional expenditure (in Rs. Lakhs per annum) over the past 20 weeks. The company A carried out a regression analysis to find out the relationship between the sales and the other variables. Input data is shown in table.

Sample Week	Sales (in Rs. Lakhs per Week)	Market Demand (in Rs. Lakhs per Week)	Number of Salesmen	Promotional Expenditure (in Rs. Lakhs per Week)	Competition Index
1	20	31	20	8	2
2	6	14	39	6	4
3	35	52	12	5	5
4	39	60	30	7	3
5	16	40	12	6	1
6	32	51	26	8	1
7	11	20	14	10	3
8	23	34	19	13	4
9	7	25	19	6	2
10	4	18	17	8	3
11	6	19	15	9	2
12	31	43	26	14	2
13	46	60	32	8	4
14	52	61	40	6	2
15	12	24	30	9	2
16	5	17	31	10	4
17	42	58	32	12	4
18	47	61	33	6	2
19	39	52	27	7	2
20	42	56	37	5	3

Dependent Variable: Sales (in Rs. Lakhs per week)

Independent Variables: Market Demand (in Rs. Lakhs per week), Number of sales men, Promotional Expenditure (in Rs. Lakhs per week) and Competition Index (1-Very Low, 2-Low, 3-Neither High Nor Low, 4-High, 5-Very High).

Null Hypothesis (H0): There is no relationship between the dependent variable (sales of the company) and the independent variables (market demand, number of sales men, promotional expenditure and the competition index).

Alternate Hypothesis (H1): A relationship exists between the dependent variable (sales of the company) and the independent variables (market demand, number of sales men, promotional expenditure and the competition index).

Table presents the output from regression analysis.

ANOVA (b)

Model	Sum of Squares	Df	Mean Square	F	Sig.
Regression	4983.378	4	1245.844	105.956	.000(a)
Residual	176.372	15	11.758		
Total	5159.750	19			

a Predictors: (Constant), Competition Index, Market Demand (in Rs. lakhs per week), Promotional Expenditure (in Rs. lakhs per week), Number of Sales Representatives

b Dependent Variable: Sales (in Rs. lakhs per week)

Model Summary

Model	R	R Square	Adjusted R Square	Std. Error of the Estimate
1	.983(a)	.966	.957	3.42902

a Predictors: (Constant), Competition Index, Market Demand (in Rs. lakhs per week), Promotional Expenditure (in Rs. lakhs per week), Number of Sales Representatives

Coefficients (a)

Model	Unstandardized Coefficients		Standardized Coefficients	T	Sig.
	B	Std. Error	Beta		
(Constant)	-20.010	4.213		-4.749	.000
Market Demand (in Rs. lakhs per week)	.883	.049	.937	17.865	.000
Number of Sales Men	.238	.095	.130	2.496	.025
Promotional Expenditure (in Rs. lakhs per week)	.351	.315	.055	1.116	.282
Competition Index	.611	.715	.041	.855	.406

a Dependent Variable: Sales (in Rs. lakhs per week)

Interpretation

The p-value of F-test is 0.000, which is less than the significance level of 0.05. Hence, we reject the null hypothesis and the model is statistically significant for prediction. It explains the existence of relationship between the dependent variable (sales of the company) and the independent variables (market demand, number of sales men, promotional expenditure and the competition index).

The R^2 (R Square) value is 0.966 and the Adjusted R^2 (Adjusted R Square) value is 0.957. It describes that 95.7 % of the total variance in the dependent variable, sales of the company, is explained by the independent variables, namely, market demand, number of sales men, promotional expenditure and the competition index. Thus, the independent variables can predict the dependent variable to a greater extent. The regression model that establishes the relationship is:

$$Y = \beta_0 + \beta_1 X_1 + \beta_2 X_2 + \beta_3 x_3 + \beta_4 x_4$$

From the output tables of the regression analysis, the relationship can be established in the form of the following equation.

Sales = -20.010 + 0.883 (Market Demand) + 0.238 (Number of sales men) + 0.351 (Promotional Expenditure) + 0.611 (Competition Index)

where,

a (intercept) = -20.010

β_1 = 0.883

β_2 = 0.238

β_3 = 0.351

β_4 = 0.611

The coefficients table indicates the significance of individual independent variables. Thus, the two variables, market demand (with p-value of 0.000) and number of sales men (with p-value of 0.025) are statistically significant in this model as their p-values are less than the significance level of 0.05. The other two variables, namely, promotional expenditure (with p-value of 0.282) and competition index (with p-value of 0.406) are not statistically significant as their p-values are greater than the significance level of 0.05. Hence, the regression model can be refined with the influence of market demand and number of sales men. The sales of the company would increase in the market if there is an increase in the market demand and the number of sales men. This increase is represented by the respective coefficients. For instance, if the market demand increases by 1 unit, then the sales would increase by 0.883 units, if the other variables remain constant. If the number of sales men increases by 1 unit, then the sales would increase by 0.238 units if the other variables remain unchanged. The same is applicable for the other two variables, namely, promotional expenditure and the competition index but they are not statistically significant. Hence, they need not be included in the regression model.

Navigation Guide

- Data must be entered in the 'Data View' page of the data sheet, as collected from the past data. (In this case, it is based on the data collected for the past 20 weeks regarding the sales, market demand, number of sales men, promotional expenditure and the competition index).
- In the 'Variable View' page, a suitable name and a label must be given for the variables. (In this example, the variables are named and labelled as 'Sales' (in Rs. Lakhs per week), 'Market Demand' (in Rs. Lakhs per week), 'Number of sales men', 'Promotional Expenditure' (in Rs. Lakhs per week) and 'Competition Index'. The values must be entered as determined. The value must be entered first, followed by the corresponding label. (In this example, Competition Index is rated on a 5 point scale and the representations are 1-Very Low, 2-Low, 3-Neither Low Nor High, 4-High, 5-Very High).
- Click 'OK' after entering the values and the corresponding labels.

Data View

regression [DataSet1] - SPSS Data Editor

File Edit View Data Transform Analyze Graphs Utilities Window Help

1 : Sales 20

	Sales	Demand	Salesmen	Promotions	Competitors	var	var	var	var	var	var
1	20.00	31.00	20.00	8.00	2.00						
2	6.00	14.00	39.00	6.00	4.00						
3	35.00	52.00	12.00	5.00	5.00						
4	39.00	60.00	30.00	7.00	3.00						
5	16.00	40.00	12.00	6.00	1.00						
6	32.00	51.00	26.00	8.00	1.00						
7	11.00	20.00	14.00	10.00	3.00						
8	23.00	34.00	19.00	13.00	4.00						
9	7.00	25.00	19.00	6.00	2.00						
10	4.00	18.00	17.00	8.00	3.00						
11	6.00	19.00	15.00	9.00	2.00						
12	31.00	43.00	26.00	14.00	2.00						
13	46.00	60.00	32.00	8.00	4.00						
14	52.00	61.00	40.00	6.00	2.00						
15	12.00	24.00	30.00	9.00	2.00						
16	5.00	17.00	31.00	10.00	4.00						
17	42.00	58.00	32.00	12.00	4.00						
18	47.00	61.00	33.00	6.00	2.00						
19	39.00	52.00	27.00	7.00	2.00						
20	42.00	56.00	37.00	5.00	3.00						
21											
22											
23											

Variable View

*regression [DataSet1] - SPSS Data Editor

File Edit View Data Transform Analyze Graphs Utilities Window Help

	Name	Type	Width	Decimals	Label	Values	Missing	Columns	Align	Measure
1	Sales	Numeric	8	2	Sales (in Rs. Lakhs per week)	None	None	8	Right	Scale
2	Demand	Numeric	8	2	Market Demand (in Rs. Lakhs per week)	None	None	9	Right	Scale
3	Salesmen	Numeric	8	2	Number of Sales Men	None	None	10	Right	Scale
4	Promotions	Numeric	8	2	Promotional Expenditure (in Rs. Lakhs per week)	None	None	10	Right	Scale
5	Competitors	Numeric	8	2	Competition Index	{1.00, Very Low}	None	11	Right	Scale
6										
7										
8										
9										
10										
11										

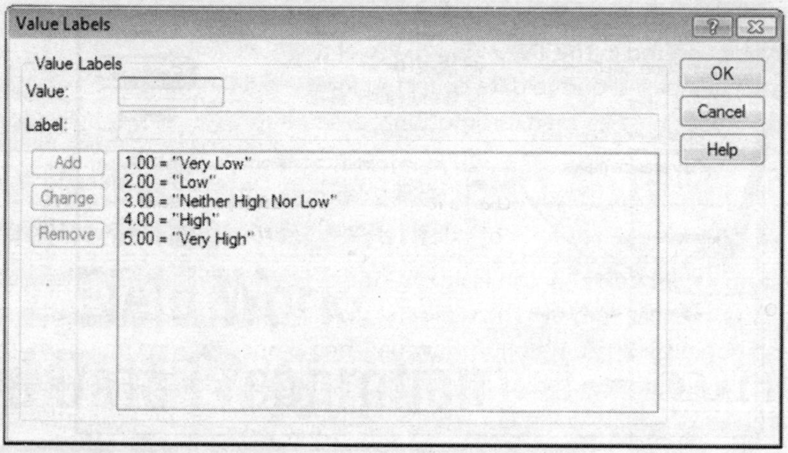

Then, the following procedure is followed:

- Select Analyse → Regression → Linear.
- Drag the dependent variable to the Dependent dialog block and the independent variables to the Independent(s) dialog block. (In this example, the variable 'Sales (in Rs. Lakhs per week)' must be dragged to the Dependent dialog block. The variables 'Market Demand (in Rs. Lakhs per week), Number of sales men, Promotional Expenditure (in Rs. Lakhs per week) and Competition Index' must dragged to the Independent(s) dialog block).
- Click 'Statistics', select 'Estimates', select 'Model Fit' and click 'Continue'.
- Click 'OK'.

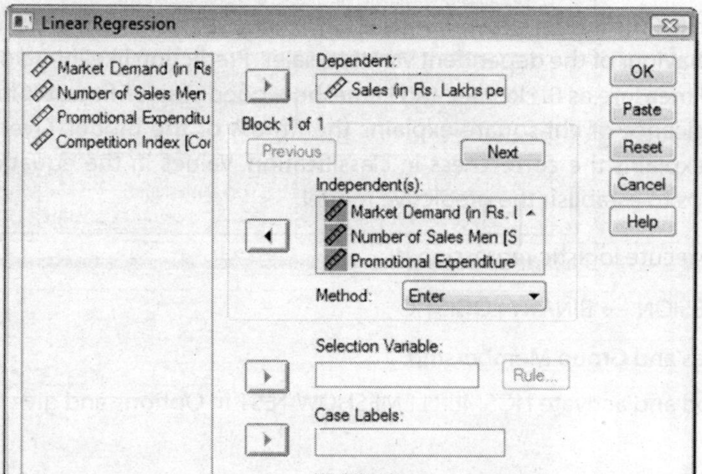

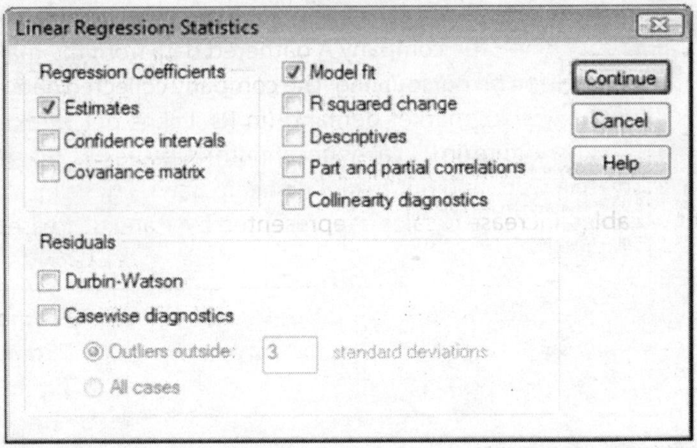

LOGISTIC REGRESSION

Linear regression is performed if the dependent and independent values are interval data. If the dependent variable is a binomial data (with two categories of data), logistic regression is performed. For example, increase or decrease in sales is the dependent variable that is predicted by the influence of several other independent variables, logistic regression is performed. It is useful for predicting the presence or absence of a characteristic or outcome based on the behaviour of independent variables. Maximum likelihood estimation (MLE) is used in logistic regression. It is similar to regression except where the dependent variable is dichotomous. For example to understand the satisfaction or dissatisfaction of consumers, to predict the existence of loyalty or not, logistic regression can be used. The coefficients can be used to estimate the odds ratios for the independent variables.

Statistical significance of the model is tested with -2 log likelihood measure. It explains the extent to which it can predict the behaviour of the dependent variable, sales. Prediction likelihood of 1, or a perfect model has -2 log likelihood measure as 0. Hosmer and Lemeshow goodness-of-fit test (Chi-square test) explains the model fit. Significance of chi-square explains the fitness of the model. Overall percentage in the classification table explains the correctness in classification. Values in the equation matrix give the 'β' coefficients that helps to establish the predictive model.

SPSS command to execute logistic regression is:

ANALYSE ⟶ REGRESSION ⟶ BINARY LOGISTIC

Save the Probabilities and Group Membership.

Select ENTER Method and activate HOSMER LEMESHOW TEST in Options and give OK.

CASE

A is a manufacturing company that sells its products in a market. The company does not have a permanent sales force. Instead, the company has outsourced its marketing and sales activities to another company, B.

Now, the management of company A has an idea of carrying out the marketing and sales activities on its own, instead of outsourcing it to B. Hence, the company A gathered data from the market regarding the past 20 weeks in order to make a decision on outsourcing. The company collected data such as sales (with increase or decrease over previous week), market demand (in Rs. Lakhs per week), number of sales representatives and promotional expenditure (in Rs. Lakhs per annum) over the past 20 weeks. The company A carried out logistic regression analysis to find out the relationship between the increase or decrease in sales and the independent variables. increase in sales is represented by '1' and decrease by '0'. Input data is shown in table.

Sample Week	Sales (increase/ decrease)	Market Demand (in Rs. Lakhs per Week)	Number of Salesmen	Promotional Expenditure (in Rs. Lakhs per Week)
1	1	31	20	8
2	1	14	39	6
3	1	52	12	5
4	0	60	30	7
5	0	40	12	6
6	1	51	26	8
7	0	20	14	10
8	0	34	19	13
9	0	25	19	6
10	0	18	17	8
11	0	19	15	9
12	1	43	26	14
13	1	60	32	8
14	1	61	40	6
15	0	24	30	9
16	1	17	31	10
17	1	58	32	12
18	1	61	33	6
19	1	52	27	7
20	1	56	37	5

Dependent Variable: Sales (with increase as '1' and decrease as '2')

Independent Variables: Market Demand (in Rs. Lakhs per week), Number of sales men, and Promotional Expenditure (in Rs. Lakhs per week).

Null Hypothesis (H_0): There is no significant relationship between increase or decrease in the sales of the company and the independent variables: market demand, number of sales men, and promotional expenditure.

Alternate Hypothesis (H_1): Increase or decrease in sales can be significantly predicted by the independent variables: market demand, number of sales men, and promotional expenditure.

Table presents the output from regression analysis.

Model Summary

Step	-2 Log likelihood	Cox & Snell R Square	Nagelkerke R Square
1	17.531(a)	.375	.506

a Estimation terminated at iteration number 5 because parameter estimates changed by less than .001.

Hosmer and Lemeshow Test

Step	Chi-square	df	Sig.
1	11.723	8	.164

Classification Table (a)

Observed			Predicted		
			SALES		Percentage Correct
			0	1	0
Step 1	SALES	0	6	2	75.0
		1	2	10	83.3
	Overall Percentage				80.0

a The cut value is .500

Variables in the Equation

		B	S.E.	Wald	df	Sig.	Exp(B)
Step 1(a)	MARKET DEMAND	.056	.041	1.927	1	.165	1.058
	SALESMEN	.146	.075	3.730	1	.053	1.157
	PROMOTIONAL EXP	-.044	.225	.038	1	.845	.957
	Constant	-4.858	2.995	2.631	1	.105	.008

a Variable (s) entered on step 1: MARKET DEMAND, SALESMEN, PROMOTIONAL EXP.

Interpretation

Statistical significance of logit regression can be understood with – 2 log likelihood measure. It explains the extent to which the dependent variable can be predicted with the independent variables. A perfect model will have the – 2 log likelihood measure of '0'. The model given is not perfect. However, the significance of prediction can be explained by Hosmer and Lemeshow goodness-of-fit test (Chi-square). This test explains the model fit. Hosmer and Lemeshow test shows a significance of 0.164 that is above 0.05 at 5 percent level of significance. The lack of significance explains that there is no significant difference between the observed and predicted values. So the model is fit for prediction.

The classification table summarizes the extent to which the model correctly classifies the dependent variables with the impact of independent variables considered. Overall 80 percent the classification of the model will be perfect. Significance of Wald's test is given in the table of 'Variables in the Equation'. Significance less than 0.05 explains that the independent variables has an influence in categorizing the sales with an increase or decrease. The variables are not significant. This is because the small size of the sample considered. As the model is fit to draw predictions, increase in the sample size will help the researchers to understand the independent variables that significantly classify the dependent variable. The logit regression model $Y = \beta_0 + \beta_1 X_1 + \beta_2 X_2 + \beta_3 x_3$ is given below.

From the variables table of logit regression analysis, the relationship can be established in the form of the following equation.

Sales (Increase/Decrease) = -4.858 + 0.056 (Market Demand) + 0.146 (Number of salesmen) - 0.044 (Promotional Expenditure)

where,

a (intercept) = -4.858

β_1 = 0.056

β_2 = 0.146

β_3 = -0.044

The variables table indicates the significance of individual independent variables. As the sample size is to less, number of sales men (with p-value of 0.053) is the only variable that is statistically significant at the level of 10 percent. The other two variables are not statistically significant as their p-values are greater than the significance level of 0.05. Hence, the increase or decrease in sales can be predicted with the number of sales men employed.

Predicted probabilities and predicted classification of sales (increase/decrease) is shown in the input file of SPSS on execution of logit regression. The input file is given below with the print screen view.

Sample Week	Sales (increase /decrease)	Market Demand (in Rs. Lakhs per Week)	Number of Salesmen	Promotional Expenditure (in Rs. Lakhs per Week)	PRE_1	PRG_1
1	1	31	20	8	.36666	0
2	1	14	39	6	.79420	1
3	1	52	12	5	.40257	0
4	0	60	30	7	.93031	1
5	0	40	12	6	.24672	0
6	1	51	26	8	.81101	1
7	0	20	14	10	.10623	0
8	0	34	19	13	.32232	0
9	0	25	19	6	.28032	0
10	0	18	17	8	.15220	0
11	0	19	15	9	.11957	0
12	1	43	26	14	.67716	1
13	1	60	32	8	.94474	1
14	1	61	40	6	.98447	1
15	0	24	30	9	.61571	1
16	1	17	31	10	.54436	1
17	1	58	32	12	.92756	1
18	1	61	33	6	.95808	1
19	1	52	27	7	.84590	1
20	1	56	37	5	.96993	1

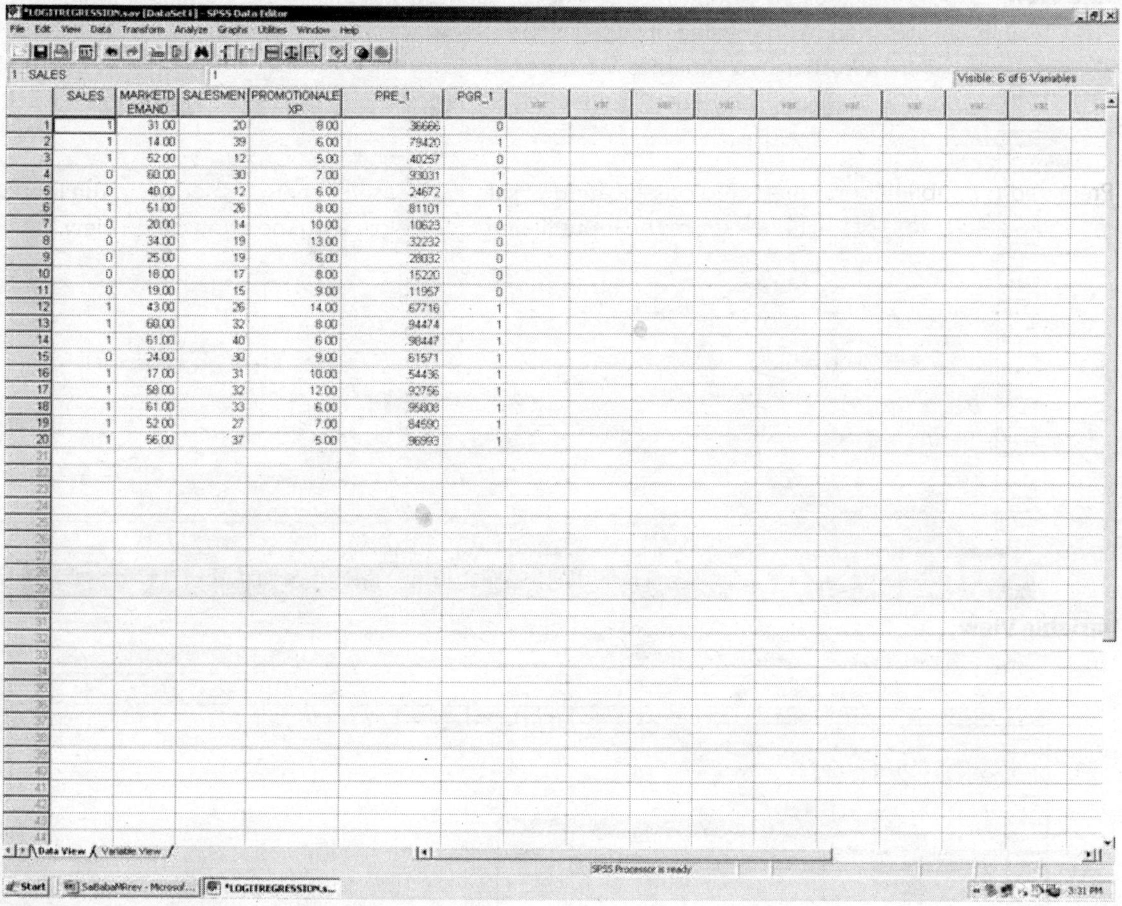

	SALES	MARKETDEMAND	SALESMEN	PROMOTIONALEXP	PRE_1	PGR_1
1	1	31.00	20	8.00	.36666	0
2	1	14.00	39	6.00	.79420	1
3	1	52.00	12	5.00	.40257	0
4	0	60.00	30	7.00	.93031	1
5	0	40.00	12	6.00	.24672	0
6	1	51.00	26	8.00	.81101	1
7	0	20.00	14	10.00	.10623	0
8	0	34.00	19	13.00	.32232	0
9	0	25.00	19	6.00	.28032	0
10	0	18.00	17	8.00	.15220	0
11	0	19.00	15	9.00	.11957	0
12	1	43.00	26	14.00	.67716	1
13	1	60.00	32	8.00	.94474	1
14	1	61.00	40	6.00	.98447	1
15	0	24.00	30	9.00	.61571	1
16	1	17.00	31	10.00	.54436	1
17	1	58.00	32	12.00	.92756	1
18	1	61.00	33	6.00	.95808	1
19	1	52.00	27	7.00	.84590	1
20	1	56.00	37	5.00	.96993	1

Navigation Guide

- Data must be entered in the 'Data View' page of the data sheet, as collected from the past data. (In this case, it is based on the data collected for the past 20 weeks regarding the increase or decrease in sales, market demand, number of salesmen, and promotional expenditure).
- In the 'Variable View' page, a suitable name and a label must be given for the variables. (In this example, the variables are named and labelled as 'Sales', 'Market Demand' (in Rs. Lakhs per week), 'Number of sales men', and 'Promotional Expenditure' (in Rs. Lakhs per week). The value must be entered first, followed by the corresponding label. (In this example, increase of sales with '1' and decrease with '0' is the label assigned for the variable 'Sales').
- Click 'OK' after entering the values and the corresponding labels.

Data View

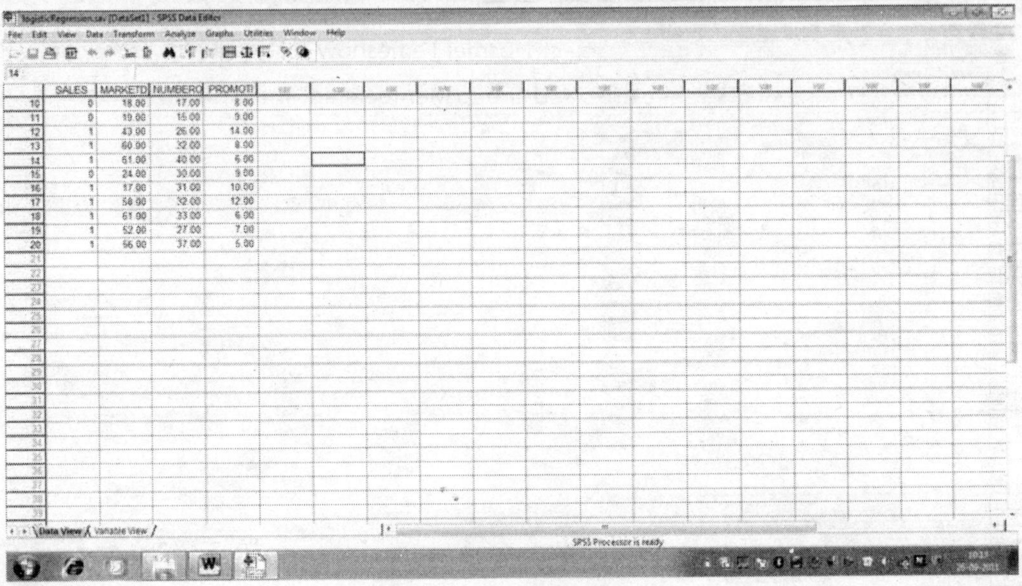

Variable View

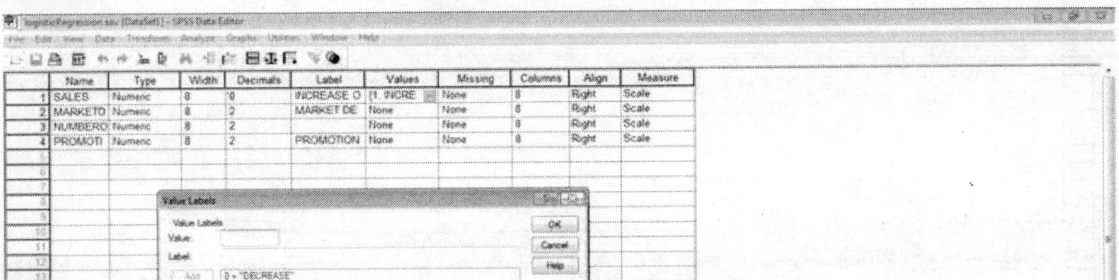

Then, the following procedure is followed:

- Select Analyse ⟶ Regression ⟶ Binary Logistic.
- Drag the dependent variable to the Dependent dialog block and the independent variables to the Independent(s) dialog block. (In this example, the variable 'Sales' must be dragged to the Dependent dialog block. The variables 'Market Demand' (in Rs. Lakhs per week), 'Number of

salesmen', and 'Promotional Expenditure' (in Rs. Lakhs per week) to the Independent(s) dialog block.

- Click 'OPTIONS', select 'Statistics', select 'Hosmer Lemeshow Test' and click 'Continue'.
- Click 'SAVE' and select Probabilities and Group Membership, and click 'Continue'.
- Click 'OK'.

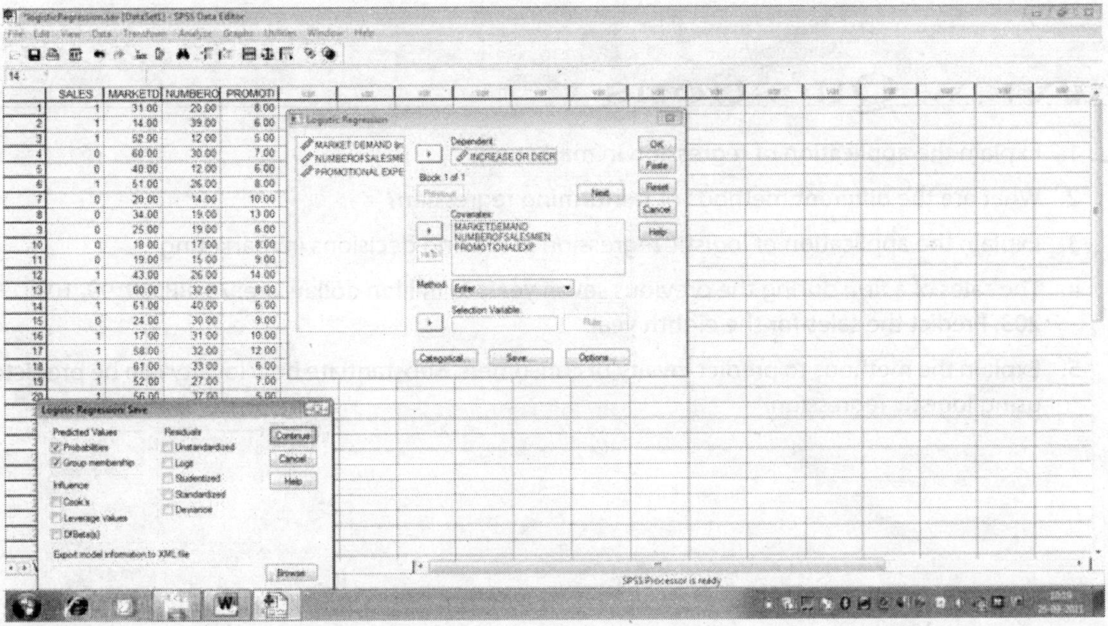

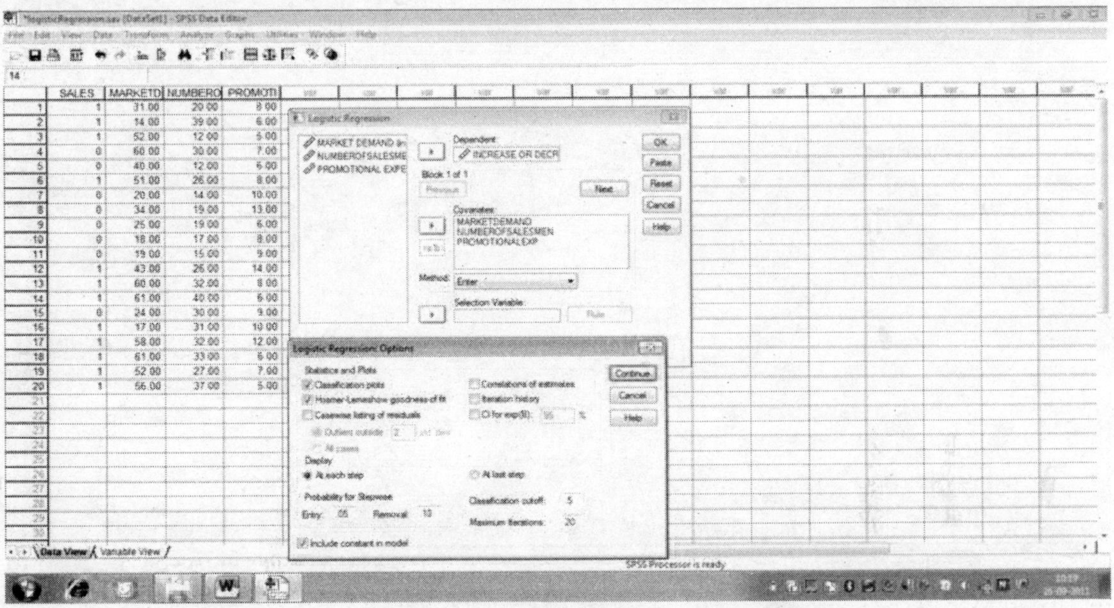

Regression works on the basic assumption that the data is metric and normally distributed. The normality of the distribution is true if the standardized residual plot is normal. If not, the predicted model will not hold good. If the dependent variable is a dichotomous variable, logistic regression is performed. If the dependent variable has more than two categories, then discriminant model is appropriate for prediction. In specific, regression models are used extensively in marketing for establishing predictive models.

Review Questions

1. Explain the application of regression in marketing.
2. What are the different methods of performing regression?
3. Explain the application of logistic regression in making decisions in marketing.
4. The sales of a firm during the previous seven years in million dollars are: 75, 88, 89, 99, 108, 111, 203. Predict the sales for the eighth year.
5. Explain the methods to predict loyalty of consumers. Substantiate how loyalty can be predicted using logistic regression.

Chapter 13

Decision Making Models

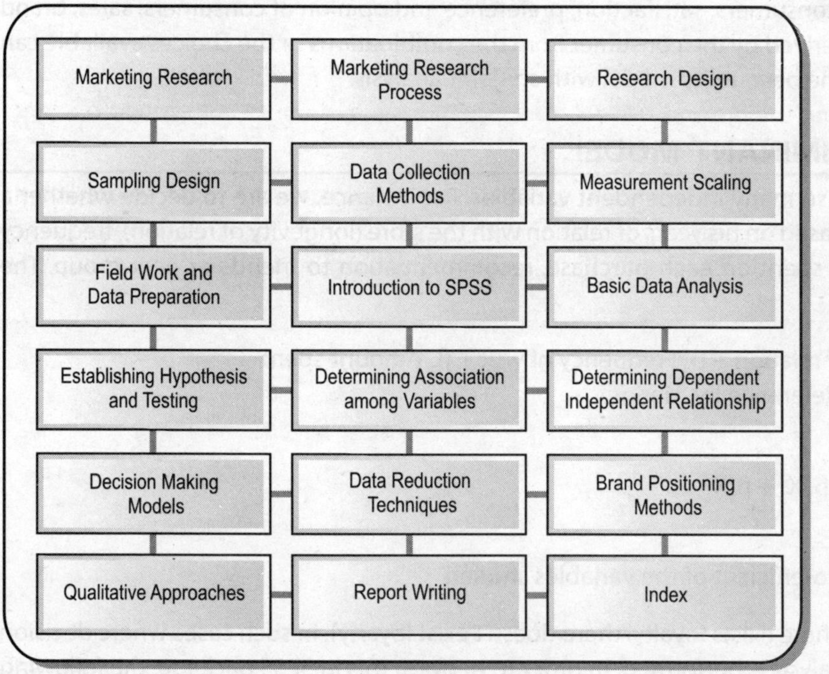

Outline

Chapter Structure

- Introduction
- Decision Making Models
- Establishing Discriminant Model
- Case
- Conjoint Analysis
- Case
- Review Questions

Chapter Overview

This chapter explains the decision making models including discriminant that classifies the respondents and categorizes in the respective subgroup; and conjoint that brings in the high utility factors to combine to yield maximum benefits for the consumers and the marketers.

INTRODUCTION

Regression, logistic regression and discriminant analysis are all decision making models applied based on the type of dependent variable. If the dependent variable has scaled data, regression is used to establish the model and predict the behaviour based on the variations in the independent variable. If the dependent variable is a dichotomous variable, logistic regression is used for the same.

DECISION MAKING MODELS

If the dependent variable has more than two categories and is a grouping variable, then discriminant analysis establishes the predictive model that helps to decide the behaviour of the dependent variable based on the fluctuations in the independent variable. These predictive models will help the marketers to understand the behaviour of consumers, satisfaction, preference and opinion of consumers, sales, brand choice, etc. Maximum utility derived by the consumer from the combinations or the choices available can help the marketers to derive the best utility model with conjoint analysis.

ESTABLISHING DISCRIMINANT MODEL

Customer loyalty depends on so many independent variables. For instance, we are to decide whether a customer is loyal or not loyal based on his years of relation with the store (longevity of relation), frequency of his visit to a store, amount spent on each purchase, recommendation to friends or peer group. The relationship can be built by:

Loyalty = $\beta_0 + \beta_1$ Longevity of relation + β_2 Frequency of visit + β_3 Amount spent on purchases + β_4 Reference by friends

this can be represented as:

$$Y = \beta_0 + \beta_1 X_1 + \beta_2 X_2 + \beta_3 X_3 + \beta_4 X_4$$

where β_0 is the constant

β_1, β_2, β_3, & β_4 are the co-efficient of the variables studied

Loyalty is a decision variable (there exists loyalty/there doesn't exist loyalty). In such cases where decision is to be made, discriminant analysis is performed. In order to perform this in SPSS package, the following command can be used.

ANALYSE → SCALE → DISCRIMINANT

In the input file, the variables are coded as follows:

Loyalty – if there exists loyalty, mark as '1; and if the loyalty does not exists, mark as '2'

Longevity of relation – the number of years the customer has relation with the store is given in years. For example, if the customer has relation with the store for 6 years, mark as '6'

Frequency – frequency of visit to a store is the number of times a customer has visited the store. It can be restricted to a year. Here we consider the total visits made for one year. If the customer has visited the store 8 times a year, we mark '8'

Amount spent – this is the average amount spent per visit measured in rupees (Rs.).

Reference – this variable is measured on a scale from 1 – 7 where '1' refers the customers dis interest in recommendation and '7' refers to the customers strong interest in referring to friends and others.

If the window of Discriminant opens, enter loyalty as grouping variable. Define the minimum and maximum values as 1 and 2 respectively. If there are three options then minimum value is 1 and maximum is 3. Enter the independent variables longevity of relation, frequency of visit, amount spent on purchases and reference made by friends. Then perform discriminant analysis.

CASE

A manufacturing company wants to promote some of its sales executives into assistant sales managers. The company does not want to promote its sales executives merely on the basis of experience or sales. Hence, the company obtained data from the other zone, regarding the performance of 20 employees in order to develop a model so that it can be used to decide about the promotion of its sales executives. The data, which was obtained from the other zone, consists of 5 parameters, namely, age of the executives, experience, average sales achieved by the executives per year (in Rs.), average number of new clients added per year by an executive and the capability of the executives. The capability is an index referring to the ability of the sales executive on the basis of performance. It is coded as [1-Low Performance, 2-High Performance]. Based on this model, the sales executives would be evaluated and their capability would be calculated. The sales executives, whose capability falls under 'High Performance', would be eligible for promotion and the others would continue as sales executives. Input data is shown in table below.

Input Table:

Sample	Capability	Age	Experience	Average Sales per Year (in Rs.)	Average Number of New Clients per Year
1	1	32	3	65000	5
2	1	30	4	49000	6
3	1	30	5	58000	7
4	2	33	2	83000	6
5	2	34	1	89000	4
6	1	29	3	69000	5
7	2	29	4	102000	8
8	1	35	5	62000	7
9	2	29	2	100000	7
10	2	30	3	95000	9
11	2	32	5	83000	10

12	1	29	3	63000	5
13	1	33	2	68000	7
14	1	26	2	65000	3
15	2	27	3	91000	7
16	1	35	3	73000	8
17	2	34	5	79000	8
18	2	32	3	77000	8
19	1	34	2	70000	9
20	2	35	5	81000	11

Null Hypothesis (H_0): There is no possibility of discrimination between the two groups with this model.

Alternate Hypothesis (H_1): The model can be used for discriminating between the two groups.

Table presents the output from Discriminant analysis.

Output Tables and Interpretation

Wilks' Lambda

Test of Function(s)	Wilks' Lambda	Chi-square	Df	Sig.
1	.232	23.359	4	.000

The p-value of chi-square test is 0.000 at n-1 (20 – 1 = 19) degrees of freedom (df). The value of 'p' is less than the significance level of 0.05 (5 percent) and even less than 0.01 (1 percent). Hence, we reject the null hypothesis. It means that the model can be used for discriminating between the two groups and it is highly significant. Wilks' Lambda value of this test is 0.232. This value always lies between 0 and 1. 0.232 is very closer to 0 and it indicates the better discriminating power of the model i.e., the model has a better power in discriminating between the two groups.

Classification Results[a]

		Capability of Sales Executive	Predicted Group Membership		Total
			Low	High	
Original	Count	Low	10	0	10
		High	0	10	10
	%	Low	100.0	.0	100.0
		High	.0	100.0	100.0

[a] 100.0% of original grouped cases correctly classified.

The classification matrix (also known as confusion matrix) indicates the ability of classification by this model. From the output table of classification matrix, we find that 100% of the existing data have been classified correctly i.e., the entire 20 objects have been classified correctly. From the column 'Low' in the table, we find that 10 objects were predicted to be in the group 'Low'. From the row 'Low' in the table, we find that all 10 objects that were predicted to be in group 'Low', have been classified into group 'Low'. From the column 'High' in the table, we find that 10 objects were predicted to be in the group 'High'. From the row 'High' in the table, we find that all 10 objects that were predicted to be in group 'High', have been classified into group 'High'. This shows that not even a single data was misclassified and hence 100% of the existing data have been classified correctly.

Standardized Canonical Discriminant Function Coefficients

Variables	Function
	1
Age of sales executive	.240
Experience of sales executive	.564
Average Sales per Year	1.165
Average number of new clients per year	-.136

From the Standardized Canonical Discriminant Function Coefficients table, we find that 4 variables, namely,

- Age of sales executive
- Experience of sales executive
- Average sales per year
- Average number of new clients per year

determine the discriminating power of the model. Among these 4 variables, average sales per year is the variable that has a better discriminating power than the other variables since it has the highest coefficient of 1.165. It is followed by experience of sales executive with the coefficient of 0.564. Age of sales executive follows experience with the coefficient of 0.240. Average number of new clients per year has the least discriminating power among the 4 variables with the coefficient of 0.136. An important thing to be noted is that only the absolute value of the coefficient must be taken into consideration while determining the discriminating power of the variables.

Canonical Discriminant Function Coefficients

Unstandardized Coefficients	Function
	1
Age of sales executive	.08534
Experience of sales executive	.43930

Average Sales per Year	.00015
Average number of new clients per year	-.07281
(Constant)	-14.805

From the Unstandardized Canonical Discriminant Function Coefficients table, the Discriminant model can be framed and the model is shown below:

Capability = -14.805 + 0.08534 (age of sales executive) + 0.43930 (experience of sales executive) + 0.00015 (average sales per year) – 0.07281 (average number of new clients per year)

This model can be used to decide whether a sales executive is eligible to be promoted as assistant sales manager or not.

Functions at Group Centroids

Capability of Sales Executive	**Function**
	1
Low	-1.725
High	1.725

Unstandardized canonical discriminant functions evaluated at group means

From the Functions at Group Centroids table, classification of a sales executive, is he eligible for promotion or not can be made. The Capability of sales executive, as shown in the table above, has a high and a low value of 1.725 and -1.725 respectively. The mid-point is 0. The Capability index of a sales executive is developed using the discriminant model. If the discriminant score i.e., Capability value is positive, then the sales executive can be classified under the group 'High' and is eligible for promotion. Consequently, if the discriminant score i.e., Capability value is negative, then the sales executive can be classified under the group 'Low' and is not eligible for promotion and would continue to serve as sales executive. For example, a sales executive, who is 35 years old, has an experience of 5 years. His average sales per is Rs. 70,000 and he adds 5 new clients per year on an average. His discriminant score i.e., Capability is calculated as follows:

Capability = - 14.805 + 0.08534 (35) + 0.43930 (5) + 0.00015 (60,000) – 0.07281 (7)

Capability = - 14.805 + 2.9869 + 2.1965 + 9 – 0.50967

Capability = - 1.13127

Thus, the sales executive falls under the category of 'Low'. Hence, the sales executive is not eligible for promotion and would continue to serve as sales executive.

For example, a sales executive, who is 32 years old, has an experience of 4 years. His average sales per is Rs. 90,000 and he adds 4 new clients per year on an average. His discriminant score i.e., Capability is calculated as follows:

Capability = - 14.805 + 0.08534 (32) + 0.43930 (4) + 0.00015 (90,000) – 0.07281 (4)

Capability = - 14.805 + 2.73088 + 1.7572 + 13.5 – 0.29124

Capability = 2.89184

Thus, the sales executive falls under the category of 'High'. Hence, the sales executive is eligible for promotion and can be promoted as assistant sales manager.

Navigation Guide

In order to enter data:

➢ Data must be entered in the 'Data View' page of the data sheet, as obtained. (In this case, it is based on the data obtained from the other zone regarding the performance of 20 sales executives. The data includes age, experience, average sales per year, average number of new clients per year and capability index).

Data View

discriminant [DataSet1] - SPSS Data Editor

File Edit View Data Transform Analyze Graphs Utilities Window Help

1 : Capability 1

	Capability	Age	Experience	AverageSales	NewClients	var	var	var	var
1	1.00	32.00	3.00	65000.00	5.00				
2	1.00	30.00	4.00	49000.00	6.00				
3	1.00	30.00	5.00	58000.00	7.00				
4	2.00	33.00	2.00	83000.00	6.00				
5	2.00	34.00	1.00	89000.00	4.00				
6	1.00	29.00	3.00	69000.00	5.00				
7	2.00	29.00	4.00	102000.00	8.00				
8	1.00	35.00	5.00	62000.00	7.00				
9	2.00	29.00	2.00	100000.00	7.00				
10	2.00	30.00	3.00	95000.00	9.00				
11	2.00	32.00	5.00	83000.00	10.00				
12	1.00	29.00	3.00	63000.00	5.00				
13	1.00	33.00	2.00	68000.00	7.00				
14	1.00	26.00	2.00	65000.00	3.00				
15	2.00	27.00	3.00	91000.00	7.00				
16	1.00	35.00	3.00	73000.00	8.00				
17	2.00	34.00	5.00	79000.00	8.00				
18	2.00	32.00	3.00	77000.00	8.00				
19	1.00	34.00	2.00	70000.00	9.00				
20	2.00	35.00	5.00	81000.00	11.00				

Variable View

➢ Open variable view and enter 'Capability, Age, Experience, Average Sales and New Clients' in the column Name. It assigns by default, the type of data, width, decimals and measure.

discriminant [DataSet1] - SPSS Data Editor

File Edit View Data Transform Analyze Graphs Utilities Window Help

	Name	Type	Width	Decimals	Label	Values	Missing	Columns	Align	Measure
1	Capability	Numeric	8	2	Capability of sales executive	{1.00, Low}...	None	10	Right	Scale
2	Age	Numeric	8	2	Age of sales executive	None	None	8	Right	Scale
3	Experience	Numeric	8	2	Experience of sales executive	None	None	10	Right	Scale
4	AverageSales	Numeric	8	2	Average Sales per Year	None	None	12	Right	Scale
5	NewClients	Numeric	8	2	Average number of new clients per year	None	None	11	Right	Scale
6										
7										
8										
9										
10										

- In the 'Variable View' page, a suitable name and a label must be given for the variables entered. (In this example, the variables are: CAPABILITY OF SALES EXECUTIVE, AGE OF SALES EXECUTIVE, EXPERIENCE OF SALES EXECUTIVE, AVERAGE SALES PER YEAR and AVERAGE NUMBER OF NEW CLIENTS PER YEAR). The value coded must be entered first, and then assign the corresponding labels. (In this example, Capability of sales executive is coded as 1-Low, 2-High). In the pull down menu of Value, code the values as follows:

  Value: 1

  Label: Low

  Click 'Add'

  Similarly add the values for the scale

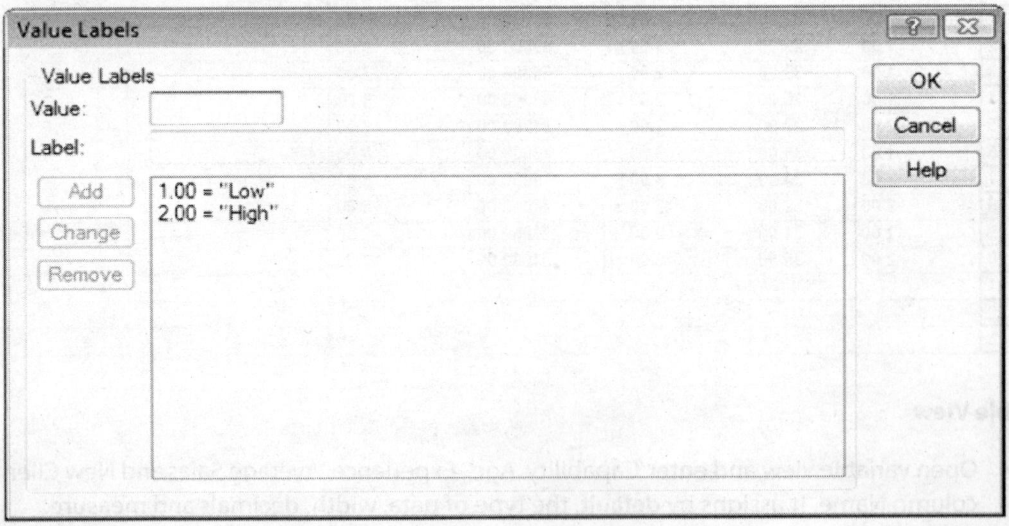

➢ Enter the values and click OK and save the input file.

Then, the following procedure is followed to perform analysis:

- Select Analyse ⟶ Classify ⟶ Discriminant Analysis.
- Drag the grouping variable to the 'Grouping Variable' dialog box. (In this example, the variable 'Capability of sales executive' must be dragged to the Grouping Variable dialog box).
- Click 'Define Range' and enter the 'Minimum' and 'Maximum' values as defined. (In this example, enter 'Minimum' as '1' and 'Maximum' as '2').

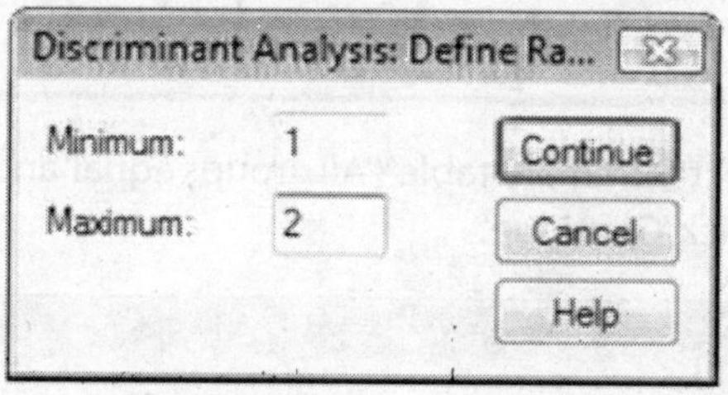

- Drag the independent variables to the 'Independents' dialog box. (In this case, the variables Age of sales executive, Experience of sales executive, Average sales per year and Average number of new clients per year are dragged to the 'Independents' dialog box). 'Enter independents together' is the default selection.

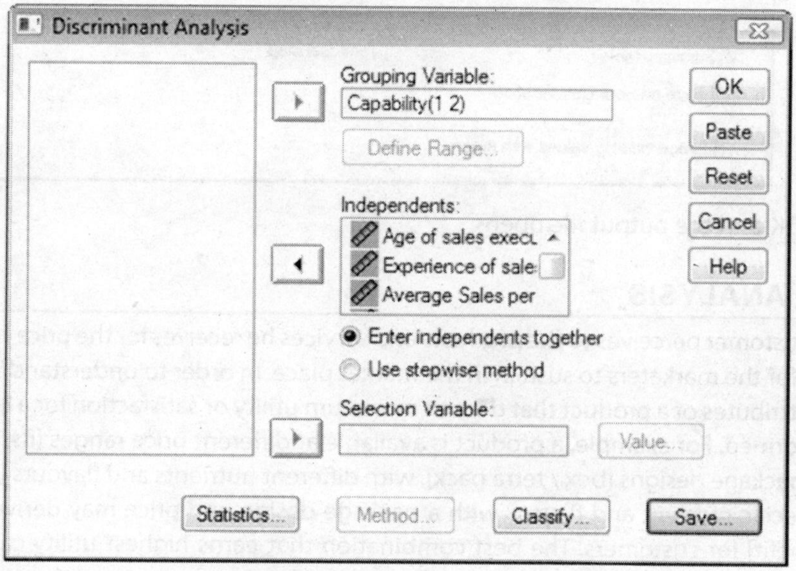

- Click 'Statistics', select 'Unstandardized' and then click 'Continue'.

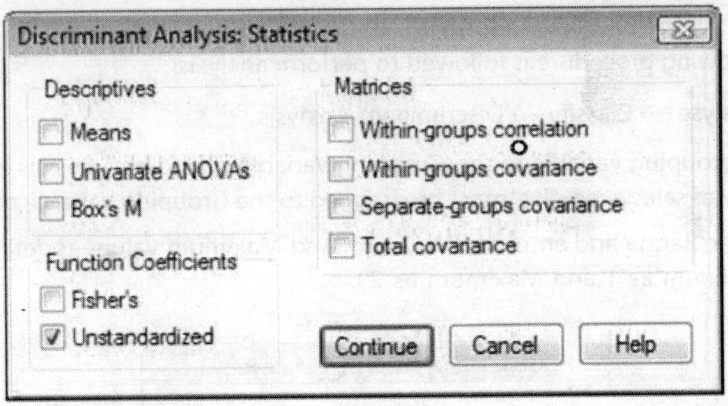

- Click 'Classification', select 'Summary table' ('All groups equal' and 'Within-groups' being the default selections) and then click 'Continue'.

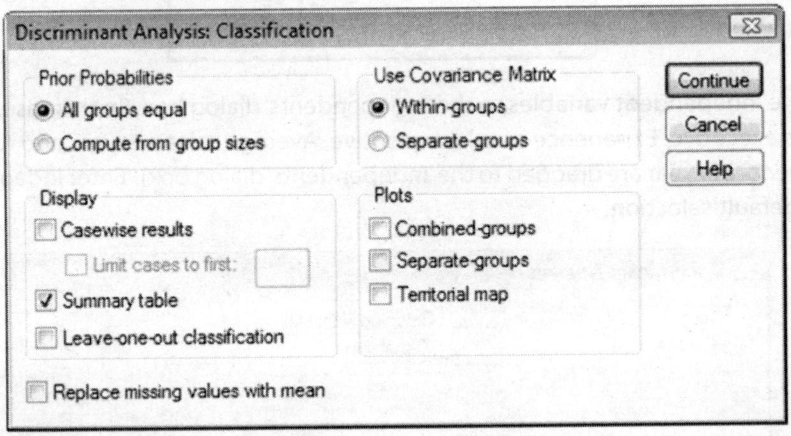

- Click 'OK' and the output file opens.

CONJOINT ANALYSIS

The value the customer perceives to the products and services he receives for the price he pay is important to understand for the marketers to sustain in the market place. In order to understand what combination of services or attributes of a product that derives maximum utility or satisfaction for a consumer, conjoint analysis is performed. For example, a product is available at different price ranges [Rs.100, Rs.120, Rs..95] with different package designs [box / tetra pack], with different nutrients and flavours [orange, apple and banana]. A specific nutrient and flavour with a package design and price may derive maximum utility [perceived benefit] for customers. The best combination that earns highest utility can be derived with conjoint analysis.

For example, in order to perform conjoint analysis, consumers are to first rank all possible combinations. The most preferred combination is ranked '1', next preferred '2' and so on. A health drink is available in three different packages [plastic container, tin, tetrapack]; three different prices [Rs.100, Rs.120, Rs.95]; with four different flavours [orange, banana, apple and pineapple]. The levels of these attributes are:

1. Package design – plastic, tin and tetra [3 levels]
2. Price – Rs.100, Rs.120, Rs.95 [3 levels]
3. Flavour - orange, banana, apple and pineapple [4 levels]

The maximum numbers of combinations that can be made with the choices given with the attributes are: 3 * 3 * 4 = 36 combinations. Respondents are to rank their choice for all these combinations and the average ranking can be taken as the input data. In order to establish the utility model using conjoint analysis, regression can be performed. 'Effects coding' can be used to perform regression. This method of coding uses dummy variables. For example, for the above attributes, the coding will be as follows:

Package Design	Var 1	Var 2
Plastic	1	0
Tin	0	1
Tetra	-1	-1

The number of variables will be n-1 where 'n' is the levels or the options available with each attribute. Similarly, the coding for the attribute Price will be:

Price	Var 3	Var 4
Rs. 100	1	0
Rs. 120	0	1
Rs. 95	-1	-1

The coding for the variable flavour will be:

Flavour	Var 5	Var 6	Var 7
Orange	1	0	0
Banana	0	1	0
Apple	0	0	1
Pineapple	-1	-1	-1

There exists 7 variables that explains different levels of the attributes and forms the independent variable for regression. The ranks given by the respondent (or the average rank of the respondents) will be the last variable, Var 8 that will be the dependent variable for the regression. The regression executed in the case will bring out the discussion of the utility derived.

CASE

A health drink is available in three different packages (plastic container, tin, tetrapack); three different prices (Rs.100, Rs.120, Rs.95); with four different flavours (orange, banana, apple and pineapple). As a marketer it is important to understand the combination of package, price and flavour that drives maximum utility for the consumers. Determine the utility of the consumers using conjoint analysis with regression run.

Coding of the input data is discussed above.

Input data is shown in table below:

Plastic is coded as '1', Tin as '2' and Tetrapack as '3'

Orange flavour is coded as '1', Banana as '2', Apple as '3' and Pineapple as '4'

S. No	Package Design (Plastic, Tin, Tetrapack)	Price (Rs.100, Rs.120, Rs.95)	Flavour (Orange, Banana, Apple, Pineapple)	Ranks
1	1	100	1	33
2	1	100	2	35
3	1	100	3	3
4	1	100	4	4
5	1	120	1	34
6	1	120	2	36
7	1	120	3	1
8	1	120	4	2
9	1	95	1	6
10	1	95	2	5
11	1	95	3	8
12	1	95	4	11
13	2	100	1	9
14	2	100	2	10
15	2	100	3	7
16	2	100	4	12
17	2	120	1	14
18	2	120	2	13

19	2	120	3	15
20	2	120	4	17
21	2	95	1	16
22	2	95	2	19
23	2	95	3	18
24	2	95	4	22
25	3	100	1	20
26	3	100	2	21
27	3	100	3	26
28	3	100	4	24
29	3	120	1	25
30	3	120	2	23
31	3	120	3	28
32	3	120	4	31
33	3	95	1	32
34	3	95	2	27
35	3	95	3	30
36	3	95	4	29

The input data collected from the questionnaire is to be coded for regression as follows:

S. No	Var 1	Var 2	Var 3	Var 4	Var 5	Var 6	Var 7	Var 8
1	1	0	1	0	1	0	0	33
2	1	0	1	0	0	1	0	35
3	1	0	1	0	0	0	1	3
4	1	0	1	0	-1	-1	-1	4
5	1	0	0	1	1	0	0	34
6	1	0	0	1	0	1	0	36
7	1	0	0	1	0	0	1	1
8	1	0	0	1	-1	-1	-1	2
9	1	0	-1	-1	1	0	0	6

10	1	0	-1	-1	0	1	0	5
11	1	0	-1	-1	0	0	1	8
12	1	0	-1	-1	-1	-1	-1	11
13	0	1	1	0	1	0	0	9
14	0	1	1	0	0	1	0	10
15	0	1	1	0	0	0	1	7
16	0	1	1	0	-1	-1	-1	12
17	0	1	0	1	1	0	0	14
18	0	1	0	1	0	1	0	13
19	0	1	0	1	0	0	1	15
20	0	1	0	1	-1	-1	-1	17
21	0	1	-1	-1	1	0	0	16
22	0	1	-1	-1	0	1	0	19
23	0	1	-1	-1	0	0	1	18
24	0	1	-1	-1	-1	-1	-1	22
25	-1	-1	1	0	1	0	0	20
26	-1	-1	1	0	0	1	0	21
27	-1	-1	1	0	0	0	1	26
28	-1	-1	1	0	-1	-1	-1	24
29	-1	-1	0	1	1	0	0	25
30	-1	-1	0	1	0	1	0	23
31	-1	-1	0	1	0	0	1	28
32	-1	-1	0	1	-1	-1	-1	31
33	-1	-1	-1	-1	1	0	0	32
34	-1	-1	-1	-1	0	1	0	27
35	-1	-1	-1	-1	0	0	1	30
36	-1	-1	-1	-1	-1	-1	-1	29

Dependent Variable: Variable 8, Rank

Independent Variables: Variables 1 to 7

Table presents the output from regression analysis.

ANOVA (b)

Model	Sum of Squares	Df	Mean Square	F	Sig.
Regression	1396.389	7	199.484	2.244	.060(a)
Residual	2488.611	28	88.879		
Total	3885.000	35			

a Predictors: (Constant), VAR00007, VAR00004, VAR00002, VAR00003, VAR00006, VAR00001, VAR00005

b Dependent Variable: VAR00008

Model Summary

Model	R	R Square	Adjusted R Square	Std. Error of the Estimate
1	.600(a)	.359	.199	9.42756

a Predictors: (Constant), VAR00007, VAR00004, VAR00002, VAR00003, VAR00006, VAR00001, VAR00005

Coefficients (a)

Model	Unstandardized Coefficients		Standardized Coefficients	T	Sig.
	B	Std. Error	Beta		
(Constant)	18.500	1.571		11.774	.000
VAR00001	-3.667	2.222	-.288	-1.650	.110
VAR00002	-4.167	2.222	-.327	-1.875	.071
VAR00003	-1.500	2.222	-.118	-.675	.505
VAR00004	1.417	2.222	.111	.638	.529
VAR00005	2.500	2.722	.170	.919	.366
VAR00006	2.500	2.722	.170	.919	.366
VAR00007	-3.389	2.722	-.231	-1.245	.223

a Dependent Variable: VAR00008

Interpretation

The p-value of F-test is 0.060, which is less than the significance level of 0.10. Hence, we reject the null hypothesis at 10 percent level of significance. The model is statistically significant for prediction. It explains the existence of relationship between the dependent variable (Rank) and the independent variables (combinations of package, price and flavour).

The Adjusted R^2 (R Square) value is 0.199. It describes that the combination of the variables package, price and design influence the ranking of the consumers to the extent of 19.9%. From the output tables of the regression analysis, the utility derived by the consumers can be established as follows:

Variables	Type	Part Utility	Utility Range (Max-Min)
Package	Plastic (1)	-3.7	7.9 – (-4.2) = 12.1
	Tin (2)	-4.2	
	Tetra (3)	7.9	
		[-(-3.7-4.2)]	
Price	Rs. 100Plastic	-1.5	1.4 – (-1.5) = 2.9
	Rs 120	1.4	
	Rs. 95	0.5	
		[-(-1.5+1.4)]	
Package	Orange (1)	2.5	2.5 – (-3.4) = 5.9
	Banana (2)	2.5	
	Apple (3)	-3.4	
	Pineapple (4)	-1.6	
		[-(2.5+2.5-3.4)]	

The coefficients table indicates the part utility of the variables. Part Utility of variable 1 and 2 are from the coefficient table and utility of third category in the same variable is given by minus of the utilities of other types. This is given in the calculation above. The utility of the category is given by difference between maximum and minimum part utility in each category.

From the utility range column, it is clear that Package is the important variable as it has the highest value. The combination that yields maximum utility is: Tetra pack with Rs. 120 and with Orange or Banana flavour. This is explained by the highest part utility in each category.

Navigation Guide

- Data must be entered in the 'Data View' page of the data sheet, as coded from the combinations data. (In this case, the combinations of three types of package, three types of prices and four flavours).
- Click 'OK' after entering the values and the corresponding labels.

Data View

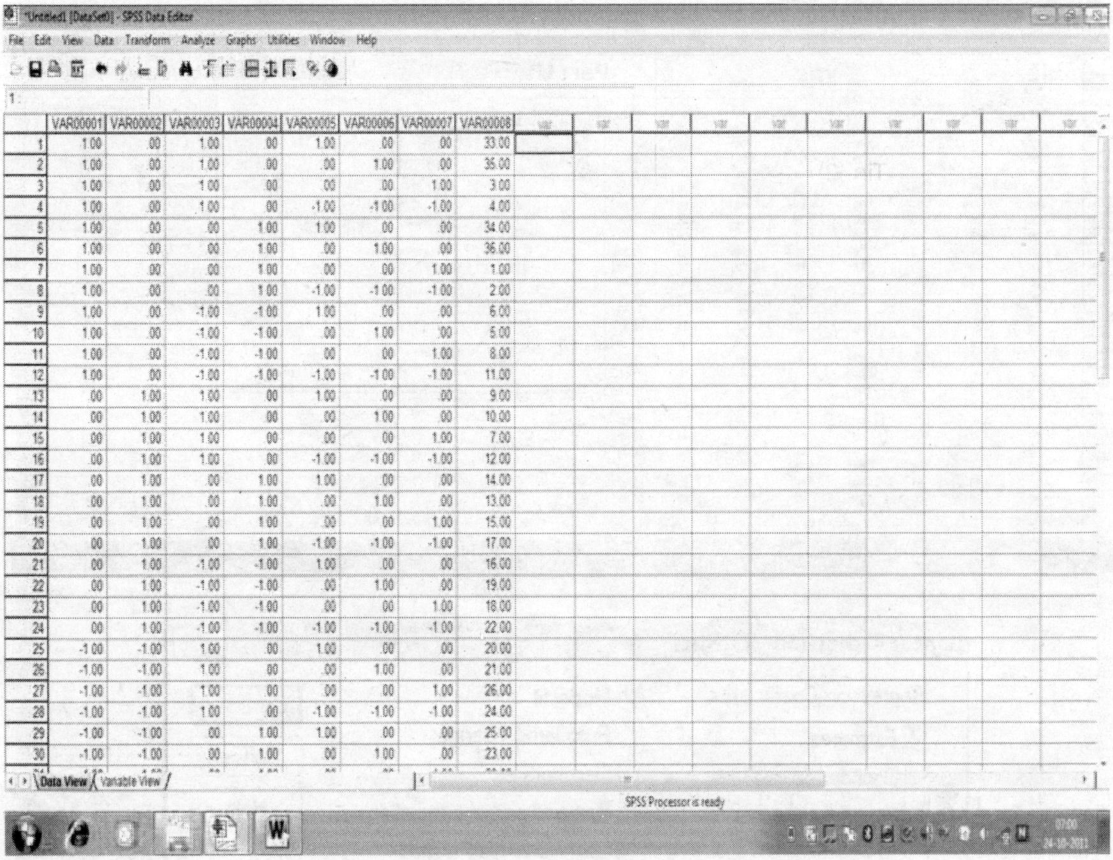

	VAR00001	VAR00002	VAR00003	VAR00004	VAR00005	VAR00006	VAR00007	VAR00008
1	1.00	.00	1.00	.00	1.00	.00	.00	33.00
2	1.00	.00	1.00	.00	.00	1.00	.00	35.00
3	1.00	.00	1.00	.00	.00	.00	1.00	3.00
4	1.00	.00	1.00	.00	-1.00	-1.00	-1.00	4.00
5	1.00	.00	.00	1.00	1.00	.00	.00	34.00
6	1.00	.00	.00	1.00	.00	1.00	.00	36.00
7	1.00	.00	.00	1.00	.00	.00	1.00	1.00
8	1.00	.00	.00	1.00	-1.00	-1.00	-1.00	2.00
9	1.00	.00	-1.00	-1.00	1.00	.00	.00	6.00
10	1.00	.00	-1.00	-1.00	.00	1.00	.00	5.00
11	1.00	.00	-1.00	-1.00	.00	.00	1.00	8.00
12	1.00	.00	-1.00	-1.00	-1.00	-1.00	-1.00	11.00
13	.00	1.00	1.00	.00	1.00	.00	.00	9.00
14	.00	1.00	1.00	.00	.00	1.00	.00	10.00
15	.00	1.00	1.00	.00	.00	.00	1.00	7.00
16	.00	1.00	1.00	.00	-1.00	-1.00	-1.00	12.00
17	.00	1.00	.00	1.00	1.00	.00	.00	14.00
18	.00	1.00	.00	1.00	.00	1.00	.00	13.00
19	.00	1.00	.00	1.00	.00	.00	1.00	15.00
20	.00	1.00	.00	1.00	-1.00	-1.00	-1.00	17.00
21	.00	1.00	-1.00	-1.00	1.00	.00	.00	16.00
22	.00	1.00	-1.00	-1.00	.00	1.00	.00	19.00
23	.00	1.00	-1.00	-1.00	.00	.00	1.00	18.00
24	.00	1.00	-1.00	-1.00	-1.00	-1.00	-1.00	22.00
25	-1.00	-1.00	1.00	.00	1.00	.00	.00	20.00
26	-1.00	-1.00	1.00	.00	.00	1.00	.00	21.00
27	-1.00	-1.00	1.00	.00	.00	.00	1.00	26.00
28	-1.00	-1.00	1.00	.00	-1.00	-1.00	-1.00	24.00
29	-1.00	-1.00	.00	1.00	1.00	.00	.00	25.00
30	-1.00	-1.00	.00	1.00	.00	1.00	.00	23.00

Then, the following procedure is followed:

- Select Analyse → Regression → Linear.
- Drag the dependent variable to the Dependent dialog block and the independent variables to the Independent(s) dialog block. (In this example, the variable 8 (Rank) is dragged to the Dependent dialog block. The variables 1 to 7 (Combinations of package, price and flavour)
- Click 'Statistics', select 'Estimates', select 'Model Fit' and click 'Continue'.
- Click 'OK'.

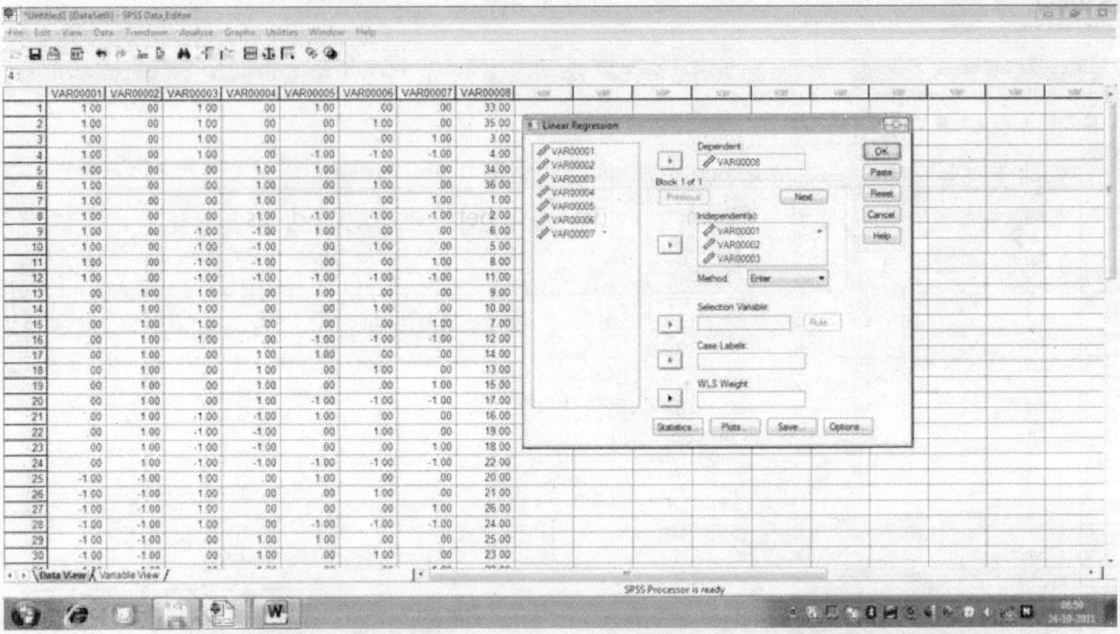

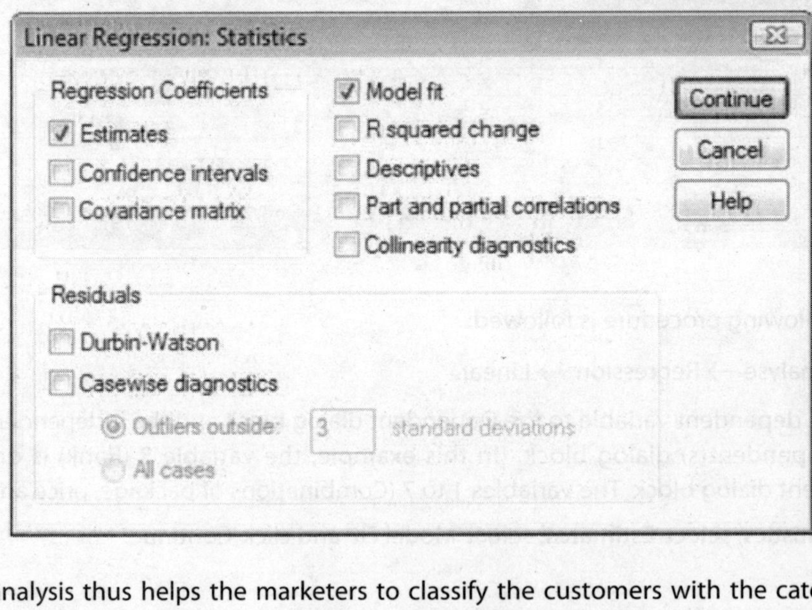

Discriminant analysis thus helps the marketers to classify the customers with the categorical variable considered. It is used in predicting the behaviour of the consumers towards the category he or she will fall. Conjoint analysis helps the marketers to understand the combination of variables that yields maximum utility for the consumers. It is applied to a greater extent to decide the composition of the products or service that brings maximum utility or satisfaction to customers.

Review Questions

1. Explain how discriminant model helps to classify the customers.
2. Determine the brand preference of customers between Nike, Adidas and Bata (coded as 1, 2, and 3 respectively) based on price, and their satisfaction with quality and service. The satisfaction is measured on a 5 point scale where '1' explains the high level of satisfaction, '2' satisfaction, '3' neutral, '4' dissatisfaction, and '5' high level of dissatisfaction. Classify the customers based on their brand choice.

SAMPLE	BRAND	PRICE	QUALITY	SERVICE
1	1	32	3	2
2	3	30	4	3
3	1	30	5	3
4	3	33	2	1
5	2	34	1	2
6	3	29	3	1
7	3	29	4	2
8	1	35	5	3
9	3	29	2	4
10	2	30	3	4
11	2	32	5	5
12	3	29	3	4
13	1	33	2	3
14	1	26	2	2
15	2	27	3	4
16	1	35	3	5
17	2	34	5	5
18	2	32	3	4
19	1	34	2	3
20	3	22	3	2
21	2	35	5	4

3. A multinational retail outlet likes to conduct a research to understand the choice of customers with three different retail formats (supermarket, hypermarket, retail chains). The choice of retail outlet may also depend on the type of city (tire 1, tire 2, tire 3); with three different service patterns (self-service, manual service, service on request). As a marketer it is important to understand the combination that drives maximum utility for the consumers. Determine the utility of the consumers using conjoint analysis with regression run.

Chapter

14

Data Reduction Techniques

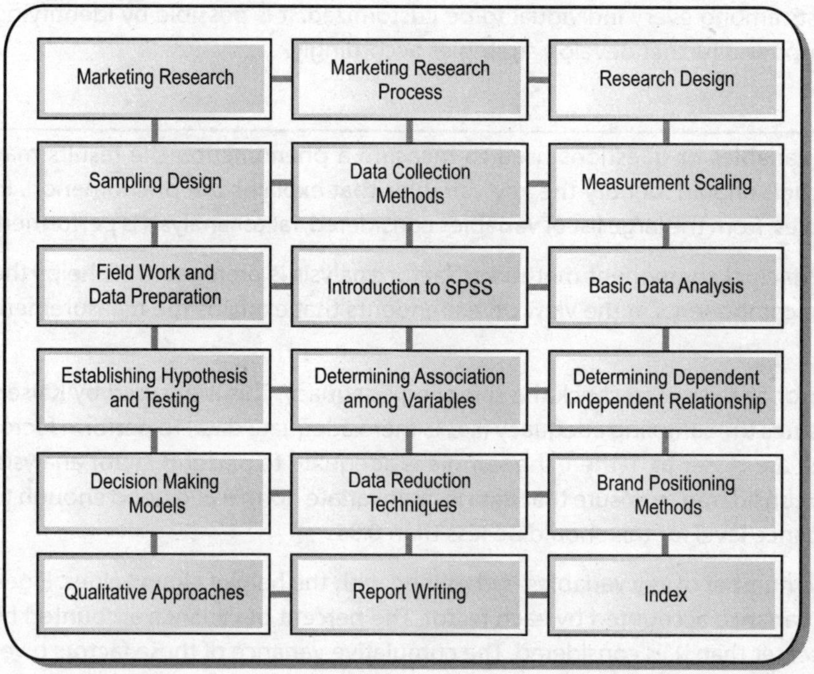

Outline

Chapter Structure

- Introduction
- Factor Analysis
- Case
- Cluster Analysis
- Case
- Review Questions

Chapter Overview

Chapter 14 explains the data reduction techniques. It includes the reduction of variables and cases with factor and cluster analysis respectively. Factor analysis is explained to identify the major factors that predict the behaviour of the study variable to a greater extent. Cluster analysis is explained to identify the segment that exists in the heterogeneous sample considered for the study.

INTRODUCTION

Huge numbers of data exist in the market place. All these data cannot be used to make decisions. Data reduction techniques help the marketers to identify the required data to be considered in making decisions. As a marketer, it may not be possible to equally consider all the variables, 10 to 20 in the market place, to make decisions. It is imperative to identify those major factors that the consumers look for. This decision can be made more logically by performing factor analysis. This technique reduces the number of variables into fewer factors that explains the study in a better way. Correlated variables are combined together into one single variable and the unrelated and unimportant variables are eliminated in the process of seeking the major factors. Cluster analysis is another data reduction technique that helps the marketers to identify the sample with few groups that in voluminous numbers. It gives clarity about the existence of small heterogeneous groups in the sample considered and the characteristics of these groups. It is important to identify the difference that exists among every individual to be customized. It is possible by identifying the characteristics of these groups and further develop strategies accordingly.

FACTOR ANALYSIS

If there exist more number of variables or questions used to measure a phenomenon the results may dilute the solution. The researchers should identify the key variables that explains the phenomenon. In order to extract these key variables, from the large list of variables considered, factor analysis is performed.

In performing factor analysis, Principal component method of factor analysis is preferred. This helps the researcher to identify the major components in the view of respondents that explains the measurement variable.

The first step in performing factor analysis is to check the sampling adequacy. This is ensured by Kaiser-Mayer-Oklin test. This test measures the sampling adequacy (i.e., is there adequate data) to perform factor analysis. If the values of this test are closer to '1' then, the sample is adequate to perform factor analysis. Bartlett Test of Sphericity is also considered to ensure that data is multivariate normal and good enough to perform factor analysis. Significance level for this should be less than 0.05.

On executing factor analysis the number of key variables is identified with the help of eigen values. Eigen values show the proportion of variance accounted by each factor. The percent of variance accounted by each factor with eigen value greater than '1' is considered. The cumulative variance of these factors gives the explanatory power of the factors extracted for the study.

Once the number of factors are extracted and their explanatory power (preferable if closer to 100) is identified, the next step is to understand what these factors are. For this purpose, rotated component matrix is considered. The rotated component matrix gives the factors extracted and loadings of each variable towards the extracted factor. The extracted factor may be a single variable or a combination of two or more variables. This is explained by the factor loadings. As a thumb rule select the variables that load 0.5 / 0.7 or more on a factor. These variables constitute the factor extracted.

CASE

An MNC wants to enter the business of manufacturing laptops for academic and business purposes. This made the company to conduct a research among the consumers regarding their expectations. As a part of the research, the company wants to identify the major factors that influence the consumers in purchasing laptop. The respondents were asked to rate their agreement in choosing a laptop with 10 variables on a 7 point scale. [1-Strongly Disagree, 7-Strongly Agree]. The variables considered are:

1. Price of the laptop must be affordable
2. Laptop must be manufactured by a reputed brand
3. Laptop must have a reasonable storage capacity
4. Laptop must have a specific warranty period
5. Speed of the processor must be high
6. Battery back-up must be there for a minimum of 2 hours
7. Laptop must be available in different colours
8. Operating System must be simple to operate
9. Cost of ownership must be minimum
10. External finishing must be stylish

Input data is shown in table below:

Input Table:

Sample	Price	Brand	Memory	Warranty	Speed	Battery	Colour	Os	Ownership	Style
1	4	1	2	4	1	2	1	1	4	2
2	1	2	6	4	5	6	1	5	3	2
3	4	2	1	4	2	1	5	2	2	5
4	2	4	4	3	4	5	3	3	4	3
5	6	3	3	5	3	3	3	3	2	3
6	1	1	5	1	4	4	2	4	2	2
7	3	5	2	2	2	2	3	2	1	4
8	7	2	1	6	2	1	2	1	4	3
9	5	2	4	5	3	3	2	3	3	2
10	2	1	6	3	5	6	2	5	4	1
11	2	4	7	3	6	6	6	6	3	2
12	3	3	3	3	4	3	3	4	3	2
13	3	2	1	2	2	2	2	2	3	1
14	1	1	2	1	1	2	3	1	4	2

15	1	5	2	1	1	2	3	1	6	3
16	1	2	2	3	2	2	2	2	2	2
17	6	3	4	5	4	3	3	3	1	4
18	1	1	1	2	1	1	2	1	6	1
19	2	1	3	2	2	3	1	2	5	1
20	2	2	3	1	2	3	6	2	2	7

Null Hypothesis (H0): The mentioned parameters do not compress into factors that are considered by consumers for purchasing laptop.

Alternate Hypothesis (H1): The mentioned parameters compress into various factors that are considered by consumers for purchasing laptop.

Tables present the output of factor analysis.

Output Tables:

KMO and Bartlett's Test

Kaiser-Meyer-Olkin Measure of Sampling Adequacy		.643
Bartlett's Test of Sphericity	Approx. Chi-Square	173.365
	Df	45
	Sig.	.000

Total Variance Explained

Component	Initial Eigenvalues			Extraction Sums of Squared Loadings			Rotation Sums of Squared Loadings		
	Total	% of Variance	Cumulative %	Total	% of Variance	Cumulative %	Total	% of Variance	Cumulative %
1	3.928	39.284	39.284	3.928	39.284	39.284	3.900	38.999	38.999
2	2.429	24.289	63.573	2.429	24.289	63.573	2.272	22.722	61.722
3	1.839	18.388	81.961	1.839	18.388	81.961	2.024	20.239	81.961
4	.800	7.997	89.958						
5	.502	5.016	94.974						
6	.274	2.738	97.712						

7	.115	1.149	98.862						
8	.060	.595	99.457						
9	.037	.372	99.829						
10	.017	.171	100.000						

Extraction Method: Principal Component Analysis.

Rotated Component Matrix (a)

Variables	Component		
	1	2	3
Price	-.181	.129	**.932**
Brand	.102	**.612**	-.013
Storage Capacity	**.966**	.022	-.059
Warranty	.118	-.099	**.941**
Processor Speed	**.966**	.103	.158
Battery Backup	**.957**	-.016	-.137
Colour	.089	**.869**	-.146
Operating System	**.975**	.079	.045
Cost of Ownership	-.220	-.585	-.425
Stylish Appearance	-.231	**.870**	.131

Extraction Method: Principal Component Analysis.

Rotation Method: Varimax with Kaiser Normalization.

a Rotation converged in 4 iterations.

Interpretation

The p-value of chi-square test is 0.000 at n-1 (20 – 1 = 19) degrees of freedom (df). The value of 'p' is less than the significance level of 0.05 (5 percent level of significance) and even less than 0.01 (1 percent level of significance). Hence, we reject the null hypothesis. It means that the mentioned parameters compress into various factors that are considered by consumers for purchasing laptop. From the KMO and Bartlett's Test table, it can be inferred that Kaiser-Meyer-Olkin Measure of Sampling Adequacy is 0.643, which means that the number of samples used for collecting data is adequate enough to carry out factor analysis.

From the Total Variance Explained table, it is clear that 3 factors have been extracted from the mentioned 10 parameters. These factors explain 81.961% of the total variance i.e., the reasons for consumers to choose a laptop is explained 81.961% by these 3 factors. Thus, 10 parameters are compressed or reduced into 3 factors. From the Rotated Component Matrix table, select those variables that has loading 0.7 or above. There are 4 variables that have high factor loadings on factor 1; 3 variables that have high factor loadings on factor 2; and 2 variables that have high factor loadings on factor 3.

The variables that have high loadings on factor 1, are given below with their loadings:

- Laptop must have a reasonable storage capacity - 0.966
- Speed of the processor must be high - 0.966
- Battery back-up must be there for a minimum of 2 hours - 0.957
- Operating System must be simple to operate - 0.975

These variables can be combined into a single factor and called **Technical Configuration**.

The variables that have high loadings on factor 2, are given below with their loadings:

- Laptop must be manufactured by a reputed brand - 0.612
- Laptop must be available in different colours - 0.869
- External finishing must be stylish - 0.870

These variables can be combined into a single factor and called **External Look**.

The variables that have high loadings on factor 3, are given below with their loadings:

- Price of the laptop must be affordable - 0.932
- Laptop must have a specific warranty period - 0.941

These variables can be combined into a single factor called **Economy**.

Thus the three major factors that consumers look into to buy a laptop are: Technical Configuration, External Look and Economy. The marketers can concentrate on these three factors to improve their sales performance.

Navigation Guide

In order to enter data:

- Data must be entered in the 'Data View' page of the data sheet, as given by the respondents. (In this case, it is based on the response given by 20 consumers for the mentioned variables on a 7 point scale [1-Strongly Disagree, 7-Strongly Agree]).

Data View

factor [DataSet1] - SPSS Data Editor

File Edit View Data Transform Analyze Graphs Utilities Window Help

26 : Price

	Price	Brand	Memory	Warranty	Speed	Battery	Colour	OS	Ownership	Style	var	var
1	4.00	1.00	2.00	4.00	1.00	2.00	1.00	1.00	4.00	2.00		
2	1.00	2.00	6.00	4.00	5.00	6.00	1.00	5.00	3.00	2.00		
3	4.00	2.00	1.00	4.00	2.00	1.00	5.00	2.00	2.00	5.00		
4	2.00	4.00	4.00	3.00	4.00	5.00	3.00	3.00	4.00	3.00		
5	6.00	3.00	3.00	5.00	3.00	3.00	3.00	3.00	2.00	3.00		
6	1.00	1.00	5.00	1.00	4.00	4.00	2.00	4.00	2.00	2.00		
7	3.00	5.00	2.00	2.00	2.00	2.00	3.00	2.00	1.00	4.00		
8	7.00	2.00	1.00	6.00	2.00	1.00	2.00	1.00	4.00	3.00		
9	5.00	2.00	4.00	5.00	3.00	3.00	2.00	3.00	3.00	2.00		
10	2.00	1.00	6.00	3.00	5.00	6.00	2.00	5.00	4.00	1.00		
11	2.00	4.00	7.00	3.00	6.00	6.00	6.00	6.00	3.00	2.00		
12	3.00	3.00	3.00	3.00	4.00	3.00	3.00	4.00	3.00	2.00		
13	3.00	2.00	1.00	2.00	2.00	2.00	2.00	2.00	3.00	1.00		
14	1.00	1.00	2.00	1.00	1.00	2.00	3.00	1.00	4.00	2.00		
15	1.00	5.00	2.00	1.00	1.00	2.00	3.00	1.00	6.00	3.00		
16	1.00	2.00	2.00	3.00	2.00	2.00	2.00	2.00	2.00	2.00		
17	6.00	3.00	4.00	5.00	4.00	3.00	3.00	3.00	1.00	4.00		
18	1.00	1.00	1.00	2.00	1.00	1.00	2.00	1.00	6.00	1.00		
19	2.00	1.00	3.00	2.00	2.00	3.00	1.00	2.00	5.00	1.00		
20	2.00	2.00	3.00	1.00	2.00	3.00	6.00	2.00	2.00	7.00		
21												
22												
23												

Variable View

Open variable view and enter 10 variables considered namely, 'Price, Brand, Memory, Warranty, Speed, Battery, Colour, OS, Ownership, and Style' in the column 'Name'. It assigns by default, the type of data, width, decimals and measure.

*factor [DataSet1] - SPSS Data Editor

File Edit View Data Transform Analyze Graphs Utilities Window Help

	Name	Type	Width	Decimals	Label	Values	Missing	Columns	Align	Measure
1	Price	Numeric	8	2	Price	{1.00, Strongl	None	8	Right	Scale
2	Brand	Numeric	8	2	Brand	{1.00, Strongl	None	8	Right	Scale
3	Memory	Numeric	8	2	Storage Capacity	{1.00, Strongl	None	8	Right	Scale
4	Warranty	Numeric	8	2	Warranty	{1.00, Strongl	None	8	Right	Scale
5	Speed	Numeric	8	2	Processor Speed	{1.00, Strongl	None	8	Right	Scale
6	Battery	Numeric	8	2	Battery Backup	{1.00, Strongl	None	8	Right	Scale
7	Colour	Numeric	8	2	Colour	{1.00, Strongl	None	8	Right	Scale
8	OS	Numeric	8	2	Operating System	{1.00, Strongl	None	8	Right	Scale
9	Ownership	Numeric	8	2	Cost of Ownership	{1.00, Strongl	None	8	Right	Scale
10	Style	Numeric	8	2	Stylish Appearance	{1.00, Strongl	None	8	Right	Scale
11										
12										
13										

➢ In the 'Variable View' page, a suitable name and a label must be given for the variables entered. (In this example, the variables are: PRICE, BRAND, STORAGE CAPACITY, WARRANTY, PROCESSOR SPEED, BATTERY BACKUP, COLOUR, OPERATING SYSTEM, COST OF OWNERSHIP, STYLISH APPEARANCE). The data must be entered as collected in the questionnaire. The value coded must be entered first, and then assign the corresponding labels. (In this example, the variables are rated on a 7 point scale: 1-Strongly Disagree, 7-Strongly Agree). In the pull down menu of Value, code the values as follows:

Value: 1

Label: Strongly Disagree

Click 'Add'

Similarly add the values for the scale.

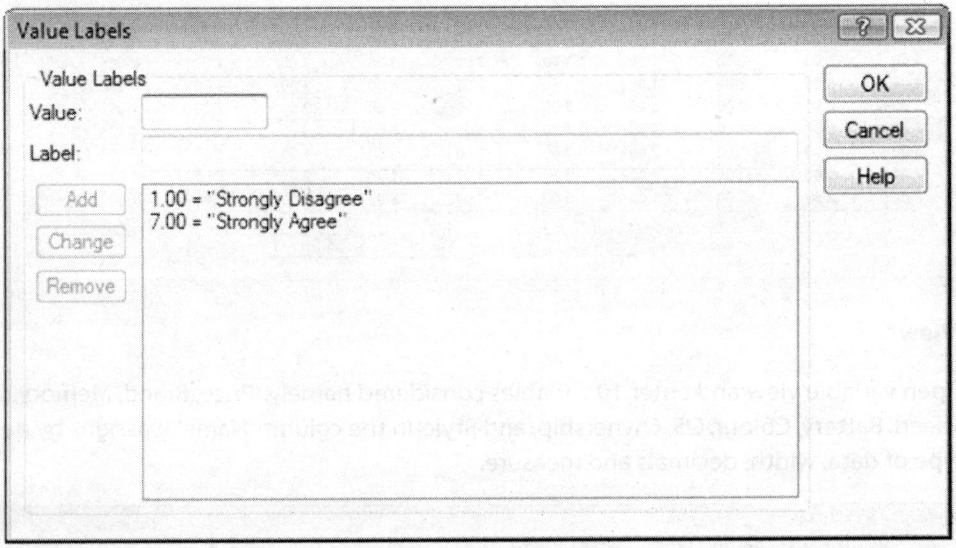

➢ Enter the values and click OK and save the input file.

Then, the following procedure is to be followed to perform factor analysis:

- Select Analyse ⟶ Data Reduction ⟶ Factor Analysis.
- Drag the variables or parameters to be tested to the Variables dialog box. (In this example, the variables ' Price, Brand, Storage Capacity, Warranty, Processor Speed, Battery Backup, Colour, Operating System, Cost of Ownership, Stylish Appearance' must be dragged to the Variables dialog box).

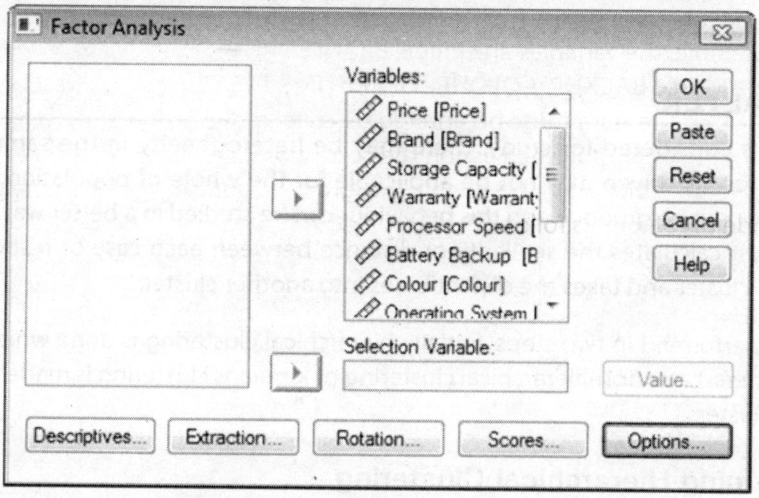

- Click 'Descriptives', select 'KMO and Bartlett's test of sphericity' ('Initial solution' being the default selection) and then click 'Continue'.

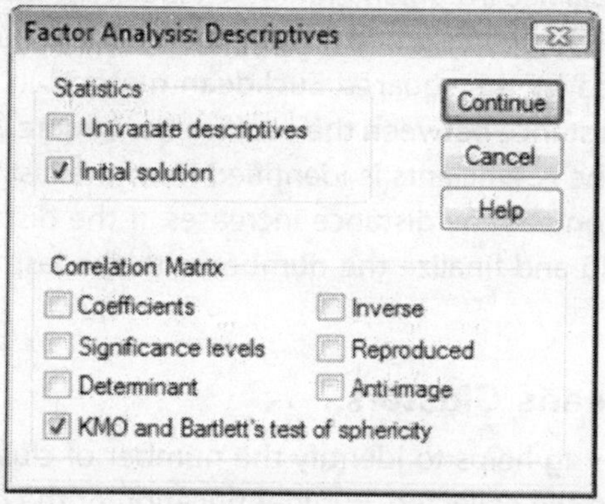

- Click 'Rotation', select 'Varimax' ('Rotated Solution' being the default selection) and then click 'Continue'.

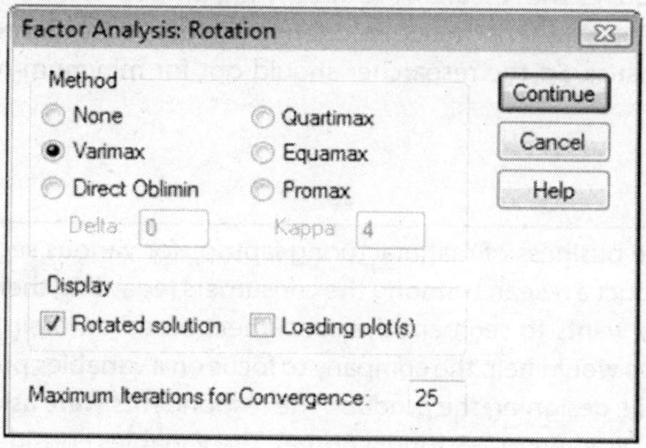

- Click 'OK' and the output file opens.

CLUSTER ANALYSIS

If a large sample is considered for study, there may be heterogeneity in the sample taken. In this circumstance, the results driven may not be applicable for the whole of population. So the similar or homogeneous cases can be grouped and this behaviour can be studied in a better way. This can be done by cluster analysis. It calculates the similarity or distance between each case or responses and groups similar cases into a cluster and takes the distant cases into another cluster.

Cluster analysis is performed in two steps. Initially hierarchical clustering is done which helps to decide the number of clusters. Later non-hierarchical clustering or k-means clustering is made to understand the behaviour of the clusters.

Step 1: Performing Hierarchical Clustering

In hierarchical clustering, SPSS groups the responses one by one. If there exists similarity, it is grouped and if there is more distance, it is split to a different cluster. The procedure continues until all cases or responses are grouped. This procedure is explained in agglomeration schedule. The mathematical procedure generally selected to have agglomeration is between-group linkage method. The number of clusters is determined based on the distance explained by the squared Euclidean method in the coefficient column of the agglomeration schedule. If the distance between the coefficients is more, unique clusters are formed. For this purpose, the difference in the coefficients is identified from the last stage with the previous stage. identify the unique clusters as long as the distance increases. If the distance or the difference reduces significantly, stop with clustering and finalize the number with the last row of the maximum distance stage.

Step 2: Performing K-Means Clusters

First stage of hierarchical clustering helps to identify the number of clusters. This gives clarity with the existence of segments in the sample collected. But identification of the characteristic of the segment is important for the marketers to make decisions based on this technique. This is done with K-Means cluster. In executing this step, it requires the researcher to specify the desired number of clusters to be formed. It is given as identified in the first stage. If more homogeneous clusters are identified from the first stage, it will have similar characteristics. So the researcher should opt for minimum number of heterogeneous clusters.

CASE

An MNC wants to enter the business of manufacturing laptops for various segments of consumers. This made the company to conduct a research among the consumers regarding their expectations. As a part of the research, the company wants to segment the consumers based on their priority measured with 10 variables. This segmentation would help the company to focus on a variables preferred among a particular segment of consumers while designing the product. The respondents were asked to rate the variables on a 7 point scale [1-Strongly Disagree to 7-Strongly Agree]. The variables considered are:

1. Price of the laptop must be as minimum as possible
2. Laptop must be manufactured by a well known brand
3. Laptop must have a reasonable storage capacity
4. Laptop must have a specific warranty period
5. Speed of the processor must be high
6. Battery back-up must be there for a minimum of 2 hours
7. Laptop must be available in different colours
8. Operating System must be easy and simple to operate
9. On-site service must be available
10. External finishing must be stylish

Input data is shown in table below:

Sample	Price	Brand	Memory	Warranty	Speed	Battery	Colour	OS	Service	Style
1	4	7	2	4	1	2	1	1	2	4
2	1	2	6	4	5	6	1	5	2	3
3	4	2	1	4	2	1	5	2	5	2
4	2	4	4	3	4	5	3	3	3	4
5	6	3	3	5	3	3	3	3	3	2
6	4	1	2	4	1	2	1	1	4	2
7	3	5	2	2	2	2	3	2	4	5
8	7	2	1	6	2	1	2	1	6	4
9	5	2	4	5	3	3	2	3	5	3
10	2	1	6	3	5	6	2	5	1	4
11	2	4	7	3	6	6	6	6	2	3
12	3	3	3	3	4	3	3	4	2	3
13	3	2	1	2	2	2	2	2	1	3
14	1	1	2	1	1	2	3	1	2	4
15	1	5	2	1	1	2	3	1	3	6
16	1	2	2	3	2	2	2	2	2	2
17	6	3	4	5	4	3	3	3	5	1
18	1	5	1	2	1	1	2	1	1	6
19	2	7	3	2	2	3	1	2	1	5
20	2	2	3	1	2	3	6	2	7	5

Tables below present the output of factor analysis.

Output Tables:

Agglomeration Schedule

Stage	Cluster Combined		Coefficients	Stage Cluster First Appears		Next Stage
	Cluster 1	Cluster 2		Cluster 1	Cluster 2	
1	2	10	6.000	0	0	13
2	5	17	7.000	0	0	5
3	15	18	8.000	0	0	9
4	13	16	8.000	0	0	7
5	5	9	8.500	2	0	12
6	4	12	10.000	0	0	13
7	13	14	12.000	4	0	15
8	1	19	14.000	0	0	10
9	7	15	14.000	0	3	10
10	1	7	22.000	8	9	15
11	3	6	22.000	0	0	12
12	3	5	26.000	11	5	14
13	2	4	26.000	1	6	16
14	3	8	28.800	12	0	17
15	1	13	33.733	10	7	17
16	2	11	35.500	13	0	19
17	1	3	57.083	15	14	18
18	1	20	60.571	17	0	19
19	1	2	69.787	18	16	0

From the Agglomeration Schedule, the difference in the coefficients is calculated in a reverse manner from 19th stage. ie. from the last. The difference is maximum between stage 17 and stage 16. There is a difference of 9.216 (69.787 – 60.571) between 1-cluster solution and 2-cluster solution (stage 19 and stage 18). Similarly, the difference of 3.488 (60.571 – 57.083) exists between 2-cluster solution and 3-cluster solution (stage 18 and stage 17). But, the maximum difference of 21.583 (57.083 – 35.500) exists between

3-cluster solution and 4-cluster solution (stage 17 and stage 16). The difference decreases after this stage. Hence, it shows that a 3 cluster solution would be the ideal solution i.e., the lower row value of the two rows corresponding to the maximum difference in the coefficient value will make the number of clusters.

Final Cluster Centers

	Cluster		
Variables	1	2	3
Price	2.10	1.67	4.86
Brand	4.10	2.33	2.14
Storage Capacity	2.20	6.33	2.57
Warranty	2.30	3.33	4.29
Processor Speed	2.00	5.33	2.43
Battery Backup	2.40	6.00	2.29
Colour	2.30	3.00	3.14
Operating System	1.90	5.33	2.14
Availability of Service	2.10	1.67	5.00
Stylish Appearance	4.20	3.33	2.71

From the Final Cluster Centers table, it can be concluded that there are 3 clusters and each cluster differ from the other by their preference towards variables. The values in the table indicate the mean values of each variable in its respective cluster. These values can be used to interpret the results and describe the characteristics of each cluster. The description is based on the 7 point scale used to collect data, where 1 represents 'Strongly Disagree' and 7 represents 'Strongly Agree'.

Cluster 1

Consumers, who belong to cluster 1 has the following characteristics:

- do not want price to be as minimum as possible
- give priority to brand name of the laptop
- do not give much importance to the storage capacity of the laptop
- do not prioritise warranty ahead of the other features
- never feel that the processor speed must be high
- never give due importance to the battery backup
- do not seek laptop in different colours
- never feel that the operating system must essentially be simple to operate

- never feel that 'on site' service is essential
- give priority to stylish appearance of the laptop

Thus, these consumers give importance to **style and appearance** of laptop.

Cluster 2

Consumers, who belong to cluster 2 has the following characteristics:

- do not want price to be as minimum as possible and give least importance to price
- never give priority to brand name
- consider storage capacity of the laptop as very important
- do not prioritise warranty ahead of the other features
- feel that the processor speed must be high
- give due importance to the battery backup and it must be minimum of 2 hours
- do not seek laptop in different colours
- feel that the operating system must essentially be simple to operate
- never feel that 'on site' service is essential
- do not give much importance to stylish appearance of the laptop

Thus, these consumers give importance to **technical configuration** of laptop.

Cluster 3

Consumers, who belong to cluster 3 has the following characteristics:

- want price to be as minimum as possible
- never give priority to brand name
- do not consider storage capacity of the laptop as very important
- do not prioritise warranty ahead of the other features but is essential to some extent
- do not consider processor speed as very important
- never give due importance to the battery backup
- do not seek laptop in different colours
- do not feel that the operating system must essentially be simple to operate
- consider 'on site' service as essential and it is very important
- do not give much importance to stylish appearance of the laptop

Thus, these consumers give importance to **price and economy** of laptop.

Number of Cases in each Cluster

Cluster	1	10.000
	2	3.000
	3	7.000
Valid		20.000
Missing		.000

The table represents the number of respondents, who belong to each cluster. 10 respondents belong to cluster 1 (style and appearance), 3 belong to cluster 2 (technical configuration) and 7 respondents fall under cluster 3 (price and economy).

Navigation Guide

In order to enter data:

- Data must be entered in the 'Data View' page of the data sheet, as given by the respondents. (In this case, it is based on the response given by 20 consumers for the mentioned variables on a 7 point scale [1-Strongly Disagree, 7-Strongly Agree]).

Data View

cluster [DataSet1] - SPSS Data Editor

File Edit View Data Transform Analyze Graphs Utilities Window Help

1 : Price 4

	Price	Brand	Memory	Warranty	Speed	Battery	Colour	OS	Service	Style	var	var
1	4.00	7.00	2.00	4.00	1.00	2.00	1.00	1.00	2.00	4.00		
2	1.00	2.00	6.00	4.00	5.00	6.00	1.00	5.00	2.00	3.00		
3	4.00	2.00	1.00	4.00	2.00	1.00	5.00	2.00	5.00	2.00		
4	2.00	4.00	4.00	3.00	4.00	5.00	3.00	3.00	3.00	4.00		
5	6.00	3.00	3.00	5.00	3.00	3.00	3.00	3.00	3.00	2.00		
6	4.00	1.00	2.00	4.00	1.00	2.00	1.00	1.00	4.00	2.00		
7	3.00	5.00	2.00	2.00	2.00	2.00	3.00	2.00	4.00	5.00		
8	7.00	2.00	1.00	6.00	2.00	1.00	2.00	1.00	6.00	4.00		
9	5.00	2.00	4.00	5.00	3.00	3.00	2.00	3.00	5.00	3.00		
10	2.00	1.00	6.00	3.00	5.00	6.00	2.00	5.00	1.00	4.00		
11	2.00	4.00	7.00	3.00	6.00	6.00	6.00	6.00	2.00	3.00		
12	3.00	3.00	3.00	3.00	4.00	3.00	3.00	4.00	2.00	3.00		
13	3.00	2.00	1.00	2.00	2.00	2.00	2.00	2.00	1.00	3.00		
14	1.00	1.00	2.00	1.00	1.00	2.00	3.00	1.00	2.00	4.00		
15	1.00	5.00	2.00	1.00	1.00	2.00	3.00	1.00	3.00	6.00		
16	1.00	2.00	2.00	3.00	2.00	2.00	2.00	2.00	2.00	2.00		
17	6.00	3.00	4.00	5.00	4.00	3.00	3.00	3.00	5.00	1.00		
18	1.00	5.00	1.00	2.00	1.00	1.00	2.00	1.00	1.00	6.00		
19	2.00	7.00	3.00	2.00	2.00	3.00	1.00	2.00	1.00	5.00		
20	2.00	2.00	3.00	1.00	2.00	3.00	6.00	2.00	7.00	5.00		
21												
22												
23												

Variable View

- Open variable view and enter 10 variables, namely, 'Price, Brand, Memory, Warranty, Speed, Battery, Colour, OS, Service, Style' in the column Name. It assigns by default, the type of data, width, decimals and measure.

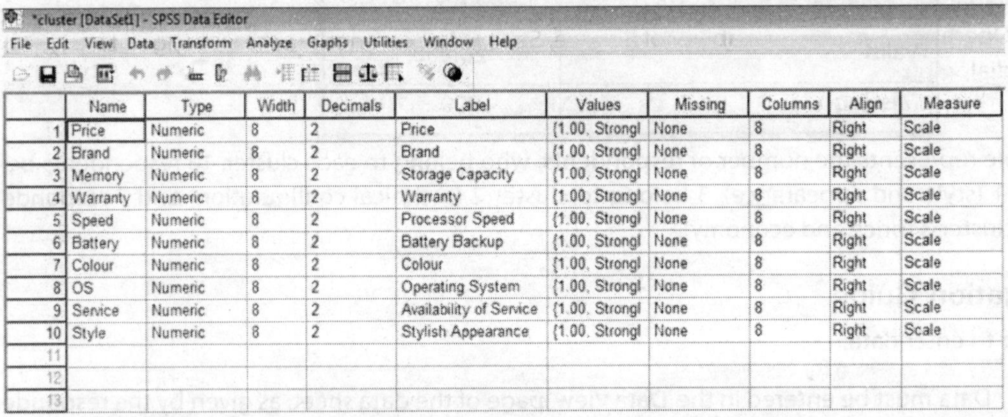

	Name	Type	Width	Decimals	Label	Values	Missing	Columns	Align	Measure
1	Price	Numeric	8	2	Price	{1.00, Strongl	None	8	Right	Scale
2	Brand	Numeric	8	2	Brand	{1.00, Strongl	None	8	Right	Scale
3	Memory	Numeric	8	2	Storage Capacity	{1.00, Strongl	None	8	Right	Scale
4	Warranty	Numeric	8	2	Warranty	{1.00, Strongl	None	8	Right	Scale
5	Speed	Numeric	8	2	Processor Speed	{1.00, Strongl	None	8	Right	Scale
6	Battery	Numeric	8	2	Battery Backup	{1.00, Strongl	None	8	Right	Scale
7	Colour	Numeric	8	2	Colour	{1.00, Strongl	None	8	Right	Scale
8	OS	Numeric	8	2	Operating System	{1.00, Strongl	None	8	Right	Scale
9	Service	Numeric	8	2	Availability of Service	{1.00, Strongl	None	8	Right	Scale
10	Style	Numeric	8	2	Stylish Appearance	{1.00, Strongl	None	8	Right	Scale
11										
12										
13										

- In the 'Variable View' page, a suitable name and a label can be assigned for the variables entered. (In this example, the variables are: PRICE, BRAND, STORAGE CAPACITY, WARRANTY, PROCESSOR SPEED, BATTERY BACKUP, COLOUR, OPERATING SYSTEM, AVAILABILITY OF SERVICE, STYLISH APPEARANCE). The data must be entered as collected in the questionnaire. The value coded must be entered first, and then assign the corresponding labels. (In this example, the parameters are rated on a 7 point scale: 1-Strongly Disagree, 7-Strongly Agree). In the pull down menu of Value, code the values as follows:

  Value: 1
  Label: Strongly Disagree
  Click 'Add'
  Similarly add the values for the scale.

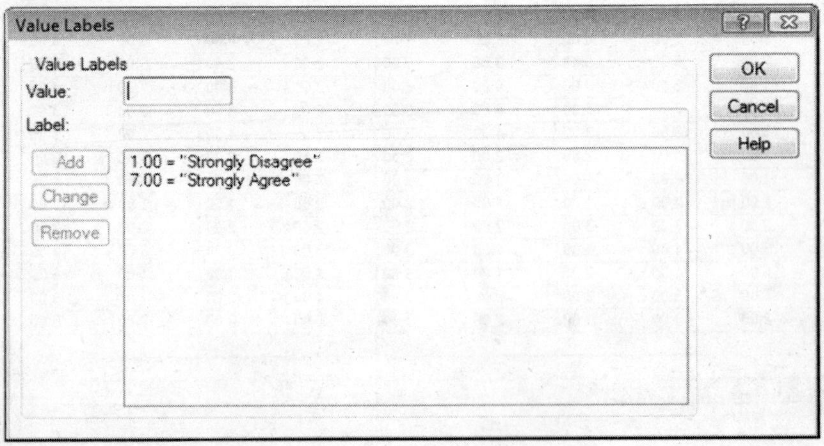

➢ Enter the values and click OK and save the input file.

Then, the following procedure must be followed to perform analysis:

- Select Analyse ⟶ Classify ⟶ Hierarchical Cluster Analysis
- Drag the variables or parameters to be tested to the Variable(s) dialog box. (In this example, the variables 'Price, Brand, Storage Capacity, Warranty, Processor Speed, Battery Backup, Colour, Operating System, Availability of Service, Stylish Appearance' must be dragged to the Variables dialog box).

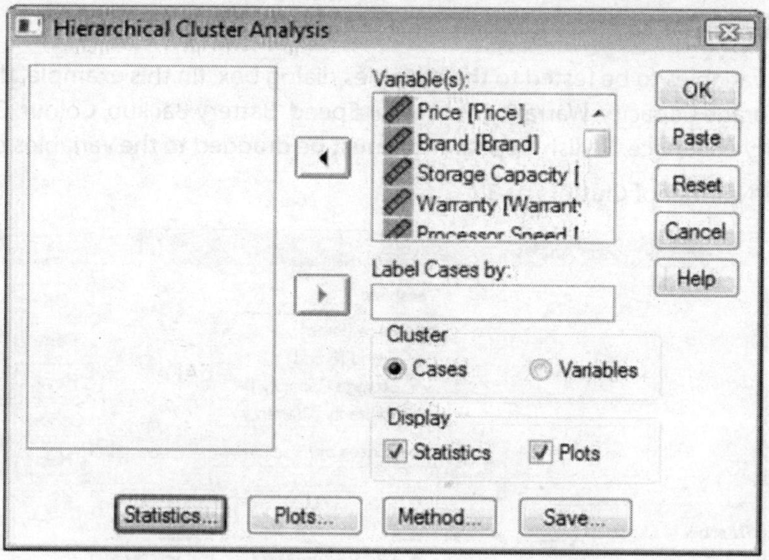

- Click 'Statistics', select 'Agglomeration Schedule' and then click 'Continue'.

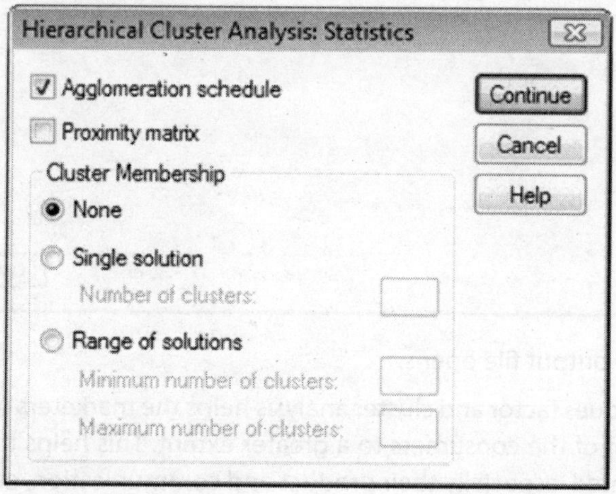

- Click 'OK' and the output file opens.

From the Agglomeration Schedule in the output table, the number of clusters can be determined. In this example, we find that the difference between the neighbouring rows, with respect to the Coefficients column, the maximum difference of 21.583 (57.083 – 35.500) exists between 3-cluster solution and 4-cluster solution (stage 17 and stage 16). The difference decreases after this stage. Hence, it shows that a 3 cluster solution would be the ideal solution i.e., the lower row value of the two rows corresponding to the maximum difference in the coefficient value.

- In order to identify the characteristics of these clusters, second stage of cluster analysis is performed by, K-Means Clustering
- Select Analyse →Classify→ K-Means Cluster Analysis
- Drag the variables to be tested to the Variables dialog box. (In this example, the variables 'Price, Brand, Storage Capacity, Warranty, Processor Speed, Battery Backup, Colour, Operating System, Availability of Service, Stylish Appearance' must be dragged to the Variables dialog box).
- Enter the 'Number of Clusters' as 3.

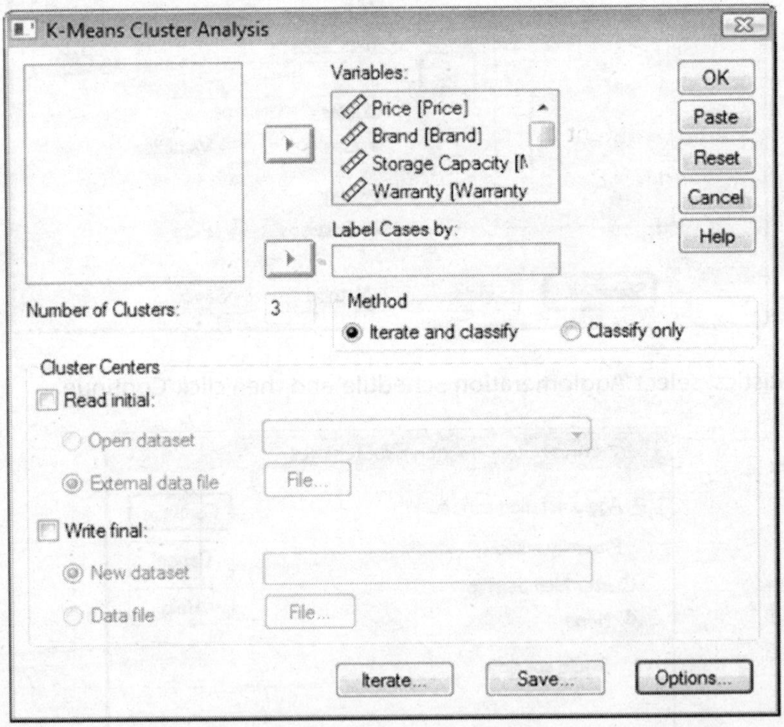

- Click 'OK' and the output file opens.

The data reduction techniques factor and cluster analysis helps the marketers to identify the few variables that predict the behaviour of the consumers to a greater extent. This helps to make decision about the strategies to be implemented, especially their product and communication, effectively. This is done with the identification of the major variables influencing the consumers and the different characteristics that exists among the sample.

Review Questions

1. What are the types of data reduction techniques?
2. Explain the application of factor analysis in marketing.
3. Explain the application of cluster analysis in identifying the segments in the market place.
4. A real estate company likes to identify the major segments and their characteristics. The data collected from 25 respondents on a 7 point scale (where 1 = completely agree, 7 = completely disagree) by the researcher on various parameters are given below. The parameters or the variables considered are:

   Var 1 – owning a house is a necessity

   Var 2 – paying high price for quality is acceptable

   Var 3 – investing in stock is risky

   Var 4 – every parent should make investment for children

   Var 5 – making investment in land is safe investment

   Var 6 – friends and family are important to make major investment decisions

   Var 7 – monthly financial obligations can be met with loan

   Var 8 – enjoying the current situation is more important

   Var 9 – advertisements play a major role to make decisions

   Var 10 – television is the major source of entertainment

   Input data is shown in table below. Execute cluster analysis to identify the segments.

Var 1	Var 2	Var 3	Var 4	Var 5	Var 6	Var 7	Var 8	Var 9
2	4	7	2	4	1	2	1	1
6	1	2	6	4	5	6	1	5
1	4	2	1	4	2	1	5	2
5	2	4	4	3	4	5	3	3
3	6	3	3	5	3	3	3	3
2	4	1	2	4	1	2	1	1
2	3	5	2	2	2	2	3	2
1	7	2	1	6	2	1	2	1
3	5	2	4	5	3	3	2	3

6	2	1	6	3	5	6	2	5
6	2	4	7	3	6	6	6	6
3	3	3	3	3	4	3	3	4
2	3	2	1	2	2	2	2	2
2	1	1	2	1	1	2	3	1
2	1	5	2	1	1	2	3	1
2	1	2	2	3	2	2	2	2
3	6	3	4	5	4	3	3	3
1	1	5	1	2	1	1	2	1
3	2	7	3	2	2	3	1	2
3	2	2	3	1	2	3	6	2
2	1	2	2	3	2	2	2	2
3	6	3	4	5	4	3	3	3
1	1	5	1	2	1	1	2	1
3	2	7	3	2	2	3	1	2
3	2	2	3	1	2	3	6	2

5. Car manufacturers like to understand the perception of consumers on a scale of 1 to 7 (where 1 = completely agree, 7 = completely disagree). The variables considered by them include price, mileage, service, comfort, technology advancement, adequate leg space, adequate space for luggage, power steering, excellent brakes, and resale value. Identify the major factors that can be recommended to the manufacturing company to concentrate. The data collected from 30 consumers is given below.

Var 1	Var 2	Var 3	Var 4	Var 5	Var 6	Var 7	Var 8	Var 9
2	1	2	2	3	2	2	2	2
2	4	7	2	4	1	2	1	1
2	1	2	2	3	2	2	2	2
3	2	7	3	2	2	3	1	2
3	2	2	3	1	2	3	6	2
2	4	1	2	4	1	2	1	1
3	6	3	4	5	4	3	3	3
1	1	5	1	2	1	1	2	1

3	2	7	3	2	2	3	1	2
3	2	2	3	1	2	3	6	2
2	4	1	2	4	1	2	1	1
2	3	5	2	2	2	2	3	2
1	7	2	1	6	2	1	2	1
3	5	2	4	5	3	3	2	3
6	2	1	6	3	5	6	2	5
6	2	4	7	3	6	6	6	6
3	3	3	3	3	4	3	3	4
2	3	2	1	2	2	2	2	2
2	1	1	2	1	1	2	3	1
2	1	5	2	1	1	2	3	1
2	1	2	2	3	2	2	2	2
3	6	3	4	5	4	3	3	3
1	1	5	1	2	1	1	2	1
3	2	7	3	2	2	3	1	2
3	2	2	3	1	2	3	6	2
2	1	2	2	3	2	2	2	2
3	6	3	4	5	4	3	3	3
1	1	5	1	2	1	1	2	1
3	2	7	3	2	2	3	1	2
3	2	2	3	1	2	3	6	2

6. Explain the usage of factor loadings to decide on the factors.

Chapter 15

Brand Positioning Methods

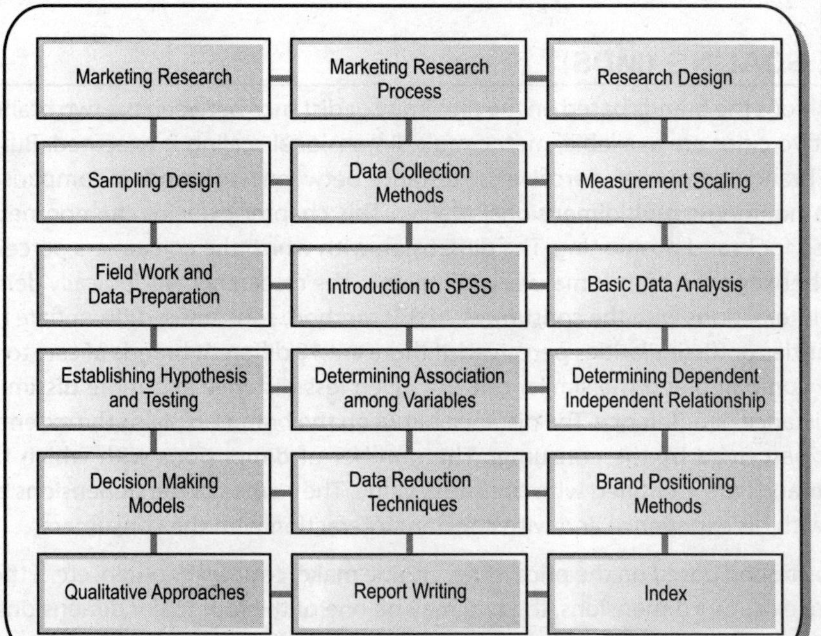

Outline

Chapter Structure

- Introduction
- Multidimensional Scaling (MDS)
- Case
- Perceptual Mapping
- Case
- Review Questions

Chapter Overview

Chapter 15 explains the brand positioning techniques adopted in marketing research. It includes positioning of the brands based on the dimensions with which it is perceived, Multidimensional Scaling; and the variables with which the brands are positioned, Perceptual Mapping.

INTRODUCTION

Brand positioning depends on the place the brand has created in the minds of the consumers. There are two techniques in research that brings out the brand positioning map: Multidimensional Scaling (MDS) and Perceptual Mapping. These techniques place the competing brands in appropriate positions or segments as perceived by the consumers. Multidimensional Scaling positions the brands based on the perceived difference that exists among the brands and Perceptual Mapping positions the competing brands based on the attributes with which it is measured. The positioning map derived by these methods helps the marketers to identify the gap that exits in the current position or segment. It also helps the exiting firms to understand how consumers perceive their brand in comparison with the competing brands in the market. It also aids them to understand those brands that are in close competition and those brands that are positioned in a different manner by the consumers.

MULTIDIMENSIONAL SCALING (MDS)

Multidimensional scaling positions the brands based on the proximity or distance between the two brands. If actual distances between two cities are available, metric multidimensional scaling is executed. But in case of the distance between brands, consumers perceive the distance between two brands in comparison with the other brands. It is a nonmetric multidimensional scaling. This chapter explains the nonmetric multidimensional scaling used for brand positioning. The dimension with which the consumers perceive the similarity or dissimilarity between the brands may vary. Ultimately, the researcher will logically derive the dimensions based on his interactions with the consumers. In this method, consumers differentiate the brands to the extent of similarities or dissimilarities perceived. If there are 10 different brands of cars to be positioned, these brands are compared and the similar one are given less distance and more dissimilar brands are rated with more distance or difference. The distance between the brands explains the extent of similarities or dissimilarities perceived by the consumer. The number of dimensions with which the consumers differentiate the brands are identified with the stress value. The names of the dimensions are identified by the researcher with his experience and with constant interaction with the consumers.

For instance, cars may be positioned based on the price, style, engine make, country or origin, etc. If the stress value shows that there exist two dimensions, the two may be one of the four major dimensions. This depends on the segment and the type of brands considered for positioning. The researcher should identify the dimensions with his continuous interactions with the respondents. The decision of the dimension is decided by the stress value that explains the good fit. If the stress value is low, the dimension is good fit to explain consumer perception as stress explains the lack of fit.

SPSS command to perform MDS:

In menu bar, ANALYSE ⟶ SCALE ⟶ MULTIDIMENSIONAL SCALING (ALSCAL)

Select all the variables in the Variable box. Default it assigns 'Data are Distances'.

In the option MODEL, select minimum and maximum dimensions. Minimum can be 2 and maximum can be 3 or 4 depending on the size of the sample and number of brands compared.

In OPTIONS, select 'Individual Subject Plots'. Then click CONTINUE to return to the main dialogue box. Click OK.

CASE

A retail outlet likes to understand the position of the eight brands of soft drinks offered in the stores. The drinks considered are: Slice, Coke, Pepsi, Sprite, Fanta, Miranda, 7-Up, and Thumsup. These brands are given in both columns and rows in matrix format with the variables 1 to 8 respectively. Consumers were asked to give the extent of similarity and dissimilarity perceived between the brands. The ordinal scale is used between '0' to '8' where '0' represent more similar and '8' explains maximum dissimilarity between the brands. Symmetrical 8x8 matrix is formed where rows and columns represent the brands. VAR 1 is Slice in both rows and columns. So the cell with VAR 1 and VAR 1 will be '0' as it is the same and not perceived with difference. But the distance perceived between VAR 1 and VAR 8 (Slice and Thumsup) is '8' that explains both the brands are perceived completely different by the consumers as the distance between these brands is high.

Input table is shown below:

	VAR 1	VAR 2	VAR 3	VAR 4	VAR 5	VAR 6	VAR 7	VAR 8
VAR 1	0	3	4	6	1	5	2	8
VAR 2	3	0	2	4	7	7	8	6
VAR 3	4	2	0	1	3	6	7	3
VAR 4	6	4	1	0	2	4	7	7
VAR 5	1	7	3	2	0	2	4	5
VAR 6	5	7	6	4	2	0	3	6
VAR 7	2	8	7	7	4	3	0	1
VAR 8	8	6	3	7	5	6	1	0

On execution of MDS, the following output tables are extracted.

Iteration history for the 3 dimensional solution (in squared distances)

Young's S-stress formula 1 is used.

Iteration	S-stress	Improvement
1	0.17394	
2	0.14273	0.0312
3	0.12809	0.01465
4	0.1216	0.00648
5	0.11974	0.00187
6	0.11863	0.00111
7	0.11787	0.00075

Iterations stopped because S-stress improvement is less than .001000

- Stress and squared correlation (RSQ) in distances
- RSQ values are the proportion of variance of the scaled data (disparities) in the partition (row, matrix, or entire data) which is accounted for by their corresponding distances.
- Stress values are Kruskal's stress formula 1.

For matrix

Stress = .07704 RSQ = .90293

Configuration derived in 3 dimensions

Stimulus Coordinates

Stimulus Number	Stimulus Name	Dimensions		
		1	2	3
1	VAR00001	-0.3287	-0.9145	1.3545
2	VAR00002	1.3882	0.981	1.0173
3	VAR00003	1.3747	0.5473	-0.0789
4	VAR00004	1.3294	-0.7491	-0.7144
5	VAR00005	-0.3525	-1.2404	-0.4614
6	VAR00006	-0.7208	-0.5625	-1.4449
7	VAR00007	-1.7631	0.2146	0.624
8	VAR00008	-0.9272	1.7238	-0.2963

Iteration history for the 2 dimensional solution (in squared distances)

Young's S-stress formula 1 is used.

Iteration	S-stress	Improvement
1	.32526	
2	.28771	.03755
3	.28022	.00749
4	.27564	.00458
5	.27173	.00390
6	.26809	.00364
7	.26581	.00228
8	.26535	.00045

Iterations stopped because S-stress improvement is less than .001000

- Stress and squared correlation (RSQ) in distances
- RSQ values are the proportion of variance of the scaled data (disparities) in the partition (row, matrix, or entire data) which is accounted for by their corresponding distances.
- Stress values are Kruskal's stress formula 1.

For matrix

Stress = .20276 RSQ = .68449

Configuration derived in 2 dimensions

Stimulus Coordinates

Stimulus Number	Stimulus Name	Dimensions	
		1	2
1	VAR00001	-.1386	-1.0645
2	VAR00002	1.3588	1.1805
3	VAR00003	1.2304	.2297
4	VAR00004	1.2265	-.7553
5	VAR00005	-.4688	-.9685
6	VAR00006	-.9277	-.6910
7	VAR00007	-1.5598	.6001
8	VAR00008	-.7207	1.4690

Iteration history for the 1 dimensional solution (in squared distances)

Young's S-stress formula 1 is used.

Iteration	S-stress	Improvement
0	.52771	
1	.51097	
2	.48167	.02929
3	.48158	.00009

Iterations stopped because

S-stress improvement is less than .001000

- Stress and squared correlation (RSQ) in distances

- RSQ values are the proportion of variance of the scaled data (disparities) in the partition (row, matrix, or entire data) which is accounted for by their corresponding distances.
- Stress values are Kruskal's stress formula 1.

For matrix

Stress = .39773 RSQ = .45711

Configuration derived in 1 dimension.

Stimulus Coordinates

Stimulus Number	Stimulus Name	Dimension
		1
1	VAR00001	.5356
2	VAR00002	1.3817
3	VAR00003	.8073
4	VAR00004	1.0865
5	VAR00005	-.5941
6	VAR00006	-.7758
7	VAR00007	-1.3561
8	VAR00008	-1.0852

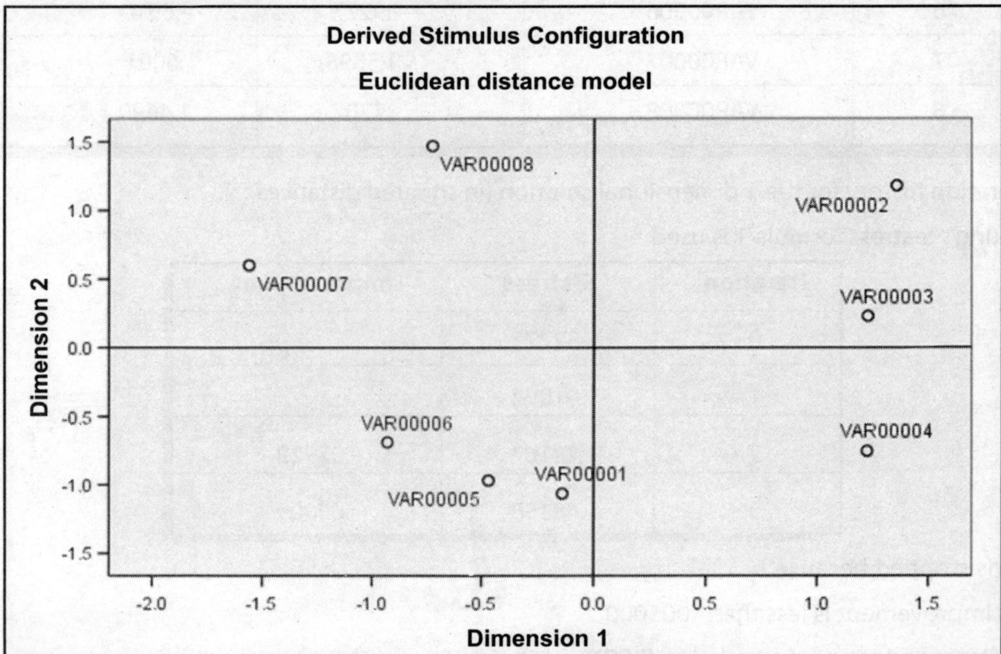

Interpretation

The output tables give one, two and three dimensional solutions. The dimensions that give the best positioning of the brands is given by the stress value of the dimensions considered. The stress values for the dimensions are:

1 - dimensional solution: 0.39773

2 - dimensional solution: 0.20276

3 - dimensional solution: 0.07704

Stress value explains the lack of fit. So the dimension that has stress value close to '0' gives better positioning of the brands. As the number of brands considered is 8, number of dimensions stated in SPSS can be 3 or 4. Our purpose of brand positioning is to understand the position of the brands with minimal dimensions. So a maximum of 3 dimensional solution is opted. The dimension with less stress value is 3. So a three dimensional solution gives a better positioning map. The name of the dimensions is derived with the expertise of the researcher and with interaction with consumers. Here, the dimensions can be:

Dimension 1: Availability

Dimension 2: Taste

Dimension 3: Brand image

Stimulus coordinate of three dimensional solution explains the strength of the brands with the dimensions. Brands Coke, Pepsi and Sprite are preferred by the consumers for its availability. Coke and Pepsi also has the strength of taste and brand image as their stimulus coordinates are higher for these dimensions also.

Navigation Guide

- Data is to be entered in the 'Data View' page of the data sheet, as given by the respondents. (In this case, it is based on the average response given by respondents for 8 brands of soft drinks based on the similarities or dissimilarities perceived between them).
- In the 'Variable View' page, brand names can be given in the names of the variables.

(In this example, the variables are retained as such).

- The values must be entered in matrix format as collected from the respondents in the questionnaire.
- Save the data file.

Data View

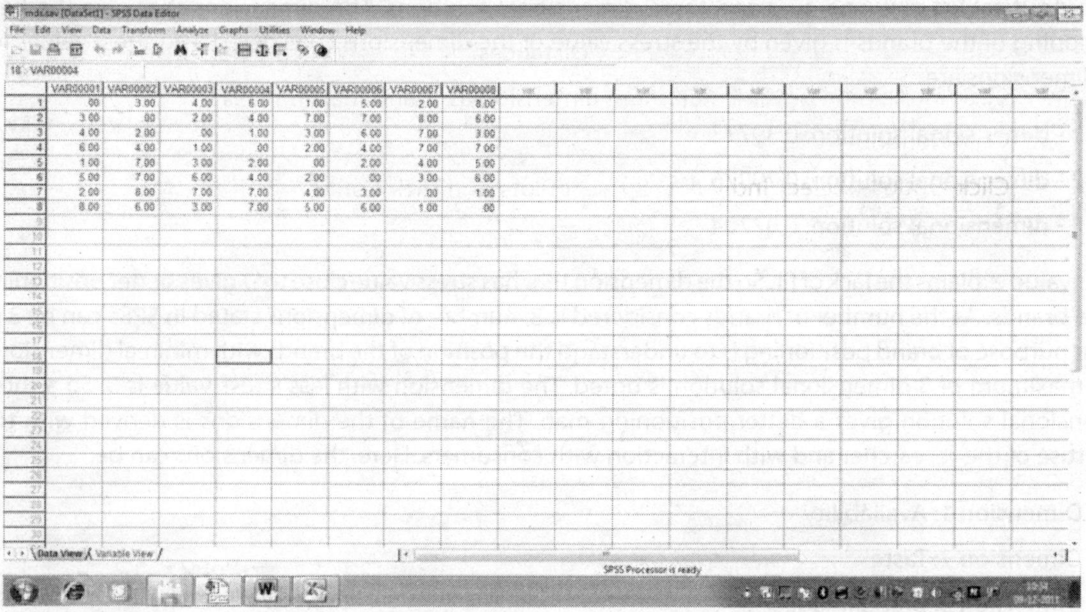

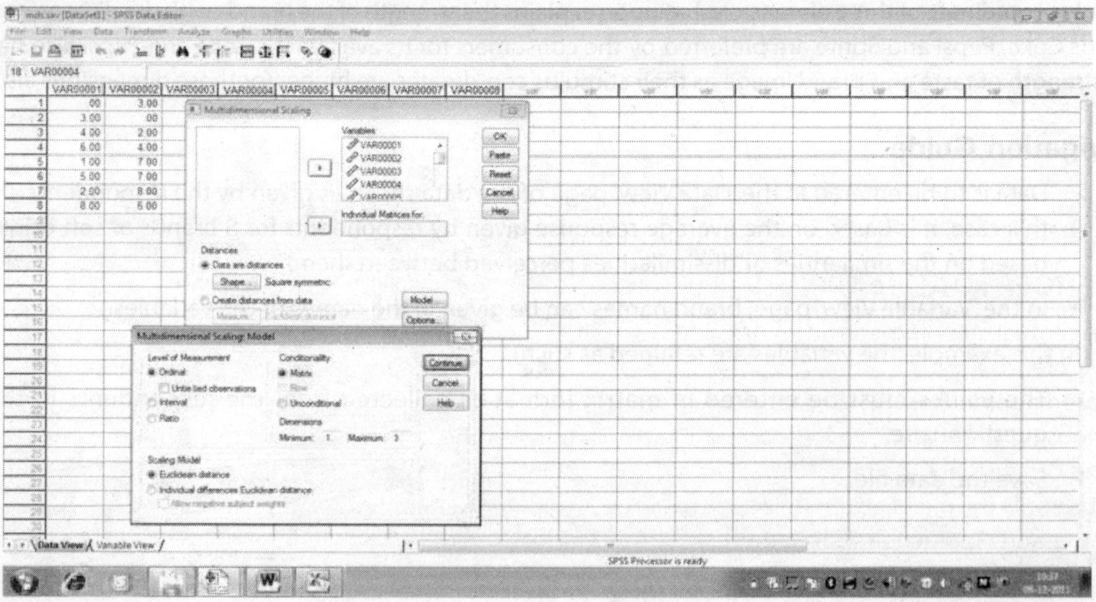

Variable View

Then, the following procedure is followed:

- Select Analyse⟶Scale⟶Multidimensional Scaling.

- Drag the variable to be tested to the Variable dialog box. (In this example, the variables are the brands names as VAR 1 to VAR 8).
- Select 'Data are Distances' in the box 'Distances'.
- Click 'Model' and give the minimum dimension as '1' and maximum as '3'.
- Click 'Continue'.
- Click 'Options', select 'Individual Subject Plots' and click 'Continue'.
- Click 'OK'.

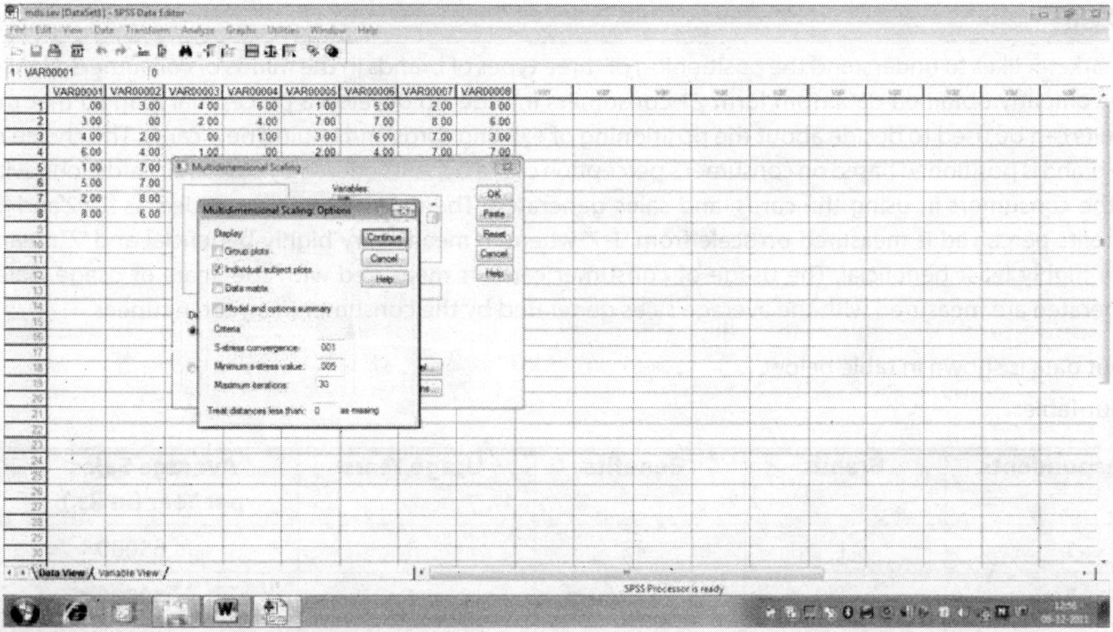

PERCEPTUAL MAPPING

Perceptual mapping is an attribute based approach where the factors or variables important to discriminate the brands are considered for positioning. Factor analysis and Discriminant analysis are other attribute based approaches. Factor analysis helps to identify the factors or attributes that consumers consider in choosing the brand. Discriminant analysis differentiates the brands based on the attributes considered. This can further be extended for positioning these brands with plots. This analysis will help the marketers to identify the major attributes considered by consumers in choosing a product or service and the position the brands has acquired based on the attributes measured. Technically this analysis can be performed with Discriminant analysis in SPSS. As a positioning map it helps to understand those brands positioned in the same segment and the variables with which the consumers weigh the brands.

SPSS command to perform Perceptual Mapping:

In menu bar, ANALYSE ⟶ CLASSIFY ⟶ DISCRIMINANT

Select all the GROUPING VARIABLE as the Brands considered. Define the range of the grouping variable by clicking the option DEFINE RANGE. Minimum value will be '1' and maximum will be '2' or any other number depending on the number of brands considered. Then click CONTINUE.

In the INDEPENDENTS box, select all the variables considered to position the brands.

Select CLASSIFY. In DISPLAY, select SUMMARY TABLE. Then, click CONTINUE.

In CLASSIFY, then select the option COMBINED GROUP PLOTS in PLOTS.

To have the attributes on the perceptual map, Standardized Coefficients can be plotted on Excel.

CASE

A marketer likes to understand the positioning of three types of brands in the minds of consumers. Hence, the company obtained data from form 21 consumers in order to develop a perceptual map so that the results can be used to decide about the positioning of existing cards and issuing new cards. The choice of the brand is positioned based on consumer's perception of the benefits offered by customer cards, longevity of the consumers in using the cards, and sales generated. The three brands are coded as '1', '2'and '3'. Benefits perceived is measured on scale from '1-7' where '1' means very highly beneficial and '7' means very highly least beneficial. The usage of consumer cards is measured with the years of usage. Sales generated are measured with the average sales generated by the consumer in a year in rupees.

Input data is shown in table below.

Input Table:

Respondents	Brands	Benefits	Usage Years	Average Sales per Year (in Rs.)
1	1	32	3	65000
2	1	30	4	49000
3	3	30	5	58000
4	2	33	2	83000
5	3	34	1	89000
6	3	29	3	69000
7	2	29	4	102000
8	1	35	5	62000
9	3	29	2	100000
10	2	30	3	95000
11	2	32	5	83000
12	1	29	3	63000
13	3	33	2	68000

14	1	26	2	65000
15	3	27	3	91000
16	1	35	3	73000
17	2	34	5	79000
18	2	32	3	77000
19	1	34	2	70000
20	2	35	5	81000
21	3	30	3	67000

Null Hypothesis (H_0): There is no significant discrimination between the position of three brands.

Alternate Hypothesis (H_1): There is significant discrimination between the three brands as positioned in the minds of the consumers.

Tables below present the output for positioning the loyalty cards.

Output Tables and Interpretation

Wilks' Lambda

Test of Function(s)	Wilks' Lambda	Chi-square	df	Sig.
1 through 2	.347	17.480	8	.025
2	.811	3.456	3	.326

The p-value of chi-square test (for test function 1) is 0.025 at n-1 (4 – 1 = 3) degrees of freedom (Df). The value of 'p' is less than the significance level of 0.05 (5 percent). Hence, we reject the null hypothesis. This explains that there is significant discrimination perceived between the two loyalty cards by the consumers. Wilks' Lambda value of this test is 0.347. This value always lies between '0' and '1'. 0.347 is closer to '0' and it indicates the better discriminating power of the model i.e., the model has a better power in discriminating between the two groups that can be further positioned clearly. The test function 2 has a wilks lambda close to '1' and the chi-square significance is also greater than 0.05. It will not discriminate the brands effectively. So the test function 1 is considered for positioning the brands based on consumers perception.

Classification Results (a)

		Brands	Predicted Group Membership			Total
			1.00	2.00	3.00	1.00
Original	Count	1.00	7	0	0	7
		2.00	0	5	2	7
		3.00	2	1	4	7
	%	1.00	100.0	.0	.0	100.0

		2.00	.0	71.4	28.6	100.0
		3.00	28.6	14.3	57.1	100.0

a 76.2% of original grouped cases correctly classified.

The classification matrix indicates the ability of classification by this model. The output table of classification matrix explains that 76.2 % of the existing data have been classified correctly.

Standardized Canonical Discriminant Function Coefficients

Variables	Function	
	1	2
Age of sales executive	.165	.204
Experience of sales executive	.683	.017
Average Sales per Year	1.013	-.640
Average number of new clients per year	.134	.713

From the Standardized Canonical Discriminant Function Coefficients table, it is clear that average sales per year is the variable that positions the brand to a greater extent followed by the experience of the sales men in the retail outlet. This is drawn with the coefficient of Function 1.

The positioning of the two cards diagrammatically is given below.

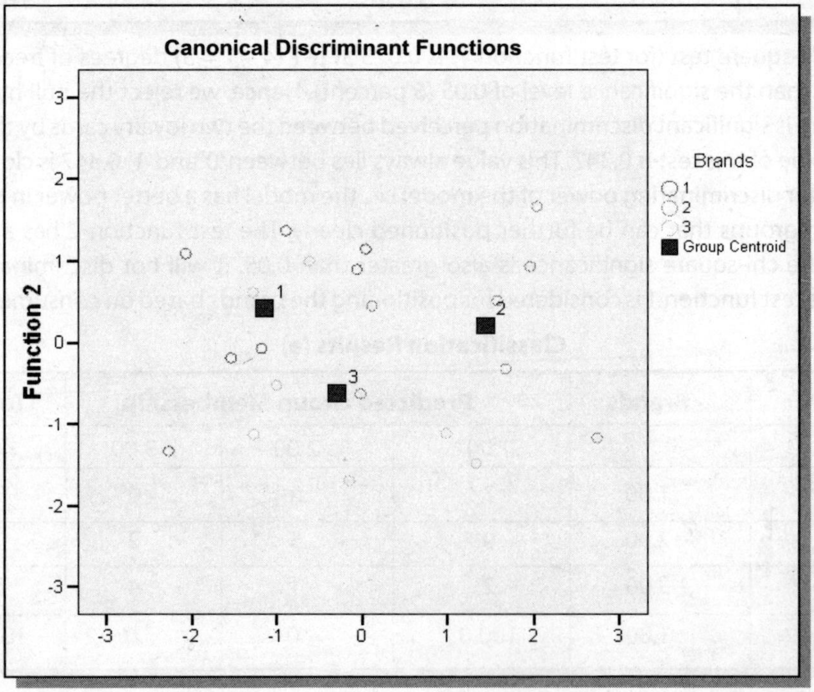

Navigation Guide

In order to enter data:

- Data must be entered in the 'Data View' page of the data sheet, as obtained. In this case, it is the data obtained from 20 respondents.

Data View

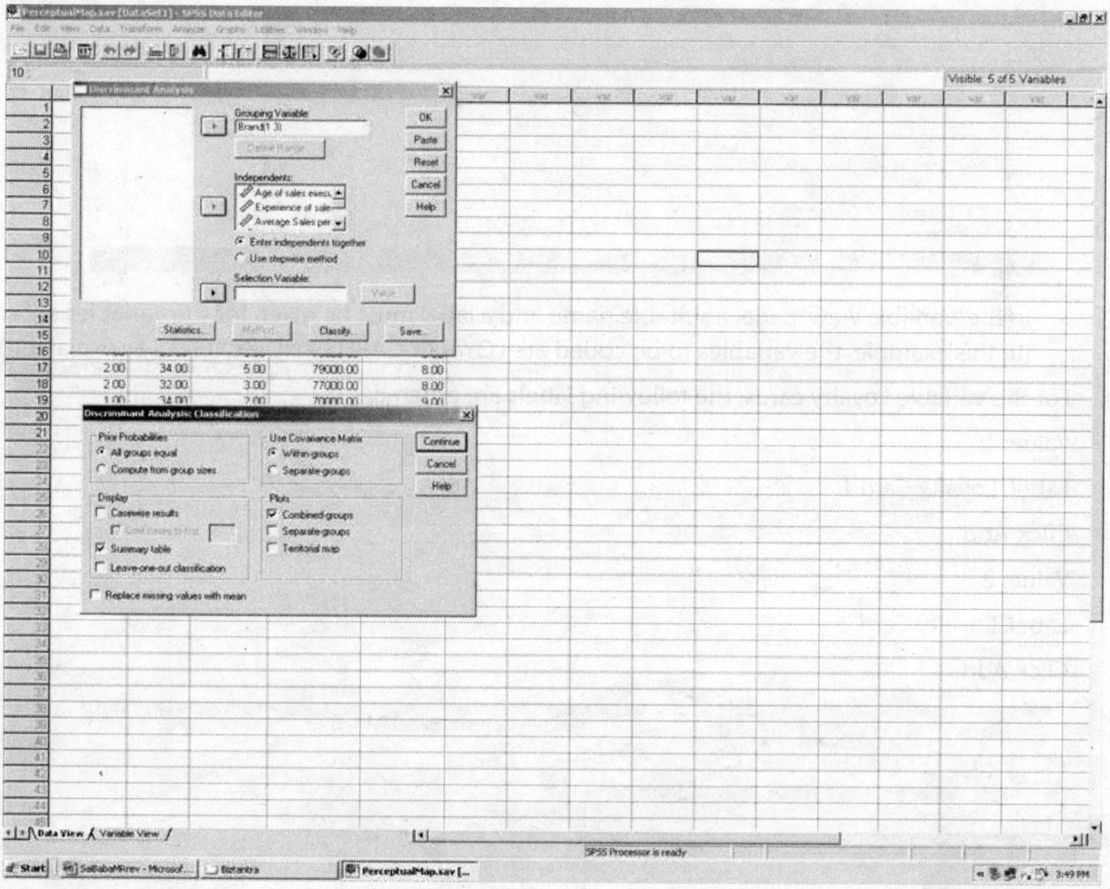

Variable View

- Open variable view and enter 'Loyalty cards, Benefits, Usage Years, and Average Sales' in the column Name. It assigns by default, the type of data, width, decimals and measure.

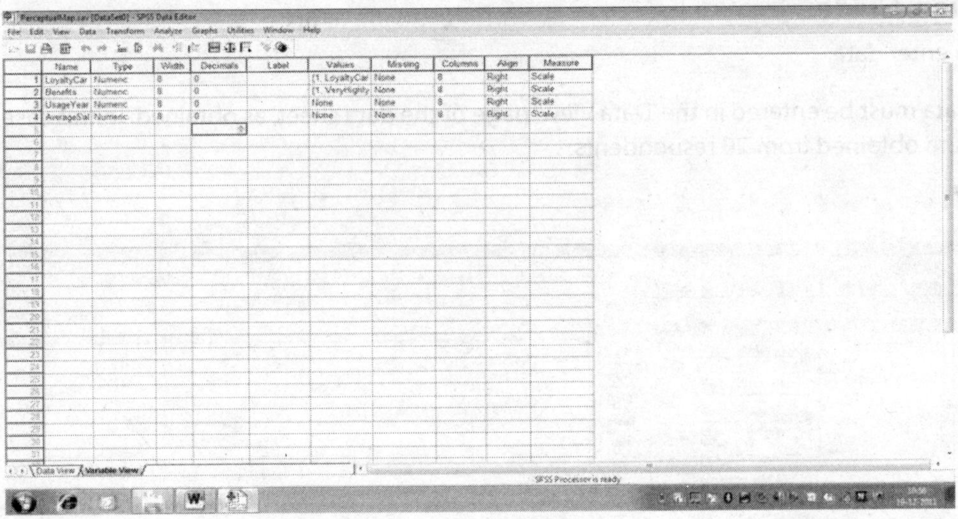

➢ In the 'Variable View' page, a suitable name and a label must be given for the variables entered. (In this example, the variables to be coded are LOYALTY CARDS AND BENEFITS as explained)

For the variable Loyalty cards, the following labels are entered:

Value: 1

Label: Loyalty Card 1

Click 'Add'

Value: 2

Label: Loyalty Card 2

Click 'Add'

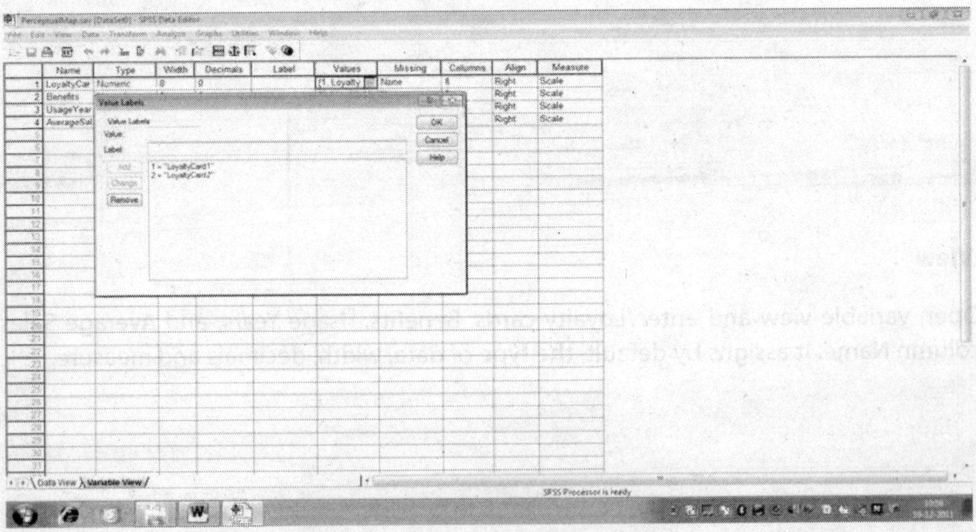

Similarly add the values for the scale for the variable, 'Benefits'

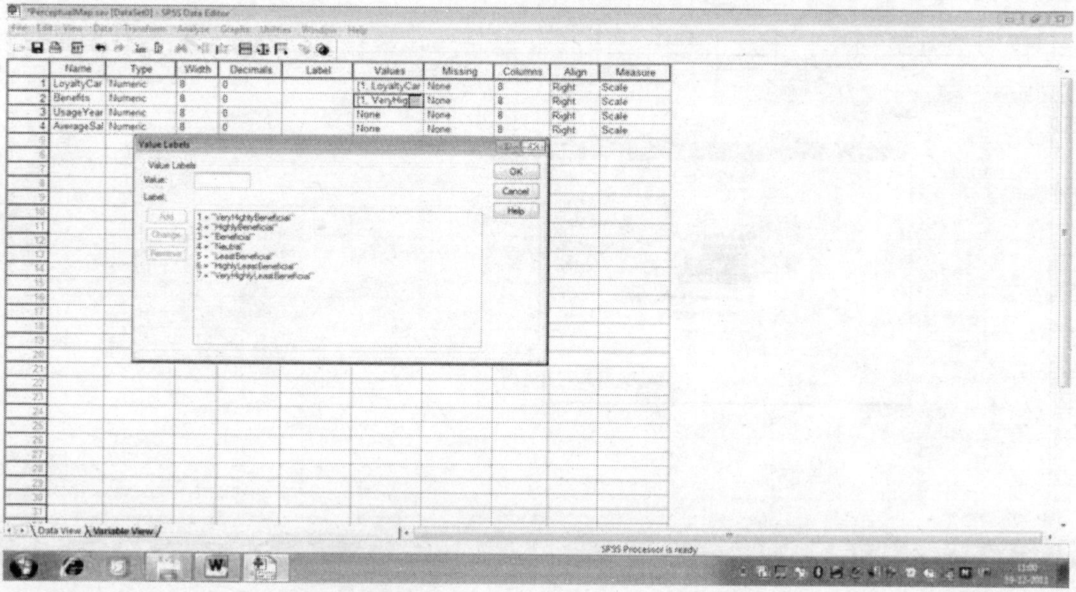

➢ Enter the values and click OK and save the input file.

Then, the following procedure is followed to perform analysis:

- Select Analyse ⟶ Classify ⟶ Discriminant Analysis.
- Drag the grouping variable to the 'Grouping Variable' dialog box. (In this example, the variable 'Loyalty Cards' is dragged to the Grouping Variable dialog box).
- Click 'Define Range' and enter the 'Minimum' and 'Maximum' values as defined. (In this example, enter 'Minimum' as '1' and 'Maximum' as '2').

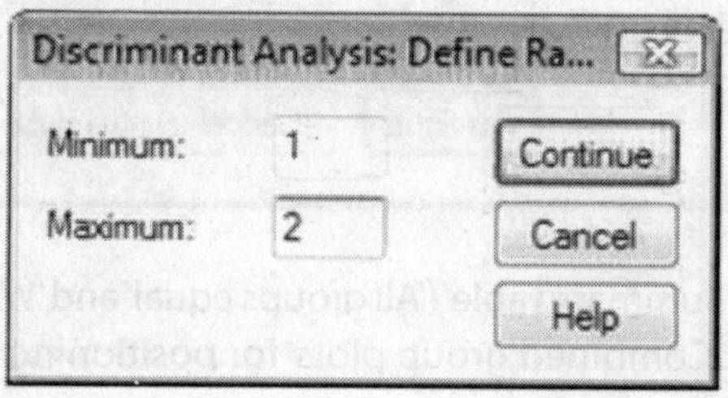

- Drag the independent variables to the 'Independents' dialog box. (In this case, the variables Benefits, Usage Years, and Average sales per year are dragged to the 'Independents' dialog box). 'Enter independents together' is the default selection.

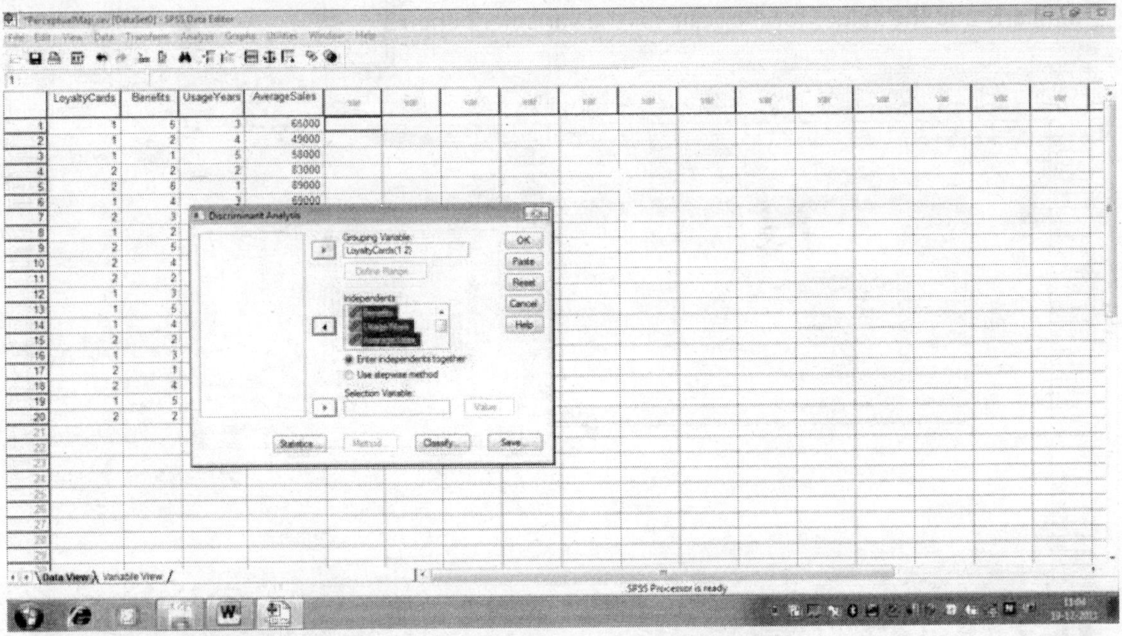

- Click 'Statistics', select 'Unstandardized' and then click 'Continue'.

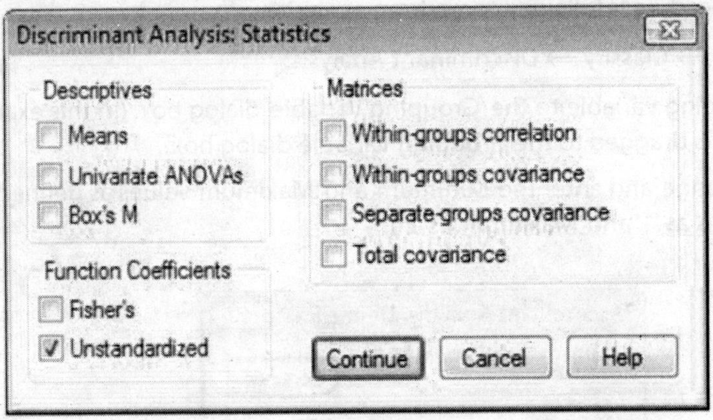

- Click 'Classification', select 'Summary table' ('All groups equal' and 'Within-groups' being the default selections) and then click 'Combined group plots' for positioning and then select 'Continue'.

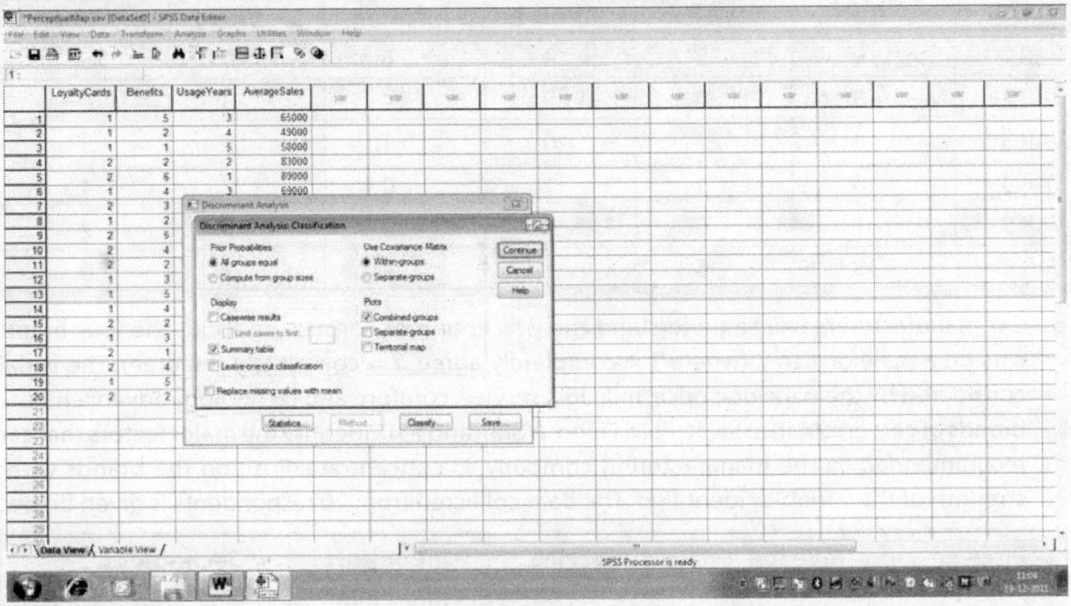

- Click 'OK' and the output file opens.

The brand positioning techniques MDS and Perceptual Mapping helps the marketers to identify the position or the place their brands have in the minds of the consumers with the existing brands in the market. This measures the effect of communication and the positioning made by the advertisements. It also identifies the segments existing brands concentrate and the gap that exists for the new players to enter.

Review Questions

1. What are the brand positioning methods?
2. Explain the usage of MDS in marketing.
3. How better is perceptual mapping than discriminant analysis in classifying the brands?
4. Explain the procedure to position the brands with Perceptual Mapping.
5. The six tooth paste brands: Colgate, Close up, Pepsodent, Cibaca, Meswak, and Babool are considered as Variables 1 to 6. These brands are compared by the respondents and marked between '0' to '6' if perceived similar to dissimilar respectively. The data collected from 10 respondents is taken average and given in the matrix below. Perform MDS to position these brands and identify the dimensions with which they are positioned by the respondents.

	VAR 1	VAR 2	VAR 3	VAR 4	VAR 5	VAR 6
VAR 1	0	3	4	6	1	5
VAR 2	3	0	2	4	3	6
VAR 3	4	2	0	1	5	3
VAR 4	6	4	1	0	2	4
VAR 5	1	3	5	2	0	2
VAR 6	5	6	3	4	2	0

6. Car manufacturers like to understand the perception of consumers about the four brands of cars on a scale of 1 to 7 (where 1 = completely agree, 7 = completely disagree). The variables considered by them include price, mileage, service, comfort, and technology advancement. The brands of cars are: Maruti Swift, Ford Fiego, A Star, and i-10. Identify the major factors that can be recommended to the manufacturing company to concentrate. Position the brands with the strength of the variables identified. The data collected from 20 respondents is given below.

Price	Mileage	Service	Comfort	Technology
2	2	3	2	2
7	2	4	1	2
2	2	3	2	2
7	3	2	2	3
2	3	1	2	3
1	2	4	1	2
3	4	5	4	3
5	1	2	1	1
7	3	2	2	3
2	3	1	2	3
1	2	4	1	2
5	2	2	2	2
2	1	6	2	1
2	4	5	3	3
1	6	3	5	6
4	7	3	6	6
3	3	3	4	3
2	1	2	2	2
1	2	1	1	2
5	2	1	1	2

Chapter

16

Qualitative Approaches

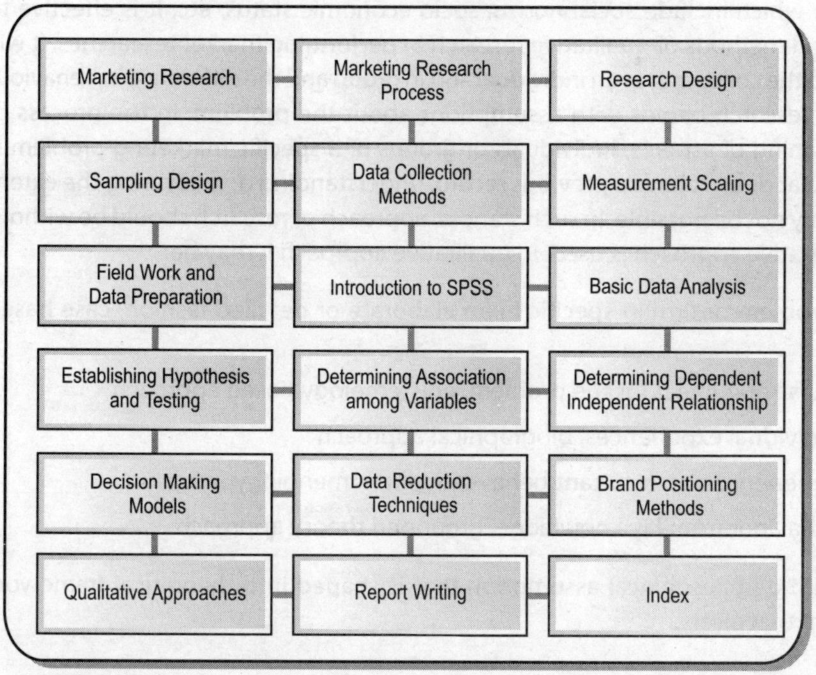

Outline

Chapter Structure

- Introduction
- Approaches in Qualitative Research
- Methods of Conducting Research
- Data Analysis and Decision Making
- Review Questions

Chapter Overview

This chapter discusses the different approaches to qualitative research – biographical research, phenomenology, theory building, ethnography and case study. The chapter also provides insight into the procedure for conducting a qualitative research, methods of data collection and data analysis to draw conclusion.

INTRODUCTION

Quantitative research techniques help to understand the characteristics of a population or predict causal relationships that exist. This is done with quantitative data collected from secondary sources or through primary sources or survey. Quantifying variation may not be possible or required in every market research situation. There may be need to describe the variation, explain the relationships, describe individual experiences or group norms. This is performed with qualitative research. It seeks to explore the phenomenon in a semi-structured and flexible approach. It has more application in an exploratory research as open ended questions are used to probe the participants. It helps in investigating complex and sensitive problems that may not have existing literature. It provides 'human side' of a problem which include opinion, belief, emotions, and relationship among individuals. Qualitative research is also effective in identifying intangible factors in a human which include social norms, socio economic status, etc. It is effective to understand the approaches and methods of qualitative research in performing market researches. It will help the researcher understand the consumer as an individual and in group and the difference in behaviour and relationships. Qualitative research begins with assumptions about the problem. In the process of research, enquiry into the meaning of aspects, individuals or groups of a specific marketing problem is made. For research problems that doesn't have a previous record, understanding or measuring the extent of the problem or its impact may not be possible. In such stances, approach of research should be without past experience. Hence a qualitative approach is used. In qualitative approach it may be:

- To understand the problem or firm in specific in an elaborate or detailed fashion, case based approach
- To understand the cause and effect for the problem, epistemology based approach
- To study based on individual experiences, biographical approach
- To understand the experience and resultant behaviour, phenomenology
- To distinguish the behaviour from lay knowledge, grounded theory approach

Qualitative Research starts with a philosophical assumption that is shaped into theoretical framework with a set of belief or paradigm that exists.

Philosophical Assumptions

Philosophical assumptions are the facts known in reality. It explains the researcher's knowledge, language, role of values and methods used for research. The philosophical assumptions that build on the qualitative research are: Ontology, Epistemology, Values, Language and Logical assumptions of research process.

- Ontological Assumptions – are those that relate to the assumptions about reality. There may exist multiple realities that can be expressed in quotes. It brings out the beliefs and experiences of the individuals participating in the study.
- Epistemological Assumptions – are the assumptions about the relationship between the researcher and the respondents. Qualitative research requires high level of participation and involvement on the part of the researcher. The extent of relationship and openness are decided by the researcher.

- Assumptions of Value – relate to the values researcher associate with himself and the study. These values will actively interpret the respondents views
- Assumptions of Language – are those related to the language used in research. It can be narrative or reported style. In case of narrative style, usage of 'I' will be common. Usage of language depends on the researchers comfort level and the terms and concepts discussed in research.
- Logical Assumptions – are the assumptions about the methods and process of doing research made based on researchers experience. It can be inductive (bottom up from reality) or deductive (top down from theory) methods of developing theories. Research questions are formulated accordingly and data collection methods are planned.

Paradigms

Assumptions of research made are then shaped with the worldwide beliefs or paradigms. Paradigms are perceived beliefs that guide action. Four worldwide views or paradigms that shape qualitative research are: Postpositivism, Constructivism, Advocacy, and Pragmatism (Creswell, 2003).

- Postpositivism – is where multiple views of participants are collected. Rigorous methods of data collection and analysis are employed to draw multiple perspectives.
- Social Constructivism – is a situation where individuals are sought opinion about the problem based on their experiences. It involves questioning approach where the focus is on the specific context in which the respondents position themselves.
- Advocacy – is more a participatory approach. Research and the respondents decide the research process collaboratively. Respondents or the participants are involved from designing the research questions, narrowing down the research problem, collecting data, analyzing and drawing solutions for the research problem.
- Pragmatism – is an approach where the researcher decides the method of research. It believes in ultimate solution to the problem. So the methods of questioning and data collection are laid down carefully by the researcher.

There are different approaches in performing qualitative research and it is discussed in the next section.

APPROACHES IN QUALITATIVE RESEARCH

Approaches in performing qualitative research can be classified under five heads. However, research may extend from any of these five approaches or take a combination of them.

1. Phenomenology

Phenomenology is a clear understanding of the phenomenon or event as experience and explained by group of individuals. This approach considers individual and their opinion about the happenings in the society or world. Experience of the participant is narrated and the effects and perception of the experience narrated is investigated. This method of research explores the individual understandings of the participants about an event or issue. It brings out the subjectivity of the reality. For instance, to understand the opinion of individuals about the controversies in an advertisement endorsed by a film actor, this method of research can be employed. Shared experience of the participants can also be collected. For instance, winning sales team, explaining the reasons for other teams to fail can be bring out the experience of the team as a whole. One important issue in this research is; the phenomenon or the event or the problem to be investigated should be clear and recent. Post positivism is the approach adopted in this research.

Semi structured one-on-one interviews are commonly conducted to collect data. Questions posed to the participants can vary based on the nature of the participant. Participants are identified with snowball sampling method or referral sampling method. Judgmental sampling can also be used. Sample of 25 to 30 participants is appropriate for this method. However, the number depends on the event and the homogeneity of the participants. They are free to express their opinion about the event and the researcher should encourage and probe them to share. Researcher should collect information on:

- What is your experience during the event?
- What situation or event has influenced them to experience something or behave in a specific manner?

These questions will bring the reasons for the experience of the individuals in a unique way. Statements or themes are developed by grouping the experiences shared by the participants. The major themes and subthemes explained by the participants are grouped by understanding the similarities, clustering and evolving the concept. Knowing common experiences will help the policy makes or service providers (insurers, educationalist, etc) to understand the perception of the group about the event.

2. Case Research

The researcher goes to the natural field setting and observes or collects the data about the problem studied. Depth of the problem is studied with exploration made about the phenomenon. Constructivism is build upon the experiences in a specific event or situation. Individual views of the participants are collected with in-depth interviews. However, existing documents, records and observation can also be the data source. For this purpose purposive sampling is generally adopted to select the right representation of the sample. The case will explain the settings in which the individual faced the event or problem. It may consider an individual or an organization or an event or a program or process. Case research addresses specific research questions in a focused manner. Cases can be described or explored or compared. So cases can be exploratory, descriptive or explanatory. It can explain the problem of a single or multiple cases. For example, case study of an individual textile firm can be researched or the case of textile mills in India can also be studied. It depends on the purpose or objective of the research. It revolves round the following questions.

- What is the experience about the event or situation?
- How the event has occurred? – the context and the background
- Who are the decision makers?

3. Biographical Research

Biographical Research explores the individual experiences. In-depth interviews are generally adopted to understand the life history of a person. It can also be continued with an observation and verification of personal documents. Biographical research takes through the life history of an individual. This research focuses on the individual and the problems faced and the conclusions arrived in a narrative manner. Self representation of an individual's life is autobiography. Biographical research is more exploratory in nature and uses diverse methodological and interpretive ways. Changes of an individual in different cultural, social or structural settings are studied. Individuals act with some reason to make meaning in the social context. One important decision the researcher has to make is the number of stories that will be discussed in the research. Single life story or number of stories can be decided based on the purpose of the research. If an individual is the only witness of an event or situation or he is the representation of a cultural group, individual life history is studied in biographical researches. If the research focuses on the problem faced by similar individuals, a sample of individuals is selected for the research. The sample can be less to the extent of three or five. This method encourages the researcher to reflect on their disposition to evolve stories about the life history in the area of research. So the researcher should be clear about the focus of the study and reasons to select a specific research. This will help them to narrow down the stories to the research theme addressed.

4. Ethnography

Ethnography is the study of social relations and behaviours that occur with groups, tea ms, organizations, and society. This approach is adopted to study the culture of consumers or behaviour of specific group of people. For instance, to understand the behaviour of members of Rotary Club / Bikers Club, ethnography research is performed. This research explains the differences in behaviour of individuals with ethnicity, geographic location or group associated. The researcher or the ethnographer identifies himself a part of the group studied to understand their behaviour. This involves ethnographer to co-exist among the population studied. Advocacy is the paradigm adopted for the research.

In case of ethnography research, purpose or opportunistic sampling method is adopted. It helps ethnographers to focus on specific features of the sample selected. Data collected from the sample is examined to understand the key issue that emerges. Inductive method is adopted to generate theoretical explanation from the data collected. Effectiveness of this method depends on the reflecting ability of the ethnographer, as being a part of the group or the society. Data for ethnographic research is collected from interviews, surveys, in-depth observation and personal experiences. Participant observation is adapted to a greater extent in ethnography researches. It helps to understand the culture that exists among the group over a period of time. The observation is done for long duration i.e. atleast for six months. This method of data collection requires expertise on the part of the ethnographer or the researcher to feel and experience the behaviour of the group, as a member of the group. For instance, to understand the reasons for the youth to buy a bike can be better understood if the researcher is a biker among the youth, sharing their experiences and believes. This approach requires maturity on the ethnographer to be in the group without making any contribution of emotional attachment. Otherwise, it will bring bias in the information collected for the research. Field notes are prepared based on the observations made. During observation, ethnographer can use informal interviews to clarify or probe the issue. In case of non-participant observation, ethnographer observes the sample or group from outside. It is done by videotaping the behaviour or recording the minutes of the meeting, diaries or photographing.

5. Grounded Theory

Grounded theory was originally developed by Glaser and Strauss in 1960. The purpose is to develop theory about a specific subject. This requires extensive ground on understanding the concept. It is an iterative process which starts with generalized approach and identifies the underlying theoretical concept and then builds on it. To develop the concept, linkages between the data and the theory are derived. It is a lengthy process involved to evolve conceptual theory from the generalized data available. Once the theory is identified, validating process begin.

Systematic observation is translated into field notes, composing with interview questions and responses. Data is collected from multiple sources (interviews, observations, secondary sources, etc.) about the subject studied. Selective or purpose sampling is adopted to select the sample. Several levels of sampling are adopted to have more samples. Groups representing different demographic characteristics can be approached. For instance, professionals, managers, employees, etc. can be approached at different stages. Once data is collected, analysis is performed in following stages:

- ***Coding*** process identifies categories of the data and groups them. Open coding is adopted initially to identify the categories and later, selective coding is performed for concept building.
- ***Memoing*** process registers the ideas, opinion and comments of the researcher evolved during different phases of research. This will help in the process of concept or theory building
- ***Integrative diagrams and sessions*** collect all the information to build the theory. Diagrams may exhibit relationship or conceptual maps or cartoons that help summarization. The research team work together to evolve meaningful conclusions.

METHODS OF CONDUCTING RESEARCH

There are various tools and techniques used to collect and analyze data for qualitative research. Some of the data collection methods are:

1. Existing Documents

Existing documents can be used to collect data for case research or biographical research. The interviews given in newspapers, magazines, journals or contents in the books can be the source of data. It is the secondary data collected for qualitative research.

Primary data collection methods for qualitative research are discussed below.

2. Observation

In this case, the observer collects the data in the field. Natural behaviour of the respondents can be recorded. It can be disguised or undisguised depending on the law in force in the country. Photographs, pictures and manual recording of the behaviour can be done to collect the data. It requires expertise on the observer to record the data objectively. It is appropriate for ethnography studies and to build grounded theories.

3. In-depth Interviews

These are generally one to one interviews conducted in a semi structured way. Data can be audio or video recorded or written by the interviewer. This is done to probe the interviewee about a specific subject. The topic will be started by the interviewer with initial questions. No rigid procedure is followed. Based on the response, further questions will be raised. So it requires expertise on the part of the interviewer to spontaneously raise questions based on the response. This is performed if individual opinion is required with the reasons and emotions. It is appropriate for biographical research, phenomenological research and case research.

4. Focus Group Discussion

This method of data collection is done if the group opinion is sought. If the topic requires other person to deliberate, then focus group discussions are preferred. Opinion of different parties involved in the problem can be enquired collectively. It is a focused interview done with a group of members. Members of the group can vary from six to ten who sit down in circles for their discussion and it is video recorded. It is important to select the right members from whom data has to be collected. Facilitator can actively participate by stimulating questions for the discussion or be a passive member, recording the discussion. Researcher has to clearly identify the purpose of the discussion, develop key issues to be discussed, plan the discussion and record it. It takes around one to two hours. Online focus group discussions are also performed. This method is useful to understand the cultural norms of a group or to collect diversified opinion of the emerging issue or about a subgroup. This method can be used in ethnography research or grounded theory. For example, to understand the role of women in buying consumer durable, focus group with different segment of women would draw reliable data for further decision.

DATA ANALYSIS AND DECISION MAKING

Data collected in the interview process is coded with an inductive approach to identify the patterns. Once data is collected, coding of the responses is performed. It starts with general coding and proceeds with focused coding. In case of focused coding, the major items identified are checked for its repetition and the concepts are drawn from the statements. Every line, sentence and paragraphs collected during interviews or in the field are reviewed to decide the appropriate code or concept. This stage of coding reduces data to make more meaningful concepts. Meaning is drawn from the raw data recorded. For this purpose, software's like Nvivo or NUD*IST can be used. If the representative sample considered is less in number, manual analysis can be performed. Some of the analyses performed with qualitative data are:

1. Content Analysis

It classifies large amount of data into understandable small units. Once the research problem is finalized, the categories or features to be focused are identified for that specific problem. Related text is summarized into a specific category. Occurrence of the established categories is further explored. For instance, a group of buyers may discuss about the celebrity endorsed for a brand. It can bring out the relevance of the celebrity to that specific brand. The discussion can be grouped under several heads, and its repetition can be reviewed to understand the results of relevance of the celebrity. Large segment of data is easily narrowed down to draw meaning and conclusion.

2. Conversation Analysis

Visual image of the respondent is clearly traced to understand the emotions behind the oral communication. This helps the researcher to understand the respondent's depth of liking or disliking for a subject. In case of ethnography research, the discussion of daily behaviour of the respondents can be better analyzed with conversation analysis. This summarizes the conversation of the respondents in a natural occurrence setting. The data is not provoked by the researcher.

3. Narrative Analysis

This method draw attention with the way a specific problem is addressed. It has a sequence or order in which the story or the problem is explained. For example, to understand the behaviour of youth in shopping mall, ethnography research can be used and narrative analysis can be performed. It brings out the story with a sequence of events, and categorizing into specific class. It brings out the meaning of the researchers opinion in a better way. How the message is narrated and the contents inbuilt in the story are important to increase the validity of this method.

4. Discourse Analysis

There are different methods of performing discourse analysis. However, it is a method of writing or speaking that constructs a specific type of knowledge with practical implications. This analysis is used to understand relationships, behaviour, etc. exerted by the consumers.

Review Questions

1. What are the pros and cons of qualitative analysis?
2. Explain the application of the approaches in qualitative research.
3. What are the methods of data collection that can be used for qualitative research?
4. Explain the data analysis methods that are appropriate for qualitative research.
5. Explain the application of focus group discussion.
6. When an ethnography research is appropriate?

Chapter 17

Report Writing

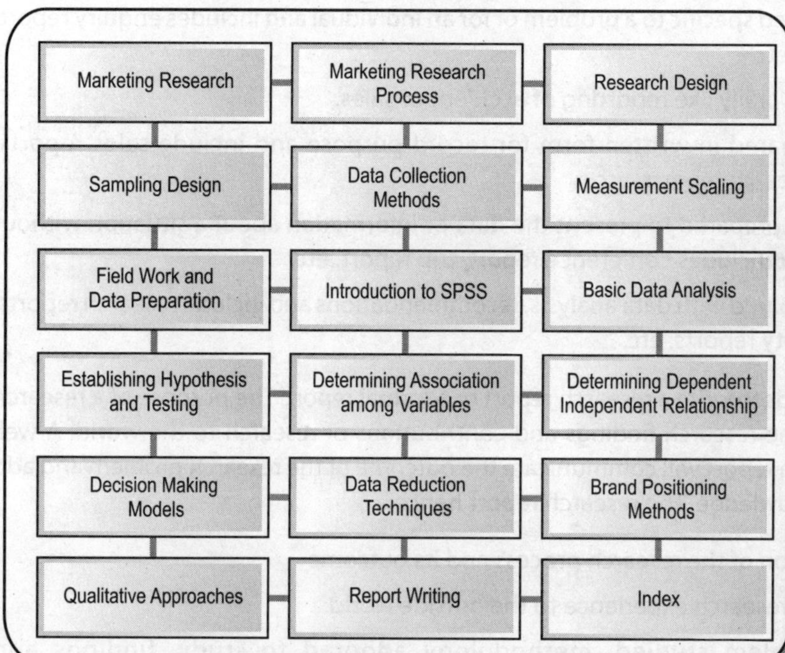

Outline

Chapter Structure

- Introduction
- Organization of the Report
- Presentation of Tables and Figures
- Research Proposal
- Review Questions

Chapter Overview

This chapter elaborates the intricacies associated with reporting the research. It deals with writing a research report for the purpose of communicating the outcome to the real world. Appropriate style for writing, presentation of tables, and figures are explained.

INTRODUCTION

A report summarizes the facts, information, opinion and any other related matters of the problem studied or situation analyzed. It communicates the work done or the results of the project or problem. It can be of any of the following types:

1. Formal reports – prepared elaborately for official purpose which includes annual reports, research reports, company reports, etc.
2. Informal reports – prepared for communicating internally which includes laboratory reports, production reports, trip reports, etc.
3. Routine reports – prepared on regular intervals which include sales reports, production reports, cost reports, etc.
4. Special reports – prepared specific to a problem or for an individual and includes enquiry report, research report, thesis, etc.
5. Oral reports – prepared orally like reporting of accident or sales.
6. Written reports – prepared in written form for record purpose and include sales reports, production reports, research reports, etc.
7. Informational reports – prepared to present the data or information about a situation without analytical perspective. It includes conference report, trip report, etc.
8. Analytical reports – prepared with data analysis, recommendations and include research reports, project reports, feasibility reports, etc.

This chapter explains the methods to write a research report or a formal report. The purpose of a research report is to bring to limelight the research findings and contributions of research to the world. A well written and presentable research report will communicate the outcome of the research problem and add value to the existing body of knowledge. The research report hence:

- Is a formal declaration of the research process and its outcome
- Communicates the research experience to the outside world
- Narrates the problem studied, methodology adopted to study, findings and recommendations.
- It is simple, specific, accurate and understandable for those who are interested with the area of research.

A research report is a base to provide solution to the problem studied, that results in formulation of strategies and policies in the area researched.

ORGANIZATION OF THE REPORT

A report is organized under several heads for the clarity of the reader. Contribution made by a research is well communicated with a formally organized report. Consistent and appropriate formatting is used for research report. It is generally written in formal language in simple present or simple past tense. Universal truths are given in simple present tense and results and observations in simple past tense. The seven C's followed in writing a report are:

1. **Complete** – plan and work comprehensively to execute
2. **Clear** – outline and design the report. Use paragraphs with unique headings and subheads and decide the layout, format, space, margin, headers and footers
3. **Concise** – limit the report for the required number of pages. Edit, condense and eliminate redundancy. Tables and illustrations can be used for writing more paragraphs
4. **Consistent** – use single voice throughout. Follow consistent verb tense and uniform spacing between headings and paragraphs
5. **Correct** – use right grammar and spelling. Edit, proof read and document all sources used
6. **Considerate** – reader friendly for the audience. Use graphs with text and colours to generate interest for the readers
7. **Convincing** – persuade the audience about the relevance of the research

BODY OF RESEARCH REPORT

Researchers can have their own style of reporting. However in general, 'Times New Roman' font style with '12' or '14' font size with double space and one inch margin on all sides is followed. Report is single sided and jargons and superlatives are not used in writing. This also depends on the requirement of the reader or the client. A research report is generally organized under the following heads:

1. Preliminary Pages

Every report will include certain preliminary pages based on the requirement. Some of them are title page, preface (acknowledgement and declaration), certificates, and table of contents, list of tables and figures, and list of abbreviations or terms used (if any).

2. Executive Summary or Abstract

This section summarizes the whole report in a logical order. It outlines purposes, methodology, findings and recommendation. It can run from half page to one page.

3. Introduction

This forms Chapter 1 for a research report and introduces the research study or the research problem. It brings out the context in which the problem or the study has emerged, clear statement of the problem, objectives or the purpose of research, hypothesis to be proved or disproved and limitations of research (if any). It outlines the background, purpose and defines terms and sets limits for research. In short, it elaborates 'what' is studied in the research.

4. Literature Review

This is generally in the second chapter which provides the review of the concepts used, theories referred and research article referred in the similar area. This is done by going through the previous research works done in the area or related area that helps the researcher to understand the variables studied for the similar problem and gaps that exists. This chapter can be arranged for reviewing concepts and theories and later for research articles referred. In the body of the report, the second name of the author with year of publishing is referred to present the reviews. The complete reference will be made available in the reference section. At the end of this chapter, an overview of the research studies and the research gap identified is presented. Specific details of the previous researches with the variables considered and methodologies used should be explained to bring out the inadequacy in the previous researches and need for the research in the specific area. In short, it explains 'why' there is a need for the research in the specific area.

5. Research Methodology

Methodology chapter can be presented separately or it can form a part of Introduction Chapter. It explains the methods adopted and research design used for doing the research. It provide information about the place of research, type of data collected, sources of data collection, tools used to collect data, population considered for study, sample selected, method adopted in sampling, and tools proposed to analyze. Validity and reliability of the scales used can be tested and presented in this chapter. It is usually written in a passive voice. In short, it elaborates 'how' the research problem is studied.

6. Data Analysis

This chapter will give the data and its analysis in a logical sequence. Generally the sequence of the objectives is preferred to bring more clarity and readability. Results drawn from the information collected are presented explaining the significance of the variables studied with proving or disproving hypothesis.

7. Findings, Recommendations and Conclusion

This chapter presents findings of the analysis. It is a summarization of the analysis preformed in the previous chapter. Based on the analysis and findings, suitable recommendations are drawn. Conclusion gives the brief statement of what was found or contribution made and what research gap exists for future research. It summarizes the results and relates it to the objectives. Implications of the research findings are presented.

8. References or Bibliography

This section gives the list of cited references. American Marketing Association (AMA) style guide is followed in providing the list of references. It can be presented at the end or every chapter or towards the end of all chapters.

9. Appendices

Questionnaires used or interview schedule can be enclosed in this section. Any relevant information for the research like maps, illustrations and charts can be presented in this section. In case of qualitative research, focus group transcripts, discussion guides can be enclosed. Each appendix will be numbered in a sequence.

PRESENTATION OF TABLES AND FIGURES

Contents of the research are presented in the report a logical order. Tables and figures give more clarity and meaning for the theory presented in the report. Tables can give the results of analysis performed. It presents the data in rows and columns and is consecutively numbered and arranged near the paragraph of discussion. Every table will be introduced with the contents to be presented in it. This is followed with presentation of tables numbered and with headings. Tables are then followed by an interpretation and discussion. Figures include graphs, charts, photograph and any other drawing. This is used to show relationships or pattern in the flow of data (e.g. Trend). Appropriate type of graph (Bar graph, Pie chart, Scatter diagram, etc) is selected to present the data. Guidelines followed in presenting tables and figures are:

- Every table and figure will be properly numbered and named.
  E.g.: Table 1: Satisfaction Level of Customers in a Retail Outlet
  Figure 1: Trend in the Satisfaction Level of Customers in a Retail Outlet
- Figures and tables are generally placed in the text where it is discussed. In some cases, they may be presented towards the end of the report
- Appropriate column labels and row labels should be given
- Units of measurement (E.g. Cost in US $) is given in the respective column
- Each table and figure should be complete by itself and gives better understanding of the data presented.
- If figures and tables are sourced from existing data / secondary source, reference of the source should be given at the end of the figures and tables and duly referred in the reference section
- Axes and key features of the graphs should be labeled.
- Format of presenting tables and figures with titles should be consistent throughout the report.

CASE

A sample table giving the data of garment exports is given below:

Quantity of Garment Exports:

Garment export from India is growing in recent years and Tirupur is a major contributor to it. There are two categories viz., knitted and woven garments in exports. The quantity of export in number of pieces is presented in Table 1.

Table 17.1: Quantity of Garment Exports: India and Tirupur (In million pieces)

YEAR	KNITTED GARMENTS			WOVEN GARMENTS		
	INDIA	TIRUPUR	%	INDIA	TIRUPUR	%
1996	537.67	257.37	47.87	647.00	0.03	Negligible
1997	632.40	294.28	46.53	669.00	4.00	Negligible
1998	682.03	338.47	49.63	655.70	7.60	1.16
1999	758.44	368.03	48.52	646.00	8.40	1.30
2000	827.68	410.36	49.58	677.10	13.90	2.05
2001	718.02	372.41	51.87	546.30	10.70	1.96
2002	652.72	345.35	52.91	578.90	10.70	1.85
2003	678.72	370.37	54.57	563.80	10.00	1.77
2004	737.57	400.48	54.30	543.80	9.40	1.73

Note: *Negligible represents less than 1 % contribution*
% refers to the percentage share of Tirupur to the exports of India

Source: *Apparel Export Promotion Council Statistics, 2004*

As shown in the table 17.1 there is an increase in export of garments during the period from 1996 to 2004 in both Tirupur and all India. The share of Tirupur in total export of knitted garments from all India was 47.87 percent in 1996, with a marginal fall in 1997 and 1999. In other years, the share increased to touch 54.30 percent in 2004. However the contribution of Tirupur to export of garments is largely in knitted category and it is negligible in woven garments in terms of physical quantity.

Tables and figures are used to add value to the text and used only if found appropriate. Needless tables and figures can always be avoided.

RESEARCH PROPOSAL

Research proposal is an official document prepared before starting of the research to communicate the research plan to the client. It is generally prepared if the research is performed for a client and if the client demands a plan and schedule of the research activity. Contents of a research proposal depend on the demand of the client. However, the following information is generally included in a proposal.

- **Introduction about the Research** – that brings out the problem with the background situation.
- **Statement of the Problem** – clear statement of the research problem studied.

- **Objectives to be Studied** – purpose of the research.
- **Scope of the Research** – application of the research and its benefits to the client.
- **Proposed Methodology** – recommended methods to be adopted to study the problem. It includes proposed research design, sample to be approached, data to be collected and the instruments employed, and tools used for analysis. It also gives the sources of data collected and techniques employed for the same.
- **Expected Findings** – findings expected from the research study is also stated.
- **Schedule of Research** – time involved in completion of every stage of research will be stated and the due date for completion of the research is stated.
- **Cost of Research** – budget required to complete the project with the researchers honorarium is given in the cost of research project. The amount expected at different time schedules is listed.
- **Research Team** – expertise of the research team with the principal investigator is given. Profile of the researcher with the experience in handling similar projects is elaborated.
- **References** – this is optional and given by the clients to support the expertise and credentials of the research team.

Review Questions

1. What are the types of report?
2. What is a research report?
3. What are the contents of a research report?
4. Prepare a research proposal to understand the satisfaction of customers with a specific brand of shampoo.
5. Do a research on student's acceptance with technology and its impact on their daily life. Prepare a formal research report and detail the results of the study.

Index

S

T

V